NATURAL
RESOURCES
MEASUREMENTS

McGRAW-HILL SERIES IN FOREST RESOURCES

Henry J. Vaux, Consulting Editor

WALTER MULFORD WAS CONSULTING EDITOR OF THIS SERIES FROM ITS INCEPTION IN 1931 UNTIL JANUARY 1, 1952

NATURAL RESOURCES MEASUREMENTS

Second Edition

Thomas Eugene Avery, Ph.D.

Texas A & M University

McGRAW-HILL BOOK COMPANY

New York   St. Louis   San Francisco   Auckland
Düsseldorf   Johannesburg   Kuala Lumpur   London
Mexico   Montreal   New Delhi   Panama   Paris
São Paulo   Singapore   Sydney   Tokyo   Toronto

FRONTISPIECE

Both esthetic and utilitarian benefits are provided by this bristlecone pine in the White Mountains of California. The age of this living tree is approximately 1,000 years. (*Laboratory of Tree-Ring Research, University of Arizona.*)

Library of Congress Cataloging in Publication Data

Avery, Thomas Eugene.
  Natural resources measurements.

  (McGraw-Hill series in forest resources)
  First ed. published in 1967 under title: Forest measurements
  Includes bibliographies.
  1. Natural resources—Measurement. 2. Forests and
forestry—Mensuration. I. Title.
  HC55.A93 1975   333.7   74-11346
  ISBN 0-07-002502-9

NATURAL RESOURCES MEASUREMENTS

1 2 3 4 5 6 7 8 9 0 DODO 7 9 8 7 6 5 4

This book was set in Times Roman by Textbook Services, Inc. The editors were Thomas A. P. Adams and James W. Bradley; the production supervisor was Leroy A. Young. New drawings were done by J & R Services, Inc. R. R. Donnelley & Sons Company, was printer and binder.

For Beverly Avery Williamson

CONTENTS

PREFACE

Emphasis on environmental education and the need for improved land management practices have resulted in an expansion of college and university programs concerned with various aspects of renewable natural resources. This book provides a framework for introductory courses devoted to the techniques of natural resources measurements. Although based on the 1967 edition of *Forest Measurements*, the scope of this text is not limited to timber estimation techniques. It has been enlarged to encompass measurements of related natural resources, including rangelands, wildlife, fisheries, water, and outdoor recreation. The seven new chapters that did not appear in the first edition also include one on dendrochronology—the technique of tree-ring dating. This volume may therefore be regarded as much a new book as it is a second edition.

Part One deals with the fundamentals of statistical methods, including simple linear regression, and with land measurements. Elementary photogrammetric techniques are also reviewed.

Part Two, on timber measurements, discusses techniques that will be of primary interest to foresters and managers of woodlands. The subject matter from the previous edition is presented in a smaller number of chapters, but the essential coverage is quite similar. Discussions of certain topics, e.g., board-foot log rules, have been reduced, while subjects such as volume-line functions and tarif tables have been added. A new chapter on inventory planning has been incorporated in place of the former chapter on continuous forest inventory. The instructor who wishes to limit his course to topics discussed in the previous edition will find these materials covered by Parts One and Two of this book.

Part Three is devoted to topics not found in the previous edition. Here, the techniques of assessing various nontimber resources are introduced, and a special section on the presentation of multiple-resource measurements is included at the end of Chap. 14. The book concludes with a chapter on tree-ring dating. Taken together, the three major segments of this book encompass a combination of resource measurement techniques that have not been previously presented in a single volume.

In preparing any technical book, one of the principal problems facing an author is that of deciding what subject matter to include and what to exclude. The opinions of those who have used earlier editions weigh heavily on such decisions, but unfortunately, such opinions often reflect opposing viewpoints. Thus the author finds himself in a dilemma, e.g., whether to expand a section such as statistical methods, leave it "as is," or delete it altogether. For the particular case in point, the review chapter on statistics was retained and slightly expanded. Conversely, an introduction to electronic computers and data processing systems has been eliminated from this edition because such rapidly changing techniques are more appropriately treated in specialized, up-to-date courses. Furthermore, since this volume introduces only elementary sampling concepts, no attempt has been made to include complex sampling schemes such as those based on probability proportional to prediction.

Also, as with the earlier edition, an attempt has been made to present the subject matter in a simple and concise fashion that is easily grasped by the student. Emphasis is on the "how and what to measure" approach, but an effort has also been made to explain *why* certain measurements are needed for resource allocation and decision-making. It is assumed that the reader will have previously studied algebra and plane trigonometry; a prior knowledge of basic statistics and sampling methods will also be helpful, although essential concepts are briefly reviewed in Chap. 2.

At the suggestion of users of the previous edition, the generalized problems at the end of each chapter have been retained. These problems have been formulated, wherever possible, for adaptation to local conditions confronting the resource manager. Thus they are presented in a context that permits no fixed or standardized solutions.

It will be noted that the use of the International System of Units (metric system) has been stressed throughout the text. The English system of measurement has been used only when logical metric units or illustrative examples were not available to the author. The two principal sections that are dependent on English measurements are those concerned with the U.S. Public Land Survey and board-foot log rules.

Wherever possible, references listed at the end of each chapter have been selected from books and articles that will, it is hoped, be *available* to students and practicing land managers. From beginning to end, it has been my primary objective to provide an introduction to measurement techniques that is both readable and useful as a reference handbook.

It would be virtually impossible to complete a book of this diversity without a considerable amount of assistance and encouragement from professional colleagues. I am especially grateful to Charles O. Minor of Northern Arizona University and David B. Thorud of the University of Arizona for their support during the preparation of this revised and expanded edition.

For contributions relating to statistical methods and sampling techniques, I wish to acknowledge the invaluable suggestions of Frank Freese, U.S. Forest Products Laboratory; Kenneth D. Ware, U.S. Forest Service; Jerome L. Clutter, University of Georgia; James P. Barrett, University of New Hampshire; and Emmett F. Thompson, Mississippi State University. Chapter 6, on site, stocking, density, and growth, was revised by Peter F. Ffolliott, University of Arizona. Several of the photographic illustrations were supplied by Charles Thomas and Harry C. Hitchcock III of Northern Arizona University.

The contents of chapters dealing with nontimber resources were based largely on suggestions or contributions from colleagues. Chapter 14, on recreational resources, was developed with the assistance of A. Jay Schultz, Northern Arizona University, and David A. King, University of Arizona. In preparing Chapter 15, on dendrochronology, I was fortunate to have assistance from the staff at the Laboratory of Tree-Ring Research, University of Arizona. Other collaborators, all from the University of Arizona, were:

Phil R. Ogden, rangeland resources
C. Roger Hungerford, wildlife resources
Boyd E. Kynard, fisheries resources
Robert L. Beschta and Peter F. Ffolliott, water resources

Certain tables in the Appendix warrant special acknowledgments. The table of square-root conversions appears by courtesy of SCM Corporation, New York. I am indebted to the Literary Executor of the late Sir Ronald A. Fisher, F.R.S., to Dr. Frank Yates, F.R.S., and to Longman Group Ltd., London, for permission to reprint Appendix Table 6 (The distribution of t) from their book, "Statistical Tables for Biological, Agricultural, and Medical Research."

Finally, a word of appreciation to all those persons who have expressed their satisfaction with the first edition of this book. It is my hope that this volume will prove even more useful to managers of renewable natural resources.

Thomas Eugene Avery

NATURAL
RESOURCES
MEASUREMENTS

Part One

Fundamentals

Chapter 1

Introduction

1-1 The Scope of Natural Resources Measurements Today's resource managers are concerned not only with timber measurements but also with inventory and estimation problems arising from the appraisal of related resources such as rangelands, wildlife, fisheries, water, and outdoor recreational areas. In many parts of North America, for example, the prime objectives of wild-land management are to provide benefits in the form of clean water supplies and to meet the outdoor recreational demands of an expanding and ever-mobile population. The fundamental techniques for assessing such diverse land resources have thus been incorporated into this book under the umbrella of natural resources measurements. A special addition is a brief chapter on dendrochronology—the technique of tree-ring dating. This introductory review was included to provide some insight into a scientific area that is wholly dependent on annual growth-ring patterns; yet it represents a technique that is virtually unknown to most foresters and resource managers.

Although a "how and what to measure" approach has been employed throughout this volume, the reader should be aware that there are many resource measurement problems for which no satisfactory solutions exist. Furthermore, there is room for considerable improvement in currently employed inventory techniques and instruments—based on *existing* knowledge. As the veteran farmer said when he refused a free extension bulletin on improved soil practices,"I ain't farming now half as well as I know how to!" During recent years, new ideas have been responsible for such practices as weight-scaling of roundwood, use of aerial photographs and other remote sensors in rangeland inventories, and predictions of visitor use on outdoor recreational sites. On the other hand, we have continued to use archaic methods and measurement units for scaling logs and inadequate or inefficient sampling techniques for estimating a host of other important resource parameters. The continued need for professional resource managers with imagination and inventiveness is obvious.

1-2 Justification for Measurements   Whenever a manager is asked to inventory a particular resource, he should be concerned not only with how and what to measure, but *why* the data is needed at all! The most common answer to this problem is that a decision must be made and that the inventory data is required to provide a sound basis in formulating that decision. Any management plan for a wild-land area implies an intent to achieve some objective, such as the production of more wood, forage, game animals, water, or recreational benefits. Once the specific management objectives are clearly defined, the answer to the question "Why measure?" should also become apparent.

Industries that depend upon wood as a raw material often have large capital investments in land and standing timber. Periodic inventories of these lands are required for tax records, for justification of management expenditures (e.g., building access roads), and for determining the amount and quality of wood available for annual utilization. In like fashion, periodic censuses of game animals or fishes may be required to justify long-term financial commitments for habitat modification and environmental improvements. When a resource manager knows exactly why an inventory is needed, he is in a much better position to devise an efficient means of collecting the required resource information.

1-3 Measurement Cost Considerations   In almost all resource inventories, cost factors are of primary importance; the manager must continually seek out more efficient methods for counting, measuring, and appraisal. The basic objective of most resource surveys is to obtain an estimate of the highest statistical precision for the lowest possible expenditure. To achieve this objective requires a sound knowledge of sampling methods, because once the specific needs of management have been determined, the resource inventory becomes essentially a sampling problem.

The measurement of various resource parameters adds no real value to the materials or benefits being assessed; therefore, such measurements are regarded as service functions rather than control functions. Measuring techniques must be subordinate to the productive or beneficial phases of an operation, for the operation itself cannot be modified just to accommodate an inventory requirement. For example, every visitor to a crowded public campground cannot be delayed and required to complete a detailed questionnaire on recreational preferences—nor can a sawmill be shut down in order to measure or weigh a recent delivery of logs. Instead, an appropriate sampling scheme must be designed and employed to obtain the essential resource measurements without disrupting normal activities.

It is an obvious though commonly overlooked fact that the amount expended for a given inventory task should be geared to the value of the products or services being measured. Also, the nearer one approaches the finished product or ultimate benefit, the greater can be the allowable cost of measurement. Thus the measurement of high-quality black walnut trees, which may be worth several thousand dollars each, justifies a much greater unit expense than the assessment of small pine trees for pulpwood. Similarly, the value of finished lumber warrants a greater inventory cost than the scaling of green logs. The resource manager who becomes "cost conscious" early in his career has an attribute that will be highly respected by his employer.

1-4 The International System of Units Most countries of the world, including those credited with the origination of the English system of measurement, have now adopted the International System of Units (SI) as their official measurement standard.[1] Use of metric weights and measures was legalized in the United States as far back as 1866; since then, there has been a gradual, voluntary changeover from the English system by industrial and scientific organizations. Therefore, wherever possible, the metric system has been used for numerical examples in this book.

The metric system was originally formulated from geodetic measurements. The fundamental unit of length, the meter, was initially described as being equal to one ten-millionth of the meridional distance from the equator to the earth's poles. The meter has since been defined in much

[1]When this chapter was written, the United States was one of the few nations of the world that had not enacted legislation requiring adoption of the International System of Units.

Table 1-1   SI Base Units

Quantity measured	Name of unit	Symbol
Length	meter	m
Mass	kilogram	kg
Time*	second	s
Electric current	ampere	A
Temperature (thermodynamic)†	kelvin	K
Luminous intensity	candela	cd
Amount of substance	mole	mol
Plane angle‡	radian	rad
Solid angle‡	steradian	sr

*Same unit as presently known under the English system.
†Air temperatures are commonly expressed in degrees Celsius, a system of measurement derived from the kelvin scale.
‡As of 1973, these were termed supplementary units.

more precise terms and is now given as a length of approximately 39.37 inches. If this appears to be an awkward value to work with, the reader is reminded that the only way to use the International System of Units effectively is to *think metric*—not in terms of conversions back to the English system. Therefore, tables are provided in the Appendix for converting in only one direction: from English to metric units.

With the SI system, there are just seven base units and two supplementary units that encompass all measurement problems; all other SI units are *derived* from these fundamental units (Table 1-1). For example, area is measured in square meters, vehicle speeds in kilometers per hour, and density in kilograms per cubic meter. Precise derivations of the base units, most of which are defined in highly scientific terms, can be found in standard engineering handbooks or in the references cited at the end of this chapter. In this book, the base units of primary concern are length, mass, time, and temperature.

Each metric unit is related to another by multiples or submultiples of 10. For instance, there are 10 millimeters (mm) in 1 centimeter (cm), 100 centimeters in 1 meter (m), and 1,000 meters in 1 kilometer (km). A special advantage of using SI units is that multiples and submultiples of various quantities are also *named* according to a system of numerical prefixes (Table 1-2). Thus a *milli*meter is 1/1,000 of a meter, while a *kilo*meter is equal to 1,000 meters. In the beginning, the student should at least become familiar with those prefixes ranging from "mega" to "micro."

1-5   Reading for Continuing Education   To attain a level of competence and to keep abreast of new developments in any profession, the aspiring scientist must develop and maintain adequate reading skills. The acquisition of knowledge merely *begins* in college, and the scientist who wishes to maintain his expertise will continue to be a student for his entire professional life.

Although basic textbooks provide a sound introduction to many subjects of interest, the latest ideas and innovations are to be found mainly in current scientific journals and monographs. Since there are literally hundreds of such periodicals to choose from, the wise student will become familiar with those in his particular subject area while he has access to university library facilities. After leaving college, he will find it desirable to acquire—and read—several scientific articles each month. And, since he is likely to be reading primarily to discover new ideas or to understand a new technique, he may also find it desirable to take one or two courses in reading comprehension. The ability to read fast and still absorb essential details is an invaluable skill in any professional field.

Most scientific journals rely heavily on voluntarily submitted papers for their publications, particularly in specialized research areas. Even though such manuscripts are subjected to rigorous technical reviews, it is widely recognized (yet rarely admitted) that journal articles often rate poorly in terms of clarity, conciseness, and general readability. Thus the resource manager who expects to comprehend and evaluate such articles must adopt a disciplined and critical reading habit for scientific literature. Fortunately, most established journals require that an abstract or summary accompany each technical article. This should be read first, followed by a rapid scanning of the entire article. Then, if the study appears to be of special interest or utility, the article should be carefully reread.

Although an abstract may obviate the necessity of making notes on

Table 1-2 Prefixes for SI Units

Multiple and submultiple	Prefix	Symbol
$1,000,000,000,000 = 10^{12}$	tera	T
$1,000,000,000 = 10^{9}$	giga	G
$1,000,000 = 10^{6}$	mega	M
$1,000 = 10^{3}$	kilo	k
$100 = 10^{2}$	hecto	h
$10 = 10$	deka	da
$0.1 = 10^{-1}$	deci	d
$0.01 = 10^{-2}$	centi	c
$0.001 = 10^{-3}$	milli	m
$0.000\ 001 = 10^{-6}$	micro	μ
$0.000\ 000\ 001 = 10^{-9}$	nano	n
$0.000\ 000\ 000\ 001 = 10^{-12}$	pico	p
$0.000\ 000\ 000\ 000\ 001 = 10^{-15}$	femto	f
$0.000\ 000\ 000\ 000\ 000\ 001 = 10^{-18}$	atto	a

each article, it is well to look for salient points. After noting the locale of the study and the author's affiliation, the reader should ask himself, What were the real objectives of this study? Next, it may be appropriate to note the laboratory procedure or statistical design employed, along with the number and type of sample units measured. Finally, any tables or graphical presentations should be studied to see whether they fully substantiate the author's principal findings or conclusions. Only by taking such an analytical approach can the reader expect to gain any real benefit from reports of specialized research.

1-6 Preparation of Technical Reports Professional resource managers are sometimes inclined to minimize the value of neat, concise, and well-written technical reports. Yet in many instances, such reports may provide the only concrete evidence of work accomplished; thus they may constitute the prime basis for judgment of field proficiency by supervisors.

It goes without saying that one must be more than an accomplished grammarian; no amount of flowing penmanship can compensate for deficiencies in fieldwork and data collection. Nevertheless, the importance of producing technically accurate and grammatically correct reports can hardly be overemphasized.

Whenever feasible, all but the most routine reports should be typewritten (double-spaced) on white bond paper. Figures and tables are preferably placed on separate pages and numbered consecutively. Line drawings, graphs, and charts should be drawn in black ink and presented on an appropriate drafting medium. Although a single format cannot be expected to meet the requirements for all reports, the following outline may prove useful for student term papers or technical reports on assigned experiments:

Title page: Title in centered caps, followed by author's name. Lower part of page should show location of study (e.g., Cripple Creek National Forest) and the date (month and year completed).

Table of contents: Chapter headings and major subdivisions of chapters should be listed, along with corresponding page numbers.

Introduction: Statement of the problem, justification and importance of the study, specific objectives, and practical considerations.

Review of previous work: A concise, critical review of published literature bearing on the problem, including a statement on the relationship of the present study to previous research.

The study area: Location of the study and a description of the area involved or population to be studied (e.g., physiography, vegetative types, site conditions, climatic factors, legal description, size of area, ownership, management or silvicultural history).

Collection of field data or laboratory procedure: For some studies, *Design of the Experiment* may be a more appropriate heading. List all data collected, arrangement of field samples, special instruments or techniques employed, illustration of field forms, size of crews, time or expense involved, and special problems encountered.

Analysis of results: Compilation of field data, statistical procedures, presentation and discussion of results.

Summary and conclusions: A brief synopsis of the study undertaken, results obtained, and implications of the findings. For some types of reports, a brief summary or abstract may be required at the beginning of the discussion, i.e., preceding the introduction.

Literature cited: Arranged in standard form according to an acceptable style manual or in conformance with requirements of a specific technical publication.

Appendix: Copies of field forms and/or original raw data are often included here. Detailed statistical formulas or computations may also be shown. The various sections of the appendix should be designated by alphabetical divisions or by use of Roman numerals.

PROBLEMS

1-1 Describe a situation (real or hypothetical) in your locality where the benefits derived from precisely measuring a product or resource would *not* be likely to justify the inventory cost incurred.

1-2 Become familiar with the International System of Units, along with derived units, symbols, and conversion factors that apply to measurements in your major field of study.

1-3 What are likely to be the principal problems of converting to SI units in your professional field? Can you suggest possible solutions to any of these problems?

1-4 Without using manufactured instruments or scales, improvise an estimation technique for determining (*a*) the height of a tree or building, (*b*) the time of day to the nearest hour, (*c*) the velocity of flow for a river, and (*d*) your position on the surface of the earth.

1-5 Refer to a recent issue of a national scientific journal. What is the preferred style for preparing references or literature citations? Do abstracts that accompany the technical articles provide *adequate* synopses of the published articles? If not, explain why not.

1-6 Locate a published article on some aspect of natural resources measurements that does *not* include an abstract. Then prepare a typewritten abstract of not more than 200 words.

REFERENCES

American Institute of Biological Sciences
  1972. *CBE style manual*, 3d ed. Washington, D.C. 297 pp., illus.
Ghosh, Sanjib K.
  1973. Reading for research. *Photogrammetric Eng.* **34:** 401-404.
Hicks, Tyler G.
  1972. Metrication manual. McGraw-Hill Book Company, New York. 30 pp., illus.
Strunk, William, Jr., and White, E. B.
  1972. *The elements of style*, 2d ed. The Macmillan Company, New York. 78 pp., illus.
U.S. Department of Commerce
  1972. The International System of Units (SI). National Bureau of Standards, Special pub. 330, Government Printing Office, Washington, D.C. 42 pp.

Chapter 2

Probability, Sampling, and Estimation

2-1 Introduction Since some readers will have taken courses in statistical methods prior to their work in natural resources measurements, this chapter is intended merely as a review of applied techniques. Emphasis is placed on the handling of routine computations and the interpreting of certain statistical quantities. Basic concepts reviewed include an introduction to statistical decision theory, the estimation of population parameters, common sampling designs, and simple linear regression. The scope of this chapter does not encompass tests of hypotheses, but those readers with previous statistical training will find it desirable to review the Student's t and chi-square tests.

Many of the calculations required for statistical analyses are routine, time-consuming tasks. Therefore, students who expect to handle large quantities of numerical data should make an effort to audit courses in computer programming and data processing systems. As a minimum, each reader should become thoroughly familiar with the operation of electronic desk calculators. Such machines are now priced at a level that makes them almost universally available. A special table for extracting square roots of numbers with desk calculators is included in the Appendix.

2-2 Rounding Off Numbers To minimize personal bias and assure a degree of consistency in computations, it is desirable to adopt a systematic technique for rounding off numbers. The necessity for such a method arises when a calculated value apparently falls exactly halfway between the units being used, i.e., when the number 5 immediately follows the digit positions to be retained.

As an example, suppose the values of 27.65 and 104.15 are to be rounded off to 1 decimal place. A commonly used rule is to ignore the 5 when the digit preceding it is an even number; thus 27.65 becomes 27.6. Conversely, if the digit preceding the 5 is an odd number its value is raised by one unit. Therefore, in the example here, 104.15 would be recorded as 104.2.

Rounding off should be done after all intermediate calculations have been completed. Intermediate calculations should be carried at least two places beyond that of the final rounded figures.

2-3 Bias, Accuracy, and Precision Although most persons have a general idea of the distinction between these three terms, it appears appropriate to define the terms from the statistical viewpoint. *Bias* is a systematic distortion arising from such sources as a flaw in measurement or an incorrect method of sampling. Measurements of 10-m units with a tape only 9.9 m long will be biased; similarly, biases may occur when a timber cruiser consistently underestimates tree heights or ocularly shifts a field plot location to obtain what he regards as a more typical sample.

Accuracy refers to the success of estimating the true value of a quantity, and *precision* refers to the clustering of sample values about their own average. A badly biased estimate may be precise, but it cannot be accurate; thus it is evident that accuracy and precision are not synonymous or interchangeable terms. As an example, a forester might make a series of careful measurements of a single tree with an instrument that is improperly calibrated or out of adjustment. If the measurements cluster about their average value, they will be precise. However, since the instrument is out of adjustment, the measured values may be biased and considerably off the true value; thus the estimate will not be accurate. The failure to attain an accurate result may be due to the presence of bias, the lack of precision, or both.

PROBABILITY AND DECISION-MAKING

2-4 Rules for Calculating Probabilities For purposes of discussion, probability may be defined as the expected relative frequency with which an event takes place "in the long run." If an observed event A is expected to occur x times in n trials, the expected probability or relative frequency is

$$P(A) = \frac{x}{n}$$

For example, if a balanced coin is tossed in an unbiased fashion, one would expect to obtain *heads* about 50 per cent of the time; i.e., the *expected* probability is 0.50. If the same coin is tossed 100 times and heads occur only 41 times, the *observed* probability or relative frequency of heads is 41/100, or 0.41. Still, the likelihood of getting *heads* on any given toss is 0.50, and "over the long run" (thousands of unbiased tosses) one would expect the observed relative frequency to closely approximate 0.50.

Coin flipping is an example of an *independent* event; i.e., the occurrence of heads or tails on one toss has no predictable effect on the outcomes of subsequent tosses. Since the expected probability of obtaining heads on a single toss is 1/2, the probability of obtaining two heads (or two tails) in a row is $1/2 \times 1/2 = 1/4$, or one chance in four. Thus for two *independent* events, the probability that both will occur is the *product* of their individual probabilities.

As another example of events that are apparently independent, assume that the probability of owning a bicycle is 0.17, the probability of having red hair is 0.04, and the probability of being a college student is 0.21. If the assumption of independence is correct, the probability that a randomly selected individual will be a red-headed college student with a bicycle is $0.17 \times 0.04 \times 0.21$ or 0.001428 (roughly 14 chances in 10,000). These events have been referred to as *apparently* independent, because truly independent happenings are difficult to establish, except by statistical design and randomization.

If the occurrence of one event A precludes the occurrence of some other event B, and vice versa, A and B are said to be *mutually exclusive*. In a single appearance at bat, a baseball player may walk or hit safely but cannot do both. If the probability of drawing a walk is 0.104 and the probability of a safe hit is 0.310, the probability that the player will *either* draw a walk *or* hit safely is $P(0.310) + P(0.104) = 0.414$ (roughly 41 chances in

100). Thus for mutually exclusive events, the probability that at least one *or* the other will occur is the *sum* of their individual probabilities.

Probabilities are always positive numbers, and they range between 0 and 1. The probability that the earth will continue to revolve on its axis for another year is unknown but assumed to be 1.0. If this is true, the probability that it will not do so is 0. Nevertheless, there are few events that can be described in such absolute terms. When the probability of an event happening is 0.75 (three times in four) the probability that it will *not* occur is $1 - 0.75$, or 0.25 (one chance in four).

Resource managers, including foresters, who employ statistical procedures must learn to accept the fact that they are dealing with probabilities and not with certainties. Even when we say that we are 95 percent confident that the volume of a timber stand falls within specified limits, there are still 5 chances in 100 that it does not!

2-5 Statistical Decision Theory   Many decisions that directly affect the management or utilization of natural resources must be made with an incomplete knowledge of the consequences. In such circumstances, the principles of statistical decision theory may offer the resource manager a rational basis for deciding among a series of alternatives or possible courses of action.

Where the occurrence of future events determines the outcome, decisions are commonly made under one of three circumstances: certainty, risk, or uncertainty. If the result of each possible action is assumed to be a single, known outcome, then the decision is made under *certainty*. If each decision alternative can lead to more than one possible outcome, and the probability of each outcome occurring can be established, the decision is made under *risk*. If such probabilities *cannot* be determined, then the decision is regarded as being made under conditions of *uncertainty*.

Although resource decisions are often treated as if they were made under conditions of certainty, a fair proportion should be regarded as alternatives selected under risk or uncertainty. Examples of such circumstances might include: whether to hire additional fire crews and lookouts on a forest in anticipation of a severe seasonal drought; whether to develop new recreational facilities in remote areas when the opposing factors of increasing tourism and limited fossil fuels required for transportation are considered; or, whether certain tracts of land should be managed for single- or multiple-resource benefits in view of the long-range returns that might be expected under varying uses and economic constraints. Such decisions *are* being made each year, and certainly some of the alternatives selected *might* have been different had decision theory been employed.

Three basic components comprise the framework of all decision-making situations: the possible states of nature, the possible decision alternatives available, and the possible outcomes or consequences resulting from various decisions. The states of nature are the factors which are beyond the control of the decision-maker, viz., those future occurrences, conditions, or events that will largely dictate the outcome of whatever decision is made. The states of nature must be expressed in such a way that they are mutually exclusive. They must also be completely "exhaustive"; i.e., all states must be included, and one of the states must occur.

The decision alternatives are those possible courses of action open to the decision-maker. These should also be stated as mutually exclusive options. The possible outcomes or consequences resulting from various combinations of decisions and states of nature are often expressed numerically in terms of money or ranked in terms of subjective utility (Davis, 1968). Here, they are presented as relative monetary returns.

2-6 Decision-making under Risk Where there are two or more states of nature and the probability of each state occurring can be determined, decisions are made under risk. Assume, for example, that you are a resource manager for a large, diversified industry. A tract of timberland has just been logged, and you are presented with these three options: replant the land to trees, convert it to rangeland for livestock, or lease it to a private hunting club on a long-term basis. Your decision will be based on an evaluation of the future markets for wood products, i.e., whether such markets are favorable, the same, or unfavorable in relation to markets for the other products. The decision alternatives, states of nature, and consequences are summarized in a pay-off matrix as follows:

Decision alternatives	States of nature, i.e., future wood markets		
	Favorable	Same	Unfavorable
	Relative monetary returns realized		
1. Replant trees	12	7	1
2. Convert to range	8	11	3
3. Lease for hunting	4	5	9

When situations of this kind are faced, a suitable criterion is to select the alternative having the highest mathematical expectation, i.e., the greatest return. It is obvious from the pay-off table that if wood markets are certain to be favorable, then trees should be replanted. If markets are certain to remain the same, the manager should convert to rangeland. And if markets are certain to be unfavorable, the rational decision would be to lease the land to the hunting club. But what if we are unsure about such future markets? A decision under *risk* can be made here, provided probabilities can be established for each state of nature. Long-term economic forecasts *might* indicate a probability of 0.50 for favorable markets, 0.30 for the same conditions prevailing, and 0.20 for unfavorable markets. Expected returns would then be computed as

Alternative 1: $0.5(12) + 0.3(7) + 0.2(1) = 8.3$
Alternative 2: $0.5(8) + 0.3(11) + 0.2(3) = 7.9$
Alternative 3: $0.5(4) + 0.3(5) + 0.2(9) = 5.3$

If the stated probabilities can be viewed as reliable, then alternative 1 (replant trees) would be the rational choice here, because this decision provides the highest *expected* return. Of course, minor variations in the stated probability values could have shown options 2 or 3 to have the most favorable expected return. Thus the discerning reader will realize that the value of such computations is dependent on the determination of acceptable probabilities for each possible state of nature. It should also be noted that such calculations do *not* automatically produce the optimum decision—they merely assist the decision-maker by providing additional data for selecting a rational course of action. Decision-making under risk may be applied to logging engineering (Dane, 1965) and to a host of other resource management problem situations.

2-7 Decision-making under Uncertainty Decision theory is a concept that is commonly concerned with models for decision-making under uncertainty, i.e., under those conditions where probabilities *cannot* be determined for each possible state of nature. Although definitive probabilities were presumed for the example of decision-making under risk, the problem described is actually a classic situation of uncertainty. To put it bluntly, it is unlikely that reliable probabilities could be established for the states of wood markets 20 to 30 years in the future.

Whereas the decision made under risk is based on the alternative with the greatest expected return, there is no universally accepted criterion for choosing a course of action under conditions of uncertainty. Instead, there are several possible rationales, each with advantages and limitations (Thompson, 1968; 1972). Among the selection criteria available to the decision-maker operating under uncertainty are the principle of rationality, minimax, minimin, and minimax regrets. While other indexes exist, these will serve to illustrate the basic reasoning involved.

2-8 The Principle of Rationality Under the principle of rationality or "insufficient reason," the decision-maker, being unable to establish probabilities for the various states of nature, assumes that each state has an equal probability of occurring. Then he selects the alternative with the most favorable average return. For the problem previously outlined, the average returns would be computed as

Alternative 1: $12/3 + 7/3 + 1/3 = 20/3 = 6.67$
Alternative 2: $8/3 + 11/3 + 3/3 = 22/3 = 7.33$
Alternative 3: $4/3 + 5/3 + 9/3 = 18/3 = 6.00$

Alternative 2 (convert to rangeland) is the optimal choice under the principle of rationality—a criterion that might be more explicitly described as the theory of equal probability. Here we have reduced the problem to a risk situation by assuming equally likely states of nature.

2-9 Minimax and Minimin One of the most commonly used criteria for making decisions in the face of uncertainty is termed *minimax*. This is the alternative favored by the confirmed pessimist. The decision-maker finds the worst possible consequence for each alternative and then selects the course of action whose worst expected return is best. In effect, he assumes that the worst will occur and attempts to make the best of it by minimizing his maximum possible loss. For the sample problem, application of the minimax criterion results in a choice of alternative 3, i.e., lease the land to a hunting club.

The *minimin* criterion assumes that the best will happen and thus selects that alternative which results in the best possible consequence. This approach, representing the opposite viewpoint from minimax, is the choice of the truly optimistic decision-maker. In the sample problem, the minimin criterion would lead to alternative 1, i.e., replant the land to trees.

2-10 Minimax Regrets The minimax regret criterion represents a slightly different approach that is sometimes substituted for minimax. By this rationale, it is assumed that *differences* in expected returns are more diagnostic than the absolute amounts. To use this criterion in decision-making, the minimum expected return for each state of nature is subtracted from all expected returns for that state. These derived consequences are known as *regrets*—hence the term *minimax regrets*. For the sample problem, the original table would now appear as follows:

Decision alternatives	States of nature, i.e., future wood markets		
	Favorable	Same	Unfavorable
	Minimax regrets		
1. Replant trees	8	2	0
2. Convert to range	4	6	2
3. Lease for hunting	0	0	8

If we apply the minimax criterion to these regrets or differences and therefore assume that the worst will happen, the choice would be alternative 2: convert to rangeland, because this alternative includes the outcome whose worst is "best." It should be noted that the use of regrets may or may not result in choosing the same alternative as the unaltered minimax criterion.

There are, of course, other criteria that can be employed for decision-making under uncertainty, but the examples demonstrate that different criteria can result in the selection of different alternatives. There is no single criterion that is superior to all others, because the choice is often dependent on the attitude and outlook of the decision-maker. However, it might be noted that the minimax criterion is commonly favored under conditions of complete ignorance regarding the various states of nature.

2-11 Subjective Probabilities It is recognized that even when the decision-maker cannot establish objective probabilities for each state of nature, he may still be able to express a professional opinion or make a logical judgment regarding the occurrence of the various states. When he *can* apply his expertise in this fashion, he is operating with partial knowledge of rather than complete ignorance about the states' occurrence. And, as stated earlier, the degree of knowledge about the states of nature determines whether a decision is rendered under conditions of certainty, risk, or uncertainty.

If the resource manager must make his decision without the benefit of experimental data regarding the possible states of nature, he may rely on his judgment and experience in developing *subjective* probabilities for each state. The concept of subjective probability will be easily grasped by anyone familiar with decisions based on "expert opinion." It may also be possible to obtain experimental data to substantiate or modify the subjective probabilities and thus improve their reliability. In any event, once the probabilities have been selected for the various states of nature, the decision problem is resolved by the same procedure as that described for making decisions under risk.

The development of subjective probabilities and utility functions used in decision-making are complex topics that cannot be completely explored in this brief introduction. And, while this section was concerned with situations where the events are independent of the choice of alternatives, there are other problems where such conditions do not hold true. For additional details on these topics, the reader is referred to texts on decision theory (e.g., Chernoff and Moses, 1959).

It has been demonstrated that decision theory can be applied to many resource management situations, *provided* the decision-maker can define his problem within the proper framework, i.e., specify the possible courses of action, states of nature, and associated outcomes or expected returns. In other words, when one is able to state the problem clearly and ask the right questions, one is well on the way toward a solution. The resource manager who can structure his problems within a decision theory framework has thus hurdled a major obstacle in the application of this technique to management decisions.

STATISTICAL CONCEPTS

2-12 Necessity for Sampling For most inventories of natural resources, it is not economically feasible to measure or count 100 percent of the population about which inferences must be made. Furthermore, the time required for complete enumerations of large populations would render the data obsolete by the time they could be amassed, collated, and summarized. As a result, some form of partial measurement or sampling is dictated. Careful measurement of a small percentage of the units in a population will frequently give more reliable information than rough estimates obtained from the entire population.

Aside from time and cost factors, sampling is also necessary when testing procedures are destructive. All seeds cannot be evaluated in germination tests because there would be none left for sowing. Similarly, all fishes cannot be dissected to study concentrations of chemical elements; otherwise there would be none left for anglers or for human consumption. In business and industry, as well as in resource management, sampling is an accepted means of obtaining information about populations that cannot be subjected to a complete census.

The ultimate objective of all sampling is to obtain reliable data from the population sampled and to make certain inferences about that population. How well this objective is met depends on items such as the rule by which the sample is drawn, the care exercised in measurement, and the degree to which bias can be avoided. Of all the techniques described in this book, the concept of sampling is perhaps the most important.

2-13 Populations, Parameters, and Variables A *population* may be defined as the aggregate of all arbitrarily defined, nonoverlapping *sample units*. If a square 0.2-hectare (ha) plot is designated as a sampling unit, then a 100-ha tract comprises a population of 500 such units.

Constants that describe the population as a whole are termed *parameters*. For the foregoing population of 500 plots, the mean number of trees per plot is one parameter. A *statistic* is a quantitative characteristic that describes a sample obtained from a population. Statistics based on unbiased samples are used to estimate population parameters. The *sample* itself is merely the aggregate of sample units from which measurements or observations are taken.

Populations are generally classed as being *finite* or *infinite*. A finite population is one for which the total number of sample units can be reliably expressed as a finite number. The number of square plots in a tract of land, catfish in a hatchery, or members in the United Nations are examples of finite populations.

Infinite populations are those in which the sample units are not denumerable (countable). Also, populations from which samples are selected and replaced after each drawing may be regarded as equivalent to infinite populations. From a practical viewpoint, all the gray squirrels in North America or all the sagebrush plants in southwestern United States may be treated as infinite populations. As described in later sections of this chapter, the distinction between these two classes of populations becomes important when a relatively large number of sample units is drawn from a finite population. In statistical notation, finite population size is denoted by N, and the number of sample units observed is indicated by n.

Without a measurable degree of variation in resource characteristics, such as fish lengths, elk weights, or tree volumes, there would be few sampling problems. Any characteristic of this nature that may vary from one sample unit to another is referred to as a *variable*. Variables that may occupy any position along a measurement scale are termed *continuous* variables. Animal weights and tree heights are conceptually continuous variables, as are air temperature, wind velocity, and atmospheric pressure. *Discrete* variables are those commonly described by simple counts (discrete integers). Most of the statistical procedures described in this chapter are applicable to continuous rather than discrete variables.

2-14 Frequency Distributions The frequency distribution defines the relative frequency with which different values of a variable occur in a population. Each population has its own distinct type of distribution. If the form of the distribution is known, it is possible to predict what proportion of the individuals are within any specified limits.

The most common distribution forms are the normal, binomial, and Poisson. The normal distribution is associated with continuous variables, and it is the form most used by resource managers. The arithmetic techniques for handling data from normally distributed populations are relatively simple in comparison with methods developed for other distributions. Regardless of the distribution followed by a given variable, the means of large samples from the distribution are expected to have a distri-

bution that approaches normality. Consequently, estimates and inferences may be based on this assumption.

ELEMENTARY COMPUTATIONS

2-15   Mode, Median, and Mean   All three of these values are
sometimes referred to as *averages*, or measures of central tendency. The
mode is defined as the most frequently appearing value or class of values
in a set of observations. The *median* is the middle value of the series of
observations when they have been arranged in order of magnitude, and
the arithmetic *mean* is simply the arithmetic average of the set of observations. For a majority of statistical analyses, the mean is the most useful
value of the three. In populations that are truly normally distributed, values for the mode, the median, and the mean are identical.

Following are length observations (in centimeters) taken on a sample
of 26 small fish. These values are listed haphazardly (as tallied) at the
left and arranged in a frequency table at the right. In the frequency table,
the indicated length is the midpoint of the class.

Haphazard listing, fish lengths			Frequency table	
			Length class	No. of fish
8	9	10	5	3
8	9	9	6	0
5	7	7	7	6
10	5	8	8	9
9	8	9	9	5
10	7	8	10	3
8	7	7		26
5	8	8		
7	8			
$n = 26$				

For this set of observations, 8 cm is the modal diameter class. This
class is easily detected in the frequency table but is less discernible in the
unorganized listing. If there had been nine fish in any other class as well as
nine in the 8-cm class, the distribution would have been termed *bimodal*.
When three or more values have the same frequency or when each value
appears only once, no apparent mode can be specified.

The *median* position is found by adding 1 to the number in the sample
and dividing by 2, that is, $(n + 1)/2$. With an odd number of observations,
the median is merely picked out as the middle ranking value. Thus in a
sample of seven observations ranked as 2, 4, 9, 12, 17, 24, and 50, the 12

is the median value. Had there been only six observations (eliminating the 50), the median *position* would have fallen between the 9 and 12. Its *value* would be recorded as the arithmetic average of these two numbers, or $(9 + 12)/2 = 10.5$. For the 26 fish lengths previously noted, the median position is $(26 + 1)/2$ or 13.5. As both the thirteenth and fourteenth values fall within the 8-cm-length class, the median value is recorded as 8 cm.

It will be noted that both median and mode are unaffected by extreme values. Thus as measures of central tendency, the median and mode may be more informative than the arithmetic mean when a few extreme values are observed.

The sample *mean* or arithmetic average, commonly designated as $\bar{x}$, is computed from

$$\bar{x} = \frac{\Sigma x}{n}$$

where Σ = sum of (over entire sample)
x = value of an individual observation
n = number of observations in sample

For the 26 fish under consideration, then, the *sample mean* is $204 \div 26 = 7.85$ cm

2-16 Standard Deviation   The standard deviation is a measure of the dispersion of individual observations about their arithmetic mean. In a normally distributed population, approximately two-thirds (68 percent) of the observations will be within ± 1 standard deviation of the mean. About 95 percent will be within 1.96 standard deviations and roughly 99 percent within 2.58 standard deviations.

The standard deviation of a population is a parameter, and it is commonly denoted by the Greek letter sigma (σ). The sample standard deviation is a statistic that is an estimate of the population parameter σ, and it is symbolized by s. Again employing the symbols previously identified, the estimated standard deviation is calculated from

$$s = \sqrt{\frac{\Sigma x^2 - (\Sigma x)^2/n}{n - 1}}$$

This is equivalent to the formula

$$s = \sqrt{\frac{\Sigma(x - \bar{x})^2}{n - 1}}$$

where $\bar{x}$ is the arithmetic mean, and $(x - \bar{x})^2$ is the squared deviation of an individual observation from the arithmetic mean.

The first formula is a shortcut version of the second and is easier to use for calculations. For the 26 measurements of fish lengths, the standard deviation is

$$s = \sqrt{\frac{1,650 - (204)^2/26}{25}} = \sqrt{\frac{49.38}{25}} = 1.41 \text{ cm}$$

If the population sampled is normally distributed, it is expected that about two-thirds of the individual sample units will fall within ± 1.41 cm of the population mean.

The *variance* of a population is merely the squared standard deviation. For sample data, the variance is denoted by s^2, and it must be computed first; then the standard deviation is derived by taking the square root of the variance as shown in the previous formula.

2-17 Coefficient of Variation The ratio of the standard deviation to the mean is known as the *coefficient of variation*. It is usually expressed as a percentage value. Because populations with large means tend to have larger standard deviations than those with small means, the coefficient of variation permits a comparison of relative variability about different-sized means. A standard deviation of 5 for a population with a mean of 15 indicates the same relative variability as a standard deviation of 30 with a mean of 90. The coefficient of variation in each instance would be 0.33, or 33 percent.

For the 26 fish measurements, the mean is 7.85, and the standard deviation is 1.41. The coefficient of variation CV from the sample is

$$CV = \frac{s}{\bar{x}} (100) = \frac{1.41}{7.85} (100) = 18\%$$

2-18 Standard Error of the Mean The standard deviation is a measure of the variation of individual sample observations about their mean. Inasmuch as individuals vary, there will also be variation among means computed from different samples of these individuals. A measure of the variation among sample means is the standard error of the mean. It may be regarded as a standard deviation among the means of samples of a fixed size n. As described in succeeding sections, the standard error of the mean can be used to compute confidence limits for a population mean or for determining sample size required to achieve a specified sampling precision.

Calculation of the standard error of the mean depends on the manner in which the sample was selected. For simple random sampling from a finite population, the formula for the estimated standard error of the mean $s_{\bar{x}}$ is

$$s_{\bar{x}} = \sqrt{\frac{s^2}{n}} \sqrt{\frac{N-n}{N}} = \frac{s}{\sqrt{n}} \sqrt{\frac{N-n}{N}}$$

The term $\sqrt{N-n}/N$ is referred to as the *finite population correction*; in this term, N denotes the population size, and n is the actual sample size. If the population is small or if the sample comprises more than 5 to 10 percent of the population, the sample mean will probably be closer to the population mean than with infinite populations. As a result, the standard error of the mean will also be smaller. Thus the finite population correction serves to reduce the standard error of the mean when relatively large samples are drawn without replacement from finite populations.

If it is assumed that the 26 sample units were drawn from a population of only 200 units, the standard error of the mean would be computed as

$$s_{\bar{x}} = \frac{1.41}{\sqrt{26}} \sqrt{\frac{200-26}{200}} = 0.28 \sqrt{0.87} = 0.28\,(0.93) = 0.26\,\text{cm}$$

This value indicates that if several samples of 26 units each were randomly drawn from the same population, the standard deviation among the sample means might be expected to be approximately 0.26 cm. The value of the finite population correction is always less than unity, but it approaches unity when the sampling intensity is very low.

If the 26 sample units had been drawn from an infinite population or from one that was quite large in relation to the sample size, the standard error of the mean would have been computed simply as

$$s_{\bar{x}} = \frac{1.41}{\sqrt{26}} = 0.28\,\text{cm}$$

2-19 Confidence Limits It is recognized that sample means vary about the true mean of the population. The establishment of confidence limits provides a method of estimating what the probability is that a given sample mean might be more than some specified distance from the true mean. The standard error of the mean and a table of t values (Appendix) are used for setting up confidence limits. For simple random samples from normally distributed populations, the confidence limits for the population mean are computed by

Mean $\pm t$ (standard error) or $\bar{x} - t\, s_{\bar{x}}$ to $\bar{x} + t\, s_{\bar{x}}$

In using the Appendix table for the distribution of t, the column labeled df refers to *degrees of freedom*, which in the case of a simple random sample will be equal to one less than the sample size (that is, $n - 1$). The columns labeled *probability* refer to the level of odds demanded. If one wishes to state that the true mean falls within specified limits unless a 1-in-20 chance has occurred, the t values in the 0.05 column are used. If one wishes to establish confidence limits at the 99-percent-probability level, the 0.01 column in the t table is used, and so forth.

For the sample problem previously described, the estimated mean was 7.85 cm, and the corrected standard error of the mean was ±0.26 cm. Because only 26 sample units were taken, there are $26 - 1$, or 25, df. The 95 percent and 99 percent t values are read from the Appendix table as 2.060 and 2.787, respectively. Confidence limits for these probabilities are as follows:

$P = 0.95$:
   $7.85 - (2.06)\,(0.26)$ to $7.85 + (2.06)\,(0.26) = 7.31$ to 8.39 cm

$P = 0.99$:
   $7.85 - (2.787)\,(0.26)$ to $7.85 + (2.787)\,(0.26) = 7.13$ to 8.57 cm

Therefore, if the 26 units were randomly selected from a normally distributed population, the true population mean lies between 7.31 and 8.39 cm, unless a 1-in-20 chance has occurred in sampling. In other words, the population mean will be included in the interval unless this random sample is one of those which, by chance, yields a sample mean so far from the true population mean that the interval constructed from it will not include the mean. Such would happen, on the average, once in every 20 samples. Similarly, unless a 1-in-100 chance has occurred, the true mean is included in the interval of 7.13 to 8.57 cm. It can be seen from these examples that the higher the probability level, the wider the confidence limits must be expanded.

The resource manager must remember that confidence limits and accompanying statements of probability account for *sampling variation only*. It is assumed that sampling procedures are unbiased, field measurements are without error, and no computational mistakes are included. If these assumptions are incorrect, confidence statements may be misleading.

2-20 Sampling Intensity To plan an inventory that is statistically and practically efficient, enough sample units should be measured to obtain the desired standard of precision—no more and no less. As an example, one might wish to estimate the mean volume per hectare of a timber stand and have a 90 percent probability of being within ± 10 m³/ha of the true mean. A formula for computing the required sampling intensity may be derived by transforming the relationship for the confidence limits on the mean. Excluding the finite population correction for the moment, the formula may be expressed as

$$n = \frac{t^2 s^2}{E^2} \quad \text{or} \quad \left[\frac{ts}{E}\right]^2$$

where E is the desired half-width of the confidence interval and other symbols are as previously described.

Solving this formula requires an estimate of the standard deviation (or variance), expressed *in the same units* as the desired precision E. This estimate may be obtained by (1) measuring a small preliminary sample of the population, or (2) using the standard deviation obtained from previous sampling of the same or a similar population. The first method is likely to be most reliable, if the expense of a preliminary survey can be accepted. In the example proposed, assume that preliminary measurement of 25 randomly selected plots provided the following data:

$n = 25$ sample units; $df = 25 - 1$, or 24
$\bar{x} = 110$ m³/ha
$s = 50$ m³/ha

The original objective was to be within ± 10 m³/ha, with a confidence probability of 90 percent. Accordingly, a t value of 1.711 is read from the Appendix table (probability column of 0.1 and 24 df). The *desired* half-width of the confidence interval, $E = 10$, is substituted in the formula, along with the estimated standard deviation:

$$n = \left[\frac{(1.711)(50)}{10}\right]^2 = (8.555)^2 = 73.2, \text{ or } 74, \text{ sample units}$$

Apparently, 74 sample units will be required to attain the desired precision. Actually the number will be less than 74 because there are 73 df now involved instead of the 24 assumed in the computation. The exact number of df can only be obtained by repeated trial-and-error solutions of the formula, because it depends on the number of sample units to be measured. Resolving the equation for the nearest value in the Appendix t table (60 df) provides this result:

$$n = \left[\frac{(1.671)(50)}{10}\right]^2 = (8.355)^2 = 69.8, \text{ or } 70, \text{ sample units}$$

The sample size is thus reduced by four as a result of the change in the degrees of freedom. An even greater reduction would have resulted if the original computation had been based on as few as 5 to 10 preliminary observations.

The foregoing determination of sample size is based on an assumption of simple random sampling from an infinite population. If the population is actually finite, and the estimated sample size represents more than a negligible proportion of the population, a further adjustment is in order. If we assume, for example, that the 70 sample units will be drawn from a population of 525 possible units, we then apply a finite population correction to the calculated sample size as follows:

$$n_f = \frac{n_i}{1 + n_i/N}$$

where n_f = required sample size, corrected for finite population
n_i = sample size calculated for infinite population
N = population size

Substituting in the formula, we have

$$n_f = \frac{70}{1 + 70/525} = 61.8, \text{ or } 62, \text{ sample units}$$

The finite population correction results in a further reduction of the sample size so that now only 62 sample units must be measured to obtain an estimate having the desired level of precision.

2-21 The Standard Error as a Percent Formulas for calculating the required sample size for simple random sampling can be written in several ways. If the standard error of the mean is expressed as a percent of the mean and an estimate of the coefficient of variation is available, the required sample size (for infinite populations) can be calculated from

$$n = \left[\frac{(t)(CV)}{\text{SE}\%}\right]^2$$

where SE% is the desired standard error, expressed as a percent of the mean, and the other symbols are as previously described.

With an estimated coefficient of variation of 50 percent, for example, one might wish to determine the number of observations needed to estimate a population mean within ± 5 percent at a probability level of 0.80. In other words, the desired half-width of the confidence interval is specified as 5 percent of the mean. From the Appendix, the t value (infinite df and probability column of 0.2) is 1.282. Therefore, the total number of sample units required to achieve the specified precision in terms of the half-width of the confidence interval is

$$n = \left[\frac{(1.282)\,(50)}{5} \right]^2 = (12.82)^2 = 164.4,\ \text{or } 165,\ \text{sample units}$$

If the sample is drawn from a finite rather than an infinite population, then the finite population correction should be applied as in the previous example. Trial substitutions in this formula will demonstrate the fact that sampling intensities are increased 4 *times* when (1) the coefficient of variation is doubled, as from 25 to 50 percent, or (2) the specified standard error is reduced by one-half. These are important facts for consideration in balancing costs and desired precision in resource inventories.

The perceptive reader will also note that land *area* is a variable which does not appear in either of the sampling-intensity formulas presented here. However, the *effect* of tract size is partially included, because large areas tend to have greater variances (standard deviations) than small areas. Where sampling variation does *not* increase proportionately with increasing tract size (as in a uniform plantation), a fixed number of sample units may provide estimates that are almost as reliable for 1,000 ha as for 25 ha.

2-22 Expansion of Means and Standard Errors In most instances, estimates of means per sample plot are multiplied by a constant to scale the estimates to a more useful basis. If a resource inventory utilizes 0.1-ha plots, for example, the mean value per plot is multiplied by 10 to place the estimate on a per hectare basis. Or, for a tract of 38 ha, the mean value per plot could be multiplied by 380 (the number of possible 0.1-ha in the tract) to estimate the total value.

The rule to remember is that expansion of sample means must be accompanied by a similar expansion of standard errors. Thus if the mean timber volume per 0.1-ha plot is 9 m^3 with a standard error of ±1.5, the mean volume per hectare is 10(9) ± 10(1.5), or 90 ± 15 m^3. For a tract of 38 ha, the total volume would be expressed as 380 (9) ± 380 (1.5), or 3,420 ± 570 m^3.

The foregoing examples presume the use of expansion factors having no error. However, sample-based estimates of area are (or should be) also accompanied by standard errors. Thus the expansion of per hectare volume to total tract volume becomes one of deriving the product of volume times area and computing a standard error applicable to this product. The computation may be illustrated by assuming *independent* inventories that produced the following estimates and standard errors for volume $\bar{V}$ and area A:

Mean volume: 90 ± 15 m³/ha
Tract acreage: 38 ± 2 ha

If these two estimates are independent (and *only* if they are), their product and its standard error may be computed by

$$\bar{V}A \pm \sqrt{V^2 s_A{}^2 + A^2 s_{\bar{V}}{}^2}$$

where $\bar{V}$ = estimated mean volume per hectare
A = estimated number of hectares
$s_{\bar{V}}$ = standard error of mean volume per hectare
s_A = standard error of area estimate

Substituting the sample problem data, the total volume and its standard error are

$$90(38) \pm \sqrt{(90)^2 (2)^2 + (38)^2 (15)^2} = 3{,}420 \pm 598 \text{ m}^3 \text{ (tract total)}$$

2-23 Effect of Plot Size on Variability At a given scale of measurement, small sample plots usually exhibit more relative variability (i.e., have a larger coefficient of variation) than large plots. The relation of plot size to variance changes from one population to another. In general, large plots tend to have less relative variability, because they average out the effect of irregular plant distributions. In uniform populations (e.g., plantations), changes in plot size have little effect on variance. In nonuniform populations, the relation of plot size to variance depends on how clumps of trees (or other plants) and open areas compare with the sizes of plots.

Although plot sizes have often been chosen on the basis of experience, the objective should be the selection of the most efficient size. Usually, this is the smallest size commensurate with the variability produced. Where the coefficient of variation has been determined for plots of a given size, the coefficient of variation for different-sized plots may be estimated by a formula suggested by Freese (1962):

$$(CV_2)^2 = (CV_1)^2 \sqrt{\frac{P_1}{P_2}}$$

where CV_2 = estimated coefficient of variation for new plot size
$\quad\quad CV_1$ = known coefficient of variation for plots of previous size
$\quad\quad\quad P_1$ = previous plot size
$\quad\quad\quad P_2$ = new plot size

If the coefficient of variation for 0.2-ha plots is 30 percent, the estimated coefficient of variation for 0.1-ha plots would be computed as

$$(CV_2)^2 = (30)^2 \sqrt{\frac{0.2}{0.1}} = 900(1.414) = 1,272.6$$

$$CV_2 = \sqrt{1,272.6} = 36 \text{ percent}$$

The coefficients of variation of 36 percent for 0.1-ha plots versus 30 percent for 0.2-ha sample units may now be compared as to relative *numbers* of plots needed. Assume, for example, that the 0.2-ha plots produced a sample mean of 20 m³/ha. The sample standard deviation is 30 percent of this value, or ±6 m³/ha. If these data lead us to believe that the required sample size will be roughly 30 units, the total number of 0.2-ha plots needed to estimate the mean volume per acre within ±2 m³ at a probability level of 95 percent ($t = 2.045$ for 29 df) is estimated as

$$n = \left[\frac{(2.045)\,(6)}{2}\right]^2 = (6.14)^2 = 37.7, \text{ or } 38, \text{ plots}$$

The reader should note that it is necessary to have the standard deviation and the allowable error in the same units before substitution in the formula. In this instance, these values are ±6 and ±2 m³/ha, respectively. For comparison with the preceding results, the standard deviation for 0.1-ha plots, expressed on a per acre basis, would be 0.36 (20) = ±7.2 m³/ha. The number of 0.1-ha plots required to meet the previous standards of precision would be

$$n = \left[\frac{(2.045)(7.2)}{2}\right]^2 = (7.36)^2 = 54.2, \text{ or } 55, \text{ plots}$$

The choice between thirty-eight 0.2-ha plots versus fifty-five 0.1-ha plots is a decision that now rests on the relative time or costs involved. Some aspects of sampling "efficiency" are discussed in the pages that follow.

COMMON SAMPLING DESIGNS

2-24   The Sampling Frame   As stated previously, the objective of all sampling is to make some inference about a population from the characteristics of the sample. The method of selecting the nonoverlapping sample units to be included in a sample is referred to as the *sampling design*, and a listing of all possible sample units that might be drawn is termed the *sampling frame*.

Establishment of a reliable sampling frame can be a difficult task. For example, if an individual campground visitor is specified as the sample unit, a registration list that includes the occupants of all entering motor vehicles may or may not comprise a satisfactory sampling frame. Those persons who enter the campground on foot or horseback would probably be excluded from such a sampling frame; other visitors might arrive at such a time that they somehow avoid the necessity of registration.

Problems can also arise when the sample unit is defined as a field plot of fixed area; such sample units are commonly employed by foresters and range managers. When the tract of land from which the sample is drawn is more or less rectangular in shape and the sample units are also rectangular (or square), then each segment of the tract can be occupied by a sample unit. And a listing of all the nonoverlapping sample units fitted together inside the tract boundaries would constitute an acceptable sampling frame. Difficulties arise, however, when *circular* sample plots are chosen as sample units. A listing of all the circular, nonoverlapping plots that can be fitted into a tract of land is not an ideal sampling frame, because those areas between adjacent plot perimeters are not subject to selection as sample units. In such circumstances—and they occur frequently—one can only hope that differences between the sampling frame and the population are inconsequential. Otherwise, inferences based on a sample drawn from the frame may not provide a realistic representation of the actual population.

After the individual sample unit and the sampling frame have been defined, it is then necessary to decide on the sampling design to be employed. Three of the basic designs often used by resource managers are systematic sampling, simple random sampling, and stratified sampling (Fig. 2-1). In the descriptions that follow, sample units are assumed to be field plots (area samples) of a uniform size and shape.

2-25   Systematic Sampling   Under this system, the initial sample unit is randomly selected or arbitrarily established on the ground; thereafter, plots are mechanically spaced at uniform intervals throughout the tract of land. For example, if a 5 percent sample is desired, every twentieth sample unit would be selected.

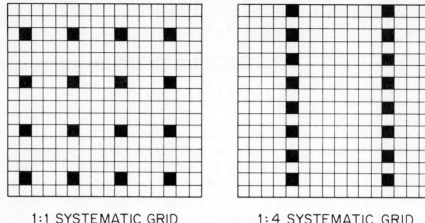

1:1 SYSTEMATIC GRID   1:4 SYSTEMATIC GRID

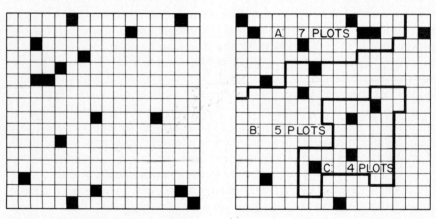

SIMPLE RANDOM SAMPLE   STRATIFIED RANDOM SAMPLE

Figure 2-1 Four possible arrangements of 16 sample plots in a population composed of 256 square plots.

Systematic sampling has been popular for assessing timber and range conditions, because (1) sample units are easy to locate on the ground, and (2) they appear to be more "representative" since they are uniformly spaced over the entire population. Although these arguments *may* be true, the drawback is that it is usually difficult—if not impossible—to estimate the variance (or standard error) for one systematic sample.

Rectangular spacings or square grid layouts may yield efficient estimates under certain conditions, but the precision can also be low if there is a periodic or cyclic variation inherent in the population. Furthermore, assessment of the precision presents a formidable problem, since simple random sampling techniques cannot be logically applied to systematic designs. An exception occurs where the elements of the population are in random order. In those rare cases where this situation exists (and can be recognized), then a systematic sample may be analyzed as a simple random sample. Nevertheless, it would be inaccurate to presume that most populations of plant communities are in random order. Thus the fact that resource managers often analyze systematic samples *as if they were randomly selected* is a violation of the basic theory. Estimates of sampling precision based on such manipulations must be regarded, at best, as approximations.

In summary, there are good defenses for systematic sampling—unfortunately, a random sampling analysis is not one of them. When an objective numerical statement of precision need not be appended to inventory estimates, however, systematic sampling may provide more information for the time (or money) expended than simple random sampling.

2-26 Simple Random Sampling All the statistical procedures previously discussed assume simple random sampling. By this approach, *every possible combination of sample units* has an equal and independent chance of being selected. This is *not* the same as simply requiring that every sample unit in the population have an equal chance of being selected. This latter requirement is met by many forms of restricted randomization and even by some systematic designs.

Allowing every possible combination of n sample units an equal chance of being selected is easily accomplished. It is only necessary that, at any state of the sampling, the selection of a particular unit be in no way influenced by the other units that have been selected or will be selected on succeeding draws. To state it another way, the selection of any given unit should be completely independent of the selection of all other units. One way to do this is to assign every unit in the population a number and to draw n numbers from a table of random digits. A modification of this technique consists of drawing random intersection points in a coordinate system based on column and row numbers designating each plot.

Sample units may be selected with or without replacement. If selection is with replacement, each unit is allowed to appear in the sample as often as it is selected. In sampling without replacement, a particular unit is allowed to appear in the sample only once. Most natural resource sampling is without replacement.

2-27 Stratified Random Sampling In stratified sampling, a population is divided into subpopulations of known size, and a simple random sample of at least two units is selected in each subpopulation. This approach has several advantages. If sample units are allocated wisely among the strata, the estimate of the population mean will be more precise than that given by a simple random sample of the same size. Also, it may be desirable to have separate estimates for each subpopulation (e.g., for different vegetative types or administrative subunits). And it may be administratively more efficient to sample by subpopulations.

A stratified random sample may combine the features of aerial and ground estimating, offering a means of obtaining timber volumes with high efficiency. Photographs are used for area determination, for allocation of field samples by volume classes, and for designing the pattern of fieldwork. For each stratum, tree volumes or other data are obtained on the ground by conventional methods. In the example that follows, emphasis is on methods of allocating a fixed number of inventory plots among the various strata recognized.

Assume, for example, that a tract of land containing 300 ha has been subdivided into five distinct timber-volume classes (strata) by interpretation of aerial photographs. Since the tract has been recently inventoried by a systematic sample of 150 field plots, it is possible to compute a preliminary approximation of the standard deviation for each stratum:

Volume class	Stratum area (ha)	Std. dev. (m³/ha)	Area × std. dev.
I	15	20	300
II	45	70	3150
III	110	35	3850
IV	60	45	2700
V	70	25	1750
Total	300	—	11,750

Assuming that a total of 150 sample units will be measured on the ground, there are two common procedures for distributing the field plots among the five volume classes. These methods are known as *proportional allocation* and *optimum allocation*.

2-28 Proportional Allocation of Field Plots This approach calls for distribution of the 150 field plots in proportion to the *area* of each type. For the five volume classes, the number of plots in each stratum would be computed as follows:

Class I: $\dfrac{15}{300}(150) = 7$ plots

Class II: $\dfrac{45}{300}(150) = 23$ plots

Class III: $\dfrac{110}{300}$ (150) $= 55$ plots

Class IV: $\dfrac{60}{300}$ (150) $= 30$ plots

Class V: $\dfrac{70}{300}$ (150) $= 35$ plots
  _____
  150 plots

One disadvantage of proportional allocation is that large areas receive more sample plots than small ones, irrespective of variation in volume per hectare. Of course, the same limitation applies to simple random and systematic sampling. Nevertheless, when the various strata can be reliably recognized and their areas determined, proportional allocation will generally be superior to a nonstratified sample of the same intensity.

2-29 Optimum Allocation of Field Plots With this procedure, the 150 sample plots are allocated to the various strata by a plan that results in the smallest standard error possible with a fixed number of observations. Determining the number of plots to be assigned to each stratum requires first a product of the area and standard deviation for each type, as derived earlier.

The number of plots to be allocated to each stratum is computed by expressing each product of "area times standard deviation" as a proportion of the product sum (11,750 in this example). Thus the 150 field plots would be distributed in the following manner:

Class   I: $\dfrac{300}{11,750}$ (150) $= 4$ plots

Class   II: $\dfrac{3,150}{11,750}$ (150) $= 40$ plots

Class III: $\dfrac{3,850}{11,750}$ (150) $= 49$ plots

Class IV: $\dfrac{2,700}{11,750}$ (150) $= 35$ plots

Class   V: $\dfrac{1,750}{11,750}$ (150) $= 22$ plots
  _____
  150 plots

No matter which method of allocation is used, field plots are located within each stratum by the method described for simple random sampling.

It will be noted that optimum allocation results in a different distribution of the field plots among the various strata. By comparison with proportional allocation, fewer plots are assigned to classes I, III, and V, i.e., those strata with relatively small standard deviations. On the other hand, more plots are allotted to classes II and IV, which were the strata with relatively large standard deviations. Thus the relative variations within the volume classes more than offset the factor of stratum area in this particular example. When stratum areas and standard deviations can be determined reliably, optimum allocation is usually the preferred method for distributing a fixed number of inventory plots.

2-30 Relative Sampling Efficiency In controlling the intensity of various sampling plans, one must fix (1) the sample size, (2) the sampling variance, or (3) the cost. The best sampling design for a given estimation problem is one which provides the desired precision (in terms of confidence limits on the estimate) for the lowest cost. Or, if the cost itself is fixed in advance of sampling, the objective is to obtain an estimate of the greatest precision for the funds available.

The relative efficiency of alternative procedures or various sampling plans may therefore be calculated from the elements of cost and precision. If the costs required to achieve the *same* level of precision (sample variance) are known for plans A and B, then the relative efficiency of the two plans may be computed as a ratio of the two expenditures. For example if plan A cost $800 and plan B achieved the same level of precision for $600, then the relative efficiency would be calculated as $800 \div 600 = 1.33$; i.e., plan B is 1.33 times as efficient as plan A.

For those situations where alternative plans do not result in the same level of precision, an index of efficiency may be computed from the survey cost per sample unit and its accompanying coefficient of variation (Freese, 1962):

$$\text{Efficiency index} = \frac{1}{(\text{cost}) (\text{CV})^2}$$

Such indices can be computed and compared for several alternative sampling plans. Since the calculation is based on a reciprocal, the plan that results in the largest index value would be regarded as the most efficient.

SIMPLE LINEAR REGRESSION

2-31 Definitions In analyzing various resource measurements, it may be important to quantify the degree of association between two or more variables. Such associations can often be examined by regression analysis. The simplest type of relationship that can exist between two quantities is one that can be represented by a straight line. Thus a *simple*, *linear regression* describes a straight-line relationship that exists between two quantities: one *dependent variable Y* and one *independent variable X*.

The quantity that is being estimated by the regression line is termed the *dependent variable*, and the quantity measured in order to predict the associated value is called the *independent variable*. When these paired quantities are shown graphically, it is conventional to plot Y values along the vertical axis (*ordinate*) of the graph and X values along the horizontal axis (*abscissa*). This would be termed a *relationship* of Y on X.

When each Y value is graphically plotted against its corresponding X value, the resulting representation is termed a *scatter diagram*. Since the purpose of such a diagram is to determine whether or not a relationship exists between the two variables, this should be the first analytical step following data collection. Careful inspection of the scatter diagram will also provide an indication of the strength of the relationship and its probable form, i.e., whether or not the association can be logically represented by a straight line.

For those rare situations where all the plotted points fall exactly on a line, a perfect linear relationship exists. Such will rarely (if ever) be the case with biological data, but the smaller the deviations from a line, the stronger the linear relationship between the two variables. Where Y values increase with X values this is termed *positive*, or *direct*, *correlation*; if Y values decrease as X values become larger, a *negative*, or *inverse*, *correlation* is said to exist. If the plotted points are not indicative of a straight-line relationship, it is sometimes possible to make a simple *transformation* of one or both of the variables so that the relationship becomes linear in form. Squaring a variable or expressing it in logarithmic terms are examples of transformations.

2-32 A Linear Equation When a linear trend exists between two variables, a regression equation of the form $\hat{Y} = a + b(X)$ may be fitted to the plotted points. In this equation, $\hat{Y}$ refers to the estimated value of the dependent variable, X is the value of the independent variable, and a and b are regression coefficients established from analysis of the data. After these coefficients have been determined, a denotes the value of the Y intercept, which is the value of Y when X equals zero; the coefficient b is the value that establishes the slope of the straight line. Therefore, a line represented by the equation $\hat{Y} = -3 + 2X$ would intercept the Y axis at an ordinal value of -3, i.e., three units below the origin of the graph. The slope coefficient of 2 means that the line would rise two units vertically along the Y axis for each unit horizontally along the X axis.

When the regression line is fitted to the plotted points by the method of "least squares," the line will pass through the point defined by the means of X and Y. The principle of least squares is that the sum of the squared deviations of the observed values of Y from the regression line will be a minimum.

2-33 A Sample Problem Suppose we observe that pine trees with large crowns appear to grow faster (i.e., have wider annual rings) than trees with small crowns. Since we would like to be able to predict the growth of trees from their relative crown sizes, we decide to use regression analysis to determine whether a strong relationship exists between the two variables. A simple random sample from the area of interest results in 62 paired measurements of tree-crown areas X and radial tree growth Y. In the tabulation that follows, crown areas are in square meters and annual radial growth is in centimeters.

Crown area (X)	Radial growth (Y)	Crown area (X)	Radial growth (Y)	Crown area (X)	Radial growth (Y)
22	0.36	53	0.47	51	0.41
6	0.09	70	0.55	75	0.66
93	0.67	5	0.07	6	0.18
62	0.44	90	0.69	20	0.21
84	0.72	46	0.42	36	0.29
14	0.24	36	0.39	50	0.56
52	0.33	14	0.09	9	0.13
69	0.61	60	0.54	2	0.10
104	0.66	103	0.74	21	0.18
100	0.80	43	0.64	17	0.17
41	0.47	22	0.50	87	0.63
85	0.60	75	0.39	97	0.66
90	0.51	29	0.30	33	0.18
27	0.14	76	0.61	20	0.06
18	0.32	20	0.29	96	0.58
48	0.21	29	0.38	61	0.42
37	0.54	50	0.53		
67	0.70	59	0.58		
56	0.67	70	0.62		
31	0.42	81	0.66		
17	0.39	93	0.69		
7	0.25	99	0.71		
2	0.06	14	0.14		

Total				3,050	26.62
Mean ($n = 62$)				49.1935	0.42935

First, the paired measurements are plotted on graph paper to determine whether there is any visual evidence of a relationship between the two variables. The resulting scatter diagram (Fig. 2-2) does indicate a general linear trend of direct correlation, and so it was decided to fit an equation of the form $\hat{Y} = a + b(X)$ to the plotted points by the method of least squares (Freese, 1967).

After selecting the model to be fitted, the next step is to calculate the corrected sums of squares and products. In the following equations, capital letters indicate uncorrected values of the variables; lowercase letters are used for the corrected values ($y = Y - \bar{Y}$).

The corrected sum of squares for Y:

$$\Sigma y^2 = \sum_{}^{n} Y^2 - \frac{\left(\sum_{}^{n} Y\right)^2}{n}$$
$$= (0.36^2 + 0.09^2 + \cdots + 0.42^2) - \frac{26.62^2}{62}$$
$$= \boxed{2.7826}$$

The corrected sum of squares for X:

$$\Sigma x^2 = \Sigma X^2 - \frac{(\Sigma X)^2}{n}$$

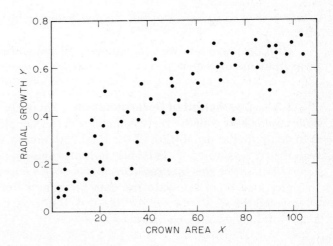

Figure 2-2 Scatter diagram of growth Y on crown area X for 62 trees.

$$= (22^2 + 6^2 + \cdots + 61^2) - \frac{3,050^2}{62}$$
$$= \boxed{59,397.6775}$$

The corrected sum of products:

$$\Sigma xy = \overset{n}{\underset{}{\Sigma}}(XY) - \frac{\left(\overset{n}{\Sigma}X\right)\left(\overset{n}{\Sigma}Y\right)}{n}$$
$$= [(22)(0.36) + (6)(0.09) + \cdots + (61)(0.42)]$$
$$- \frac{(3,050)(26.62)}{62}$$
$$= \boxed{354.1477}$$

According to the principle of least squares, the best estimates of the regression coefficients (a and b) are obtained as follows:

$$b = \frac{\Sigma xy}{\Sigma x^2} = \frac{354.1477}{59,397.6775} = 0.005962$$

$$a = \bar{Y} - b\bar{X} = 0.42935 - (0.005962)(49.1935) = 0.13606$$

Substituting these estimates in the general equation gives

$$\hat{Y} = 0.13606 + 0.005962X$$

where $\hat{Y}$ is used to indicate that we are dealing with an estimated value of Y.

With this equation, we can estimate the annual radial growth $\hat{Y}$ from measurements of crown area X.

2-34 Coefficient of Determination   There are several methods of determining how well the regression line fits the sample data. One method is to compute the proportion of the total variation in Y that is associated with the regression on X. This ratio is sometimes called the *coefficient of determination*, or the *squared correlation coefficient (r^2)*.

First, we must calculate the sum of squares due to the regression (also called the *reduction sum of squares*). Referring back to the determination of coefficient b, we have:

$$\text{Reduction SS} = \frac{(\Sigma xy)^2}{\Sigma x^2} = \frac{(354.1477)^2}{(59,397.6775)} = 2.1115$$

Next, the total variation in Y is estimated by $\Sigma y^2 = 2.7826$ (as previously calculated), and

$$\text{Coefficient of determination } (r^2) = \frac{\text{Reduction SS}}{\text{Total SS}} = \frac{2.1115}{2.7826} = 0.76$$

A common means of interpreting the r^2 value is that "76 percent of the variation in Y is associated with X. Or, in this particular example, 76 percent of the variation in radial growth can be "explained" by measurements of crown area.

2-35 Hazards of Interpretation A strong correlation between two variables (e.g., an r^2 of 0.90 or greater) implies only that the variables are closely associated. Such correlations are *not* evidence of a cause-and-effect relationship; in many instances, both quantities may be directly affected by a third element that has not been taken into consideration. For example, if prices for both pork and eggs rise at similar rates, one might find a high correlation between these two values over a period of time. However, instead of one price *causing* the other to rise, both prices are probably being pushed upward by a third factor, such as general increases in the cost of producing farm products.

Since many completely unrelated variables can be associated by "nonsense correlations," the necessity for rational thinking in data collection is of paramount importance. Before attempting to employ regression analysis, the resource manager should have sound biological reasons for associating changes in one quantity with those in another quantity. Unless reliable and representative data are collected through use of an unbiased sampling plan, regression analysis may prove to be a futile exercise.

Finally, it should be again stressed that the preceding discussion has dealt only with simple linear regression, i.e., the treatment of one dependent and one independent variable. Frequently, however, the dependent variable is related to more than one independent variable. If this relationship can be estimated by using *multiple regression* analysis, it may allow more precise predictions of the dependent variable than is possible by a simple regression. The general model for a multiple regression is

$$\hat{Y} = a + b(X_1) + c(X_2) + \cdots$$

where a, b, and c are regression coefficients that are estimated from analysis of the data. Details for handling multiple regression analysis are not treated in this chapter but may be found in most textbooks on statistical methods.

PROBLEMS

2-1 Describe an inventory procedure or measurement technique in your professional field that is likely to be (*a*) biased or (*b*) inaccurate due to lack of precision. How would you correct these deficiencies?

2-2 Give an example of two events (excluding those in games of chance) that are apparently independent of each other.

2-3 For a recently cutover area, you must decide whether to establish a new crop of trees (or other plants) by one of three methods: natural regeneration, aerial seeding, or maching-planting of two-year-old seedlings. The pay-off matrix is as follows:

Decision alternatives	Expected rain in following 60 days (mm)		
	51 +	26–50	0–25
	Relative returns (over costs) realized		
1. Natural regeneration	10	6	0
2. Aerial seeding	7	8	2
3. Plant seedlings	2	4	9

Your decision will be made under *risk*; i.e., it will be based on the amount of rain expected during the first 60 days after a chosen course of action has been taken.

First, modify the pay-off table (if necessary) to conform with local conditions. Then, on the basis of past weather records, determine the probability of precipitation for the states of nature. Finally, compute the various expected returns and make your decision on the basis of the most favorable expectation.

2-4 Draw a simple random sample of at least 30 observations from a biological population in your field of interest. Then, (*a*) place the 95 percent confidence limits on the sample mean, and (*b*) compute the total number of sample units that would be required to estimate the population mean within ±5 percent at a confidence probability of 90 percent. (*Note:* Remember to apply the finite population correction, if applicable.)

2-5 Select a local tract of land that can be subdivided into three or more strata according to vegetation, soil types, or timber volumes. Then design ground inventories to estimate some population parameter by (*a*) systematic sampling, (*b*) simple random sampling, and (*c*) an optimum allocation of field plots based on stratified random sampling. Use the *same number and size* of field plots for all three sampling designs. Compare results and relative efficiencies of the three systems.

2-6 By simple random sampling, obtain paired measurements of two variables that you believe to be linearly correlated. If a scatter diagram indicates that a straight-line relationship exists, then (*a*) fit a simple linear regression to the plotted points by the method of least squares, and (*b*) compute the coefficient of determination for the association. (*Note:*   If a linear relationship is not indicated by the scatter diagram, attempt to transform one or both variables so that the trend of plotted points becomes a linear one.)

REFERENCES

Chernoff, Herman, and Moses, Lincoln E.
1959. *Elementary decision theory.* John Wiley & Sons, Inc., New York. 364 pp., illus.

Cochran, William G.
1963. *Sampling techniques,* 2d ed. John Wiley & Sons, Inc., New York. 413 pp., illus.

Dane, C. W.
1965. Statistical decision theory and its application to forest engineering. *J. Forestry* **63**:276-279.

Davis, James B.
1968. Forest fire control decision making under conditions of uncertainty. *J. Forestry* **66**:626-631.

Freese, Frank
1967. Elementary statistical methods for foresters. *U.S. Dept. Agr. Handbook* 317, Government Printing Office, Washington, D.C. 87 pp., illus.

————

1962. Elementary forest sampling. *U.S. Dept. Agr. Handbook* 232, Government Printing Office, Washington, D.C. 91 pp.

Mendenhall, William
1971. *Introduction to probability and statistics,* 3d ed. Wadsworth Publishing Company, Inc., Belmont, CA. 466 pp., illus.

Thompson, Emmett F.
1972. Some approaches for considering uncertainty in forest investment decisions. *Virginia Poly. Inst., Pub. FWS*-1-72, pp. 9-17.

————

1968. The theory of decision under uncertainty and possible applications in forest management. *Forest Sci.* **14**:156-163.

Chapter 3

Land Measurements
And Photogrammetry

3-1 Introduction Although the resource manager will rarely be responsible for original property surveys, he may be called upon to retrace old lines, locate property boundaries, and measure land areas. To handle these tasks, the manager should become familiar with the fundamentals of land surveying, mapping, and photogrammetry. He should also have a knowledge of the systems of land subdivision found in his particular region. For those readers without previous training in plane surveying or photogrammetry, this chapter provides a concise review of elementary techniques.

Surveying is the art of making field measurements that are used to determine the lengths and directions of lines on the earth's surface. If a survey covers such a small area that the earth's curvature may be disregarded, it is termed *plane surveying*. For larger regions, where the curvature of the earth must be considered, *geodetic surveys* are required. Under most circumstances, the resource manager is concerned with plane surveying, viz., the measurement of distances and angles, the location of boundaries, and the estimation of areas. The term *photogrammetry* refers to the science of making these and other measurements on aerial photographs.

Since most of the examples in this book are presented in metric units, it would be desirable to express land measurements accordingly. However, even when SI units are adopted in the United States, it is likely that our long-established land subdivision systems will be among the last measurements to be converted. Descriptions of the U.S. Public Land Survey are therefore in English units because townships and sections are more logically tied to square chains and acres than to square meters and hectares. Tables in this chapter and in the Appendix will facilitate conversions of distances and areas to metric units; fortunately, angular measurements are essentially the same for both systems of units.

The fundamental unit of linear measurement for the survey of public lands is the Gunter's chain of 66 ft (20.12 m). The chain is divided into 100 equal parts that are known as links; each link is thus 0.66 ft, or 7.92 in., in length. Distances on all U.S. Government Land Surveys are measured in chains and links. The simple conversion from chained dimensions to acres is one reason for the continued popularity of this measurement standard. Areas expressed in square chains can be immediately converted to acres by dividing by 10. Thus a tract 1 mile square (80 chains on a side) contains 6,400 square chains, or 640 acres (Table 3-1).

DISTANCES AND ANGLES

3-2 Pacing Horizontal Distances Pacing is perhaps the most rudimentary of all techniques for determining distances in the field; nonetheless, accurate pacing is an obvious asset to the land appraiser who must determine distances without the aid of an assistant. With practice and frequent measured checks, an experienced pacer can expect to attain an accuracy of 1 part in 80 when traversing fairly level terrain.

The pace is commonly defined as the average length of two natural

Table 3-1 Conversions for Several Units of Area Measurement

Square feet	Square chains	Acres	Square miles	Square meters	Hectares	Square kilometers
4,356	1	0.1	0.000156	404.687	0.040469	0.000405
43,560	10	1	0.0015625	4,046.87	0.404687	0.004047
27,878,400	6,400	640	1	2,589,998	258.9998	2.589998
107,638.7	24.7104	2.47104	0.003861	10,000	1	0.01
10,763,867	2,471.04	247.104	0.386101	1,000,000	100	1

steps; i.e., a count is made each time the same foot touches the ground.[1] A natural walking gait is recommended because this pace can be most easily maintained under difficult terrain conditions. One should never attempt to use an artificial pace based on a fixed step length such as exactly 1 m. Experienced pacers have demonstrated that the natural step is much more reliable.

In learning to pace, a horizontal distance should be staked on level or typical terrain. This course should be paced over and over until a consistent gait has been established. Uniform pacing is difficult in mountainous terrain, because measurement of horizontal rather than slope distance is the prime objective. Steps are necessarily shortened in walking up and down steep hillsides, and special problems are created when obstructions such as deep stream channels are encountered. Thus some individual technique must be devised to compensate for such difficulties.

The inevitable shortening of the pace on sloping ground can be handled by repeating the count at certain intervals, as 1,*2, 2,* 3, 4, 5, *6, 6,* and so on. Or, if pace lengths are cut in half, counts may be restricted to every other pace. For obstructions that cannot be traversed at all (such as streams and rivers), the distance to some well-defined point ahead can be ocularly estimated; then a nonpaced detour can be made around the obstacle.

Paced distances should always be field-recorded as horizontal distances in chains or meters—not in terms of actual paces. When accurate mental counts become tedious, a reliable pacing record can be kept by a written tally or by using a hand-tally meter. The importance of regular pacing practice cannot be overstressed; without periodic checks, neither accuracy nor consistency can be expected.

3-3 Chaining Horizontal Distances   The term *chaining* refers to the operation of measuring the horizontal distance between two points. Two persons, a head chainman and a rear chainman, are needed for accurate measurement with a steel tape. On level terrain, the chain can be stretched directly on the ground. If 11 chaining pins are used, one is placed at the point of origin, and the head chainman moves ahead with 10 pins and the "zero end" of the chain. If the head chainman carries the compass, he must keep himself and the chain on the correct bearing line at all times; otherwise, it is the rear chainman's duty to keep his partner on a straight and proper course.

A good head chainman paces the length of the tape so that he can an-

---

[1]Some persons prefer to count *every* step as a pace. Advantages claimed for this technique are (1) less chance of losing count, (2) fewer problems with fractional paces, and (3) easier adjustments for slope.

ticipate when he has moved to the approximate chaining interval. When the head chainman uses his last pin, 10 tape intervals will have been covered. The rear chainman then passes the 10 pins he has collected to the head chainman for continuing the measurement. A distance of 12 chains and 82 links is recorded as 12.82 chains.

In rough terrain, where the chain is held high off the ground, plumb bobs may be used at each end to aid in proper pin placement and accurate measurement of each interval. On steep slopes, it may be necessary to "break chain," i.e., to use only short sections of the tape for holding a level line. Experienced persons can expect an accuracy of 1 part in 1,000 to 1 in 2,500 by careful chaining of horizontal distances.

Precautions must be observed in chaining to avoid loops or tangles that will result in a broken or permanently "kinked" tape. The ends of the tape should be equipped with leather thongs, and the loss of chaining pins can be minimized by tying colored plastic flagging to each. Chains should be lightly oiled occasionally to prevent rust and should be properly coiled when not in use.

The principal sources of error in chaining are (1) allowing the chain to sag instead of keeping it taut at the moment of measurement, (2) incorrect alignment, i.e., not keeping on the proper compass bearing, (3) mistakes in counting pins, and (4) reading or recording the wrong numbers.

3-4 Stadia Measurement of Horizontal Distances This technique requires a level or transit equipped with parallel cross hairs (stadia wires) and a leveling or stadia rod. Distances are measured by sighting through the instrument and observing how much of the vertically held rod appears to be included between the two horizontal cross hairs. The stadia cross hairs are usually fixed so that when the rod is 100 units of distance from the instrument, the interval between the stadia hairs as read on the level rod is one unit. For example, a reading of 1.38 on the rod would be recorded as 138 units of distance.

The accuracy of stadia measurement depends on the distance measured and the precision of the instrument. For distances up to about 100 m, experienced surveyors can expect an accuracy of about 1 part in 300 to 1 in 400. Additional details on the stadia method may be found in textbooks on plane surveying.

3-5 Nomenclature of the Compass In elemental form, a compass consists of a magnetized needle on a pivot point, enclosed in a circular housing that has been graduated in degrees. Because the earth acts as a huge magnet, compass needles in the Northern Hemisphere point in the direction of the horizontal component of the magnetic field, commonly termed *magnetic north*. If a sighting base is attached to the compass housing, it is then possible to measure the angle between the line of sight and the position of the needle. Such angles are referred to as magnetic *bearings*, or *azimuths*.

Bearings are horizontal angles that are referenced to one of the quadrants of the compass, viz., NE, SE, SW, or NW. Azimuths are comparable angles measured clockwise from due north, thus reading from 0 to 360°.[1] Relationships between bearings and azimuths are illustrated in Fig. 3-1. It will be seen that a bearing of N60°E corresponds to an aximuth of 60°, while a bearing of S60°W is the same as an azimuth of 240°. The angle formed between magnetic north and true north is called *magnetic declination*, and allowance must be made for this factor in converting magnetic bearings and azimuths to true angular readings.

3-6 Magnetic Declination Corrections may be required for either *east* or *west* declination, the former when magnetic north is east of true north and the latter when it is west of true north. Charts illustrating magnetic declination are issued periodically by the National Ocean Survey. On such maps, points having equal declination are connected by lines known as *isogons*. The line of zero declination (no corrections

----

[1]Some organizations, notably military agencies, measure azimuth angles clockwise from due south instead of due north.

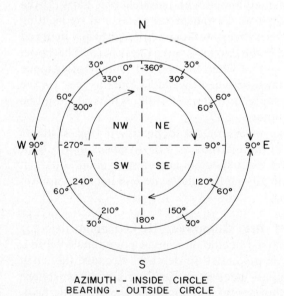

AZIMUTH - INSIDE CIRCLE
BEARING - OUTSIDE CIRCLE

Figure 3-1 Relationship of compass bearings and azimuths.

required) passing through the eastern section of the United States is called the *agonic line*. It should be noted that areas east of the agonic line have west declination, while areas west of the agonic line have east declination.

As of 1960 the agonic line was shifting westward at a rate of approximately 1 min/year. In some regions, however, the change in declination is as high as 4 to 5 min annually. It is therefore important that current declination values be used in correcting magnetic bearings. Where reliable data cannot be obtained from isogonic charts, the amount of declination can be determined by establishing a true north-south line through observations on the sun or Polaris. The magnetic bearing of this true line provides the declination for that locality. As an alternative to this approach, any existing survey line whose true bearing is known can be substituted.

3-7 Allowance for Declination In establishing or retracing property lines, angles should preferably be recorded as *true* bearings or azimuths. The simplest and most reliable technique for handling declination is to set the allowance directly on the compass itself. Thus the graduated degree circle must be rotated until the north end of the compass needle reads true north when the line of sight points in that direction. For most compasses, this requires that the graduated degree circle be turned counterclockwise for east declination and clockwise for west declination.

When there is no provision for setting the declination directly on the compass, the proper allowance can be made mentally in the field, or magnetic bearings may be recorded and corrected later in the office. For changing magnetic azimuths to true readings, east declinations are added, and west declinations are subtracted. Thus if a magnetic azimuth of 105° is recorded, and the declination is 15° east, the true azimuth would be 120°.

Changing magnetic bearings to true bearings is slightly more confusing than handling azimuths because declinations must be added in two quadrants and subtracted in the other two. The proper algebraic signs to be used in making such additions or subtractions are illustrated in Fig. 3-2.

Accordingly, if a magnetic bearing of S40°E is recorded, and the declination is 5° west, the true bearing, obtained by addition, would be S45°E. In those occasional situations where true bearings and azimuths must be converted back to magnetic readings, all algebraic signs in Fig. 3-2 should be reversed.

3-8 Use of the Compass Whether hand or staff compasses are used, care must be exercised to avoid local magnetic attractions such as wire fences, overhead cables, and iron deposits. In running a traverse,

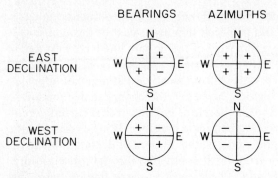

Figure 3-2 Algebraic signs for changing magnetic bearings and azimuths to true angles.

"backsights" of 180° should be taken to check all compass bearings. When such backsights fail to agree with foresights and no instrument errors can be detected, it is likely that some form of local attraction is present. Here it may be necessary to shorten or prolong the bearing line in question so that a new "turning point" outside the attraction area can be used for the compass setup. Compasses having needles immersed in liquid (dampened compasses) are generally less susceptible to local attractions than nondampened types.

Most good compasses are provided with a means of clamping the needle in a fixed position while the instrument is being transported. After each bearing is read, the needle should be tightened before moving to a new compass position; adherence to this practice will save considerable wear on the sensitive needle pivot point. To ensure accurate compass readings, novices must be cautious to see that (1) the compass is perfectly level, (2) the sights are properly aligned, (3) the needle swings freely before settling, and (4) all readings are taken from the *north end* of the needle. Hand-compass shots should not normally exceed 5 chains (or 100 m), and staff compass sights should be limited to about 10 chains (or 200 m) per setup.

COLONIAL LAND SUBDIVISION

3-9 Metes and Bounds Surveys A sizable segment of the United States, notably in the original 13 colonies, was subdivided and passed into private ownerships prior to the inauguration of a system for disposal of public lands in 1785. Many of these early land holdings were marked off and described by "metes and bounds," a procedure sometimes facetiously referred to as leaps and bounds.

The term *mete* implies an act of metering, measuring, or assigning by measure, and *bounds* refers to property boundaries or the limiting extent of an ownership. In some instances, older metes and bounds surveys may consist entirely of descriptions rather than actual measurements, e.g., "starting at a pine tree blazed on the east side, thence along a hedgerow to a granite boulder on the bank of the Wampum River, thence along the river to the intersection of Cherokee Creek . . . , etc." Fortunately, most metes and bounds descriptions are today referenced by bearings, distances, and permanent monuments. Even so, parcels of land are shaped in unusual and seemingly haphazard patterns, and a multitude of legal complexities can be encountered in attempting to establish the location of a disputed boundary along an old stone fence that disintegrated 50 years ago. Descriptions of metes and bounds surveys can ordinarily be obtained from plat books at various county court houses.

THE U.S. PUBLIC LAND SURVEY

3-10 History Most of the United States west of the Mississippi River and north of the Ohio River, plus Alabama, Mississippi, and portions of Florida have been subdivided in accordance with the U.S. Public Land Survey (Fig. 3-3). The first law governing public land surveys was enacted by Congress in 1785. That part of the Northwest Territory which later became the state of Ohio was the experimental area for the development of the rectangular system. The original intent was to establish *townships* exactly 6 miles square, followed by subdivision into 36 sections of exactly 1 mile square each. At first, no allowance was made for curvature of the earth, and numerous problems resulted. However, survey rules were revised by later acts of Congress, and the present system evolved as a culmination of these changes.

Adoption of a rectangular system marked the transition from metes and bounds surveys that prevailed in most of the colonial states to a logical and rational method for describing the public lands. Surveyors responsible for the earliest public land surveys were faced with such obstacles as crude instruments, unfavorable or dangerous field conditions, and changing survey rules. Consequently, survey lines and corners in the field were not always located with the desired precision. To eliminate litigation and costly resurveys, the original corners as established on the ground legally stand as the true corners, regardless of irregularities or inconsistencies.

3-11 The Method of Subdivision The origin of a system begins with an *initial point*, usually established by astronomical observation. Passing through and extending outward from the initial point is a true

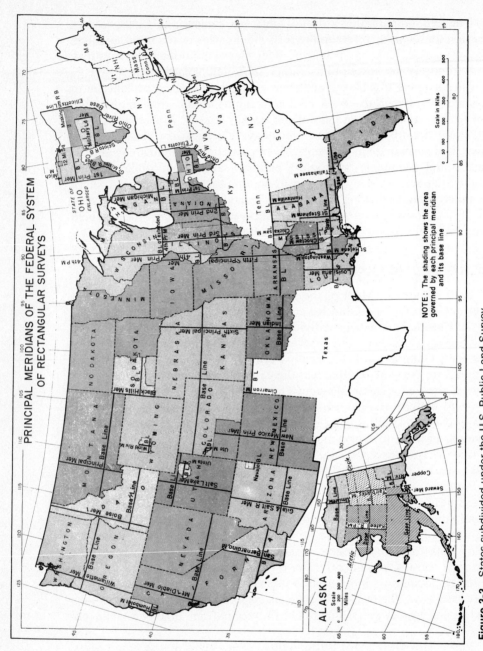

Figure 3-3 States subdivided under the U.S. Public Land Survey. (*U.S. Department of the Interior.*)

north-south line known as a *principal meridian* and a true east-west *base line* that corresponds to a parallel of latitude. These two lines constitute the main axes of a system, and there are more than 30 such systems in existence. Each principal meridian is referenced by a name or number, and the meridian is marked on the ground as a straight line. The base line is curved, being coincident with a geographic parallel. Starting at the initial point, the area to be surveyed is first divided into *tracts* approximately 24 miles square, followed by subdivision into 16 *townships* approximately 6 miles square and then into 36 sections approximately 1 mile square. An idealized system is shown in Fig. 3-4.

3-12 The 24-Mile Tracts At intervals of 24 miles north and south of the base line, *standard parallels* are extended east and west of the principal meridian. These parallels are numbered north and south from the base line, as "first standard parallel north," and so on. At 24-mile intervals along the base line and along all standard parallels, *guide meridians* are run on *true north* bearings; these lines thus correspond to geographic meridians of longitude. Each guide meridian starts from a standard corner on the base line or on a standard parallel and ends at a closing corner on the next standard parallel to the north. Standard parallels are never crossed by guide meridians. Guide meridians are numbered east and west from the principal meridian, as "first guide meridian east," and so forth.

The tracts are 24 miles wide at their southern boundaries, but because guide meridians converge, they are less than 24 miles wide at their northern boundaries. As a result, there are two sets of corners along each standard parallel. *Standard corners* refer to guide meridians north of the parallel, while *closing corners* are those less than 24 miles apart which were established by the guide meridians from the south closing on that parallel. Convergence of meridians is proportional to the distance from the principal meridian; the offset of the second guide meridian is double that of the first, and that of the third guide meridian is three times as great. Of course, actual offsets on the ground may differ from theoretical distances because of inaccuracies in surveying.

3-13 Townships The 24-mile tracts are divided into 16 townships, each roughly 6 miles square, by north-south *range lines* and east-west *township lines*. Range lines are established as true meridians at 6-mile intervals along each standard parallel and are run due north to the next standard parallel. Township lines are parallels of latitude that join township corners at intervals of 6 miles on the principal meridian, guide meridians, and range lines. Since range lines converge northward just as guide meridians do, the width of a township decreases from south to

TOWNSHIP GRID

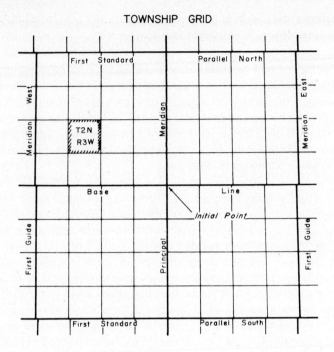

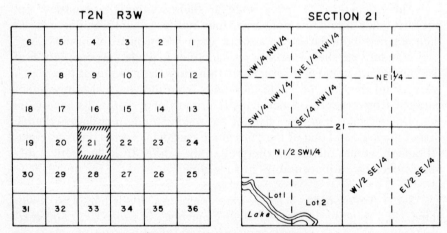

Figure 3-4 Idealized subdivision of townships and sections.

north, the shape is trapezoidal rather than square, and the area is always less than the theoretical 36 sq miles.

The survey of townships within the 24-mile tract begins with the southwest township and continues northward until the entire west range is completed; then it moves to the next range eastward and again proceeds from south to north. Townships are numbered consecutively northward and southward from the base line and eastward and westward of the principal meridian. As illustrated in Fig. 3-4, T2N, R3W denotes a township that is 6 miles north of the base line and 12 miles west of the principal meridian.

3-14 Establishment of Sections and Lots Beginning in the southeast corner of a township, sections of approximately 640 acres are formed by running lines 1 mile apart parallel to eastern range lines and 1 mile apart parallel to southern township lines. By starting in the southeastern part of the township, irregularities are thrown into the northern and western tiers of sections in each township. Survey lines are first run around section 36, then 25, 24, 13, 12, and 1. The township subdivision thus starts at the eastern boundary and proceeds from south to north, establishing one tier of sections at a time. Sections are numbered as in Fig. 3-4.

Survey corners actually established on the ground include section corners and quarter corners, the latter being set at intervals of 40 chains for subdividing the sections into 160-acre tracts. These quarter sections may later be further divided into 40-acre parcels known as *forties*. A complete land description begins with the smallest land parcel and covers each division in order on a size basis; the specific principal meridian involved is also part of the description. Thus the forty comprising the most northwesterly portion of section 21 (Fig. 3-4) would be described as $NW\frac{1}{4}$ $NW\frac{1}{4}$ S.21, T2N, R3W, 5th P. M. To derive the approximate number of acres in a subdivision, the area of the section is multiplied by the product of the fractions in the legal description. From the previous example, $\frac{1}{4} \times \frac{1}{4} \times 640 = 40$ acres.

Accumulation of irregularities in northern and western tiers of sections often results in parcels of land that have an area considerably less than the 40 or 160 acres intended. Such subdivisions may be individually numbered as *lots*. Also, navigable streams and large bodies of water encountered on survey lines are meandered by running traverses along their edges. *Meander corners* set during such surveys may result in the recognition of additional irregularly shaped *lots* that commonly range from 20 to 60 acres in size.

3-15 Survey Field Notes Complete sets of field notes describing public land surveys can be obtained from the U.S. General Land Office in Washington, D.C., and from most state capitals. Field notes are public records, and only a nominal charge is made for copying them. They include bearings and distances of all survey lines, descriptions of corners, monuments and bearings objects, and notes on topography, soil quality, and forest cover types.

Field notes are essential for locating lost or obliterated survey corners from bearings objects or "witness trees." On original surveys, such objects were identified and located by recording a bearing and distance *from the corner to the object*. As a result, lost corners may be reestablished by reversing all bearings and chaining the specified distances from witnesses or bearings objects. Specific procedures for relocating original survey lines and corners are detailed in the U.S. Department of Interior's "Manual of Instructions for the Survey of the Public Lands of the United States."

FIELD MAPS AND AREA ESTIMATES

3-16 A Closed Compass Traverse For purposes of this discussion, it is assumed that the primary objectives of a field survey are to locate the approximate boundaries of a tract and to determine the area enclosed. Where there are no ownership disputes involved, a simple closed traverse made with staff compass and steel tape will often suffice for the purposes stated. For most surveys, three persons comprise a minimum crew, and a fourth may be used to advantage. The party chief serves as a compassman and notekeeper, two others measure horizontal distances, and the fourth member handles a range pole at each compass station.

The most reliable property corner available is selected as a starting point; the traverse may be run clockwise or counterclockwise around the tract from this origin. Backsights and front sights should be taken on each line and numbered stakes driven at all compass stations. Immediately upon completion of the traverse, *interior angles* should be computed. If bearings have been properly read and recorded, the sum of all the interior angles should be equal to $(n - 2) \times 180°$, where n is the number of sides in the traverse.

After interior angles have been checked, the traverse should be plotted on graph paper at the largest convenient scale. If horizontal distances between stations have been correctly taped, the plotted traverse should approximately "close." Exact closures cannot be expected with compass traverses; errors of closure of up to 1 part in 80 are considered permissible. Greater errors may require that field work be repeated.

With the traverse plotted to scale on graph paper, the enclosed area can be determined graphically. For example, at a scale of 50 m/cm, each square centimeter would represent 2,500 m², or 0.25 ha. The total area is found by counting all such squares that are included in the traverse. Where less than one-half of a square is inside the tract boundary, it is ignored; squares bisected by an exterior line are alternately counted and disregarded. The method is fast and reasonably accurate when traverses are plotted at large scales and when finely subdivided graph paper is employed.

3-17   Plane-Table Surveying   This is a method of field mapping where field work and plotting are done simultaneously. A plane table is merely a drawing board mounted on a tripod so that it can be leveled and directionally oriented. Drawing paper is attached to the top of the board for field mapping. Sightings are made with an instrument termed an *alidade*, which may be moved from place to place on the table. A simple, open-sight alidade consists of two sighting vanes attached to each end of a metal ruler 15 to 25 cm long. When the alidade is pointed toward an object, the *direction* of the line of sight is drawn on the paper by marking along the linear base of the instrument. Relative positions of objects are located by intersections of sightings made from two or more plane-table setups or field positions.

To illustrate the use of the plane table for mapping in a field boundary, assume that points *A* and *B* are located on the ground at a known distance apart. The points are transferred to scale on the paper attached to the plane table. The table is first set up over point *A* and oriented so that the line of sight along line *AB* on the paper corresponds to the line from *A* to *B* on the ground. Alidade sights are then taken to the corners of the field, and the appropriate lines or rays are drawn in lightly on the paper. The table is then set up over point *B* and oriented with respect to point *A*. Sights are again taken on the corners of the field and rays drawn in. The intersections of corresponding rays from *A* and from *B* locate the four corners; thus the field boundaries can be drawn in between each of the corners.

The plane table is not intended for highly precise work, but good results may be obtained by careful observers. It is particularly useful for plotting indefinite details, such as roads, streams, and field boundaries. Since a plane table survey is plotted as it progresses, mistakes in recording field measurements are avoided. And since the area being mapped is always in plain view, it is easy to see what information is required. The greatest disadvantages are that plane tables are awkward to move about, and plotting work cannot be done under inclement weather conditions. Plane-table surveys can be used for area estimation, but the precision of the estimate will usually be lower than that obtained from closed compass traverses.

3-18   Dot Grids   If a piece of clear tracing material were placed over a sheet of graph paper and pin holes punched at all grid intersections, the result would be a dot grid. Thus dot grid and graphical methods of area determination are based on the same principle; dots *representing* squares or rectangular areas are merely counted in lieu of the squares themselves. The principal gain enjoyed is that fractional squares along tract boundaries are less troublesome, for the nondimensional dot determines whether or not the square is to be tallied. If an area is mapped at a scale of 100 m/cm, this is equivalent to 10,000 m^2/cm^2, or 1 ha/cm^2. Thus for a grid having 4 dots per square centimeter, each dot will represent 0.25 ha.

Dot grids are commonly used to approximate areas on vertical aerial photographs as well as on maps. If the terrain is essentially level and print scales can be accurately determined, this technique provides a quick and easy method of area estimation. However, in regions of rough topography, area measurements should be made on maps rather than directly on photographic prints.

The number of dots to be counted per square centimeter depends on the map scale employed, size of area involved, and precision desired. Grids commonly used may have from 4 to more than 100 dots per square centimeter. For tracts of less than 1,000 ha, it is generally desirable to use a dot-sampling intensity that will result in a conversion of about 4 to 10 dots per hectare. Where time permits, it is recommended that an *average* dot count be obtained by several random orientations of a grid over the same area. Each drop of the systematic grid may be regarded as a simple random sample of one; thus 10 random drops would provide $n - 1$, or 9, *df* for statistical calculations.

3-19   Planimeters   A planimeter is composed of three basic parts: a weighted polar arm of fixed length, a tracer arm hinged on the unweighted end of the polar arm, and a rolling wheel that rests on the map and to which is attached a vernier scale.

In use, the pointer of the instrument is run around the boundaries of an area in a *clockwise* direction; usually the perimeter is traced two or three times for an average reading. From the vernier scale, the area in *square centimeters* (or other units) is read directly and converted to desired area units on the basis of the map scale. Prolonged use of the planimeter is somewhat tedious, and a steady hand is essential for tracing irregular tract boundaries.

It is often useful to check planimeter estimates of area by use of dot grids, and vice versa. Relative accuracy of the two methods can be approximated by measuring a few tracts of known area. Since individual preferences vary, it may also be informative to compare the *time* required for each estimation technique.

3-20 Topographic Maps Topographic quadrangle maps have been prepared for sizable areas of the United States by various governmental agencies. Persons concerned with land surveying often find such maps useful in retracing ownership lines, planning inventories, and estimating areas. Current indexes showing map coverage available in each of the 50 states may be obtained free by writing to:

Map Information Office
U.S. Department of the Interior
Geological Survey
Reston, VA   22092

When available, topographic quadrangle sheets at a scale of 1:24,000 usually provide the greatest amount of detail. For areas west of the Mississippi River, including all of Louisiana and Minnesota, maps are available from:

U.S. Geological Survey
Distribution Section
Federal Center
Denver, CO   80225

For areas east of the Mississippi River, including Puerto Rico and the Virgin Islands, orders should be placed at this address:

U.S. Geological Survey
Distribution Section
Washington, D.C.   20242

Maps of Hawaii may be ordered at either address. Mail orders must be accompanied by payment in advance. Other sources of topographic quadrangle maps are the Tennessee Valley Authority, Maps and Surveys Branch, Chattanooga, Tennessee; the Mississippi River Commission, U.S. Army Corps of Engineers, Vicksburg, Mississippi; and the National Ocean Survey, U.S. Department of Commerce, Washington, D.C.

The national topographic map series includes quadrangles and other map series published by the Geological Survey. A map series is a family of maps conforming to the same specifications or having some common unifying characteristic such as scale. Adjacent maps of the same quadrangle series can generally be combined to form a single large map. The principal map series and their essential characteristics are:

Map series	Scale	Standard quadrangle size (latitude-longtitude)
$7\frac{1}{2}$ min	1:24,000	$7\frac{1}{2} \times 7\frac{1}{2}$ min
Puerto Rico $7\frac{1}{2}$ min	1:20,000	$7\frac{1}{2} \times 7\frac{1}{2}$ min
15 min	1:62,500	15×15 min
Alaska 1:63,360	1:63,360	16×20 to 36 min
U.S. 1:250,000	1:250,000	$1 \times 2°$
U.S. 1:1,000,000	1:1,000,000	$4 \times 6°$

Maps of Alaska and Hawaii may vary from the foregoing standards. The first all-metric topographic maps published by the Geological Survey cover portions of Alaska. Map scale has been set at 1:25,000 and contour intervals are 5, 10, or 20 m. Distances, spot elevations, and similar data are shown in both metric and English units.

PHOTOGRAMMETRY

3-21 Types of Aerial Photographs As a general rule, resource managers are primarily concerned with *vertical photographs*, i.e., those taken with an aerial camera pointed straight down toward the earth's surface. Consecutive exposures in each flight line are overlapped about 60 percent to allow three-dimensional study with a stereoscope. Although few (if any) aerial photographs are truly vertical views, they are usually presumed to be vertical when exposures are tilted no more than 3°. Unless otherwise specified, the terms *photo* and *photograph* as used in this book will denote vertical aerial photographs.

Oblique photographs are exposures made with the camera axis pointed at an angle between the vertical and the horizon. Although obliques are useful for panoramic views, they are not easily adapted to stereoscopic study; hence they are seldom used for inventory purposes.

Mosaics are assembled by cutting, matching, and pasting together portions of individual vertical exposures; the result is a large photograph that appears to be a single print. Controlled mosaics, i.e., those compiled at a uniform scale from ground reference points, provide good map approximations. Since controlled mosaics are quite expensive and cannot be viewed three-dimensionally, their use by resource managers is limited.

3-22 Aligning Prints for Stereoscopic Study Photographic flights are planned so that prints will overlap about 60 percent of their width in the line of flight and about 30 percent between flight strips. For effective stereoviewing, prints must be trimmed to the nominal 23 × 23 cm size, preserving the four fiducial marks at the midpoint of each of the edges. The principal point PP is located by the intersection of lines drawn from opposite sets of fiducial marks. The conjugate principal points (CPPs), or points that correspond to PPs of adjacent photos, are located by stereoscopic transfer from overlapping prints. Each photo thus has one PP and two CPPs, except that prints at the ends of flight lines have only one CPP.

To align the photographs for steroscopic study, a print is selected and fastened down with shadows toward the viewer. The adjacent photo is placed with its CPP about 5.5 cm from the corresponding PP on the first photo. With flight lines superimposed, the second photo is positioned. A lens stereoscope is placed with its long axis parallel to the flight line and with the lenses over corresponding photo images. In this way an overlapping strip about 5.5 cm wide and 23 cm long can be viewed by moving the stereoscope up and down the overlap area (Fig. 3-5).

Emphasis in this section is on photo-scale determinations and elementary measurements. In subsequent chapters, the use of aerial photographs for estimating timber volumes and classifying vegetation is discussed. Readers interested in a more comprehensive coverage of photogrammetric methods should consult the references cited.

3-23 Determining Photographic Scales The vertical aerial photograph presents a true record of angles, but measures of horizontal distances vary widely with changes in ground elevations and flight altitudes. The nominal scale (as 1:20,000) is representative only of the datum, an imaginary plane passing through a specified ground elevation above sea level. Calculation of the average photo scale will increase the accuracy of subsequent photo measurements.

Aerial cameras in common use have focal lengths of 85 to 610 mm. This information, coupled with the altitude of the aircraft above ground datum, makes it possible to determine the representative fraction RF, or natural scale:

$$RF = \frac{\text{focal length (m)}}{\text{flying height above ground (m)}}$$

The exact height of the aircraft is rarely known to the interpreter, however, and photo scale is more often calculated by this proportion:

$$RF = \frac{\text{photographic distance between two points (m)}}{\text{ground or map distance between same points (m)}}$$

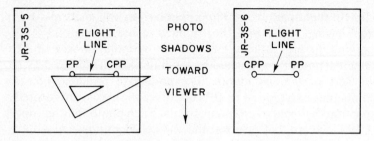

A. PRELIMINARY PHOTO ORIENTATION

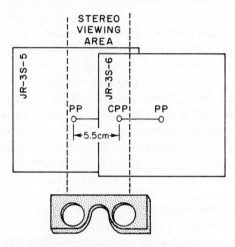

B. FINAL PHOTO ALIGNMENT

Figure 3-5 Alignment of 23 × 23 cm prints for viewing with a lens stereoscope.

As an example, the distance between two road intersections might be measured on a vertical photograph as 0.12 m. If the corresponding ground distance is measured as 1,584 m, the representative fraction would be computed as

$$RF = \frac{0.12}{1,584} = \frac{1}{13,200} \text{ or } 1:13,200$$

It is not essential to calculate the scale of every photograph in a flight strip. In hilly terrain, every third or fifth print may be used; in flat topography, every tenth or twentieth may be used. Scales of intervening photos can be obtained by interpolation.

3-24   Length and Area Estimates   The calculated photo scale of 1:13,200 may also be expressed as 132 m/cm, 0.132 km/cm, 7.576 cm/km, and so on. By using such conversions, it is possible to make quick estimates of object sizes directly on the aerial photograph. Lengths of buildings or property lines can be approximated, tree-crown diameters can be placed into size classes, and stratum areas can be estimated for applications of stratified random sampling.

For example, a river that measures 0.25 cm on the photograph would be approximately 132(0.25), or 33, m wide. And, since each square centimeter on the photo would encompass 17,424 m^2, or 1.74 ha, a pasture that measures 2.5 by 3.0 cm (7.5 cm^2) would contain 1.74(7.5), or 13.05, hectares. Although measurements made directly on photographs are sometimes less reliable than map determinations, they can be sufficiently precise for inventory planning and stratification purposes.

3-25   Using Photos for Field Travel   Although photographic flights are planned to run either north-south or east-west, few prints will be oriented precisely with the cardinal directions. If one wishes to travel cross country with the aid of a vertical photograph, it is usually necessary to first establish a line of known compass direction on the print. This reference line may be transferred to the photo from existing maps or located directly on the ground by taking the compass bearing of any straight-line feature, e.g., a road or field edge.

Once the reference line is drawn on the photograph, it should be extended so that it intersects the proposed line of cross-country travel. The angle between the two lines is then measured with a protractor to establish the bearing of the travel route. If one wishes to travel to a specific point or field plot along the proposed line, the photo scale should be determined as precisely as possible; then the travel distance can be determined directly on the print with a metric scale.

3-26   The Parallax Formula   To determine heights of objects on stereopairs of photographs, it is necessary to measure or estimate (1) absolute stereoscopic parallax and (2) differential parallax. *Absolute stereoscopic parallax*, measured parallel to the line of flight, is the algebraic difference of the distances of the two images from their respective principal points. Except in mountainous terrain, the average photo base length is ordinarily used as an approximation of absolute stereoscopic parallax. It is measured as the mean distance between the PP and CPP for an overlapping pair of photographs.

Differential parallax is the difference in the absolute stereoscopic parallax at the top and the base of the object, measured parallel to the flight line. The basic formula for conversion of parallax measurements on aerial photographs is

$$h = (H) \frac{dp}{P + dP}$$

where h = height of measured object
H = height of aircraft above ground datum
P = absolute steroscopic parallax at base of object being measured
dP = differential parallax

If object heights are to be determined in meters, the height of the aircraft must also be in meters. Absolute stereoscopic parallax and differential parallax must be expressed in the same units; ordinarily, these units will be in millimeters and hundredths.

3-27 Parallax Measuring Devices Differential parallax (dP) is usually measured stereoscopically with a parallax wedge or with a stereometer employing the "floating-mark" principle; use of the stereometer is detailed here.

The typical stereometer (or "parallax bar") has two lenses attached to a metal frame that houses a vernier and a graduated metric scale. The left lens contains a fixed reference dot; the dot on the right lens can be moved laterally by means of the vernier. The stereometer is placed over the stereoscopic image parallel to the line of flight (Fig. 3-6). The right-hand dot is moved until it fuses with the reference dot and appears as a single dot resting on the ground, and the vernier reading is recorded to the nearest 0.01 mm. Then the vernier is turned until the fused dot appears to "float" at the elevation of the top of the object. A second vernier reading is taken, and the difference between the two readings is the differential parallax (dP). This value can be substituted in the parallax formula without conversion if the absolute parallax (P) is also expressed in millimeters.

As an example, assume that the two stereometer readings for a building were 10.75 mm (ground) and 9.63 mm (top). The differential parallax is therefore 1.12 mm. If we have an average photo base (P) of 91.44 mm and an aircraft flying height of 3,600 m, the height of the building would be computed as

$$h = (3,600) \frac{1.12}{91.44 + 1.12} = 43.56 \text{ m}$$

Figure 3-6 Lens stereoscope with attached stereometer. The cylinder on the base is revolved to move the right-hand lens and create a floating dot. (*Courtesy of Zeiss-Aerotopograph.*)

Once the photographic specifications are fixed, the expected precision of height measurement is largely dependent on the stereoscopic perception of the individual interpreter. At photo scales of 1:10,000 to 1:15,000, skilled interpreters can determine the heights of clearly defined objects within ± 2 to 3 m. Measurement precision tends to improve as photo scales become larger, i.e., as aircraft heights above the ground datum decrease.

PROBLEMS

3-1 Establish a pacing course and determine (*a*) your number of paces per kilometer, and (*b*) your number of paces per chain (or other land unit).

3-2 Design and construct a simple sighting tube with parallel cross hairs for stadia measurement. Use this stadia device with a leveling rod to measure several horizontal distances; then compare results with taped measurements of the same lines.

3-3 Orient a staff compass with true north. Why are the positions of east and west reversed on the face of the compass? What is the exact magnetic declination for your locality? What was it 50 years ago? Can you locate and explain any areas of unusual "local attraction"?

3-4 Visit the nearest property records repository in your locality. Prepare a facsimile of either (*a*) a plat and description of a metes and bounds survey or (*b*) a sample page of field notes from a GLO plat book. If feasible, supplement this data with a recent aerial photograph of the same locality. Then prepare a report on land use and ownership changes that have taken place since the original land survey.

3-5 Run a closed compass traverse (or plane-table survey) around a small parcel of land. Plot the boundaries on graph paper and determine the area by the graphical method.

3-6 Delineate several tracts of known area on a map. Then make area estimates for the tracts by using several dot grid intensities and a planimeter. Compare times required and accuracies obtained for the various methods.

3-7 Using aerial photographs from your own locality, determine the average scale (*a*) as a representative fraction, (*b*) in centimeters per kilometer, and (*c*) in hectares per square centimeter. Then establish a line of known compass bearing on the photographs.

3-8 Determine the heights of 10 trees, buildings, or other objects from parallax measurements. After completion of photographic estimates, obtain ground measurements of the same objects with an Abney level or other hypsometer. Compare results, and explain reasons for differences noted.

REFERENCES

American Society of Photogrammetry
  1960. *Manual of photographic interpretation.* George Banta Company, Inc., Menasha, WI. 868 pp., illus.

Avery, T. E.
  1970. Photo-interpretation for land managers. Eastman Kodak Company, Pub. M-76, Rochester, NY. 26 pp., illus.

  _____

  1968. *Interpretation of aerial photographs,* 2d ed. Burgess Publishing Company, Minneapolis. 324 pp., illus.

Davis, R. E., Foote, F. S., and Kelly, J. W.
  1966. *Surveying: Theory and practice,* 5th ed. McGraw-Hill Book Company, New York. 1,096 pp., illus.

U.S. Department of the Army
  1964. *Elements of surveying.* Tech. Manual TM 5-232, Government Printing Office, Washington, D.C. 247 pp., illus.

U.S. Department of Commerce
  1962. Magnetic poles and the compass. Serial 726, Coast and Geodetic Survey, Government Printing Office, Washington D.C. 9 pp., illus.

U.S. Department of the Interior
  1973. *Manual of instructions for the survey of the public lands of the United States.* Government Printing Office, Washington, D.C. 333 pp., illus.

Wilson, Robert L.
  1969. *Elementary forest surveying and mapping.* O.S.U. Bookstores, Inc. Corvallis, OR. 165 pp., illus.

Part Two

Timber
Measurements

Chapter 4

Measuring Standing Trees

4-1 Abbreviations and Symbols In almost every scientific discipline, there are periodic attempts to standardize the nomenclature, symbols, and abbreviations associated with various quantities. Forestry is no exception, as evidenced by the references cited at the end of this chapter. However, those who advocate uniform symbolism rarely seem to look beyond their own narrow areas of scientific interest. As a result, symbols adopted for one discipline may have entirely different connotations in another scientific field.

The problem of abbreviations and symbols becomes particularly difficult in a book of this nature where measurement techniques from several disciplines tend to overlap, and where both English and metric units are involved. Therefore, a system of priorities must be established. For this volume, the International System of Units (SI) receives top priority, followed by common statistical notations, and McGraw-Hill technical composition standards. After these requirements are met, definitions and symbols are based on terminology recommended by the Society of American Foresters (1971) and the International Union of Forestry Research Organizations (1959).

Thus the symbol f will mean frequency and *not* form factor, g will designate grams and *not* basal area at 1.3 m, and k will refer to kilo (thousand) and *not* to form quotient. The term *cords* will not be abbreviated, because cd is the SI symbol for luminous intensity (candela). A notable exception to the foregoing rules is the use of h as a symbol for height. Since this symbol has been so widely advocated in forestry litera-ture, it has been retained even though it is also the SI designation for hour. Where hour is used, it will be spelled out.

In accordance with the publisher's standards, abbreviations and sym-bols for measurement units are used without periods, except when they spell a word (e.g., in. for inch). With these provisions in mind, the more common symbols and abbreviations employed in Part Two are as follows:

ba	basal area
baf	basal-area factor (point-sampling)
bd ft	board feet
CFI	continuous forest inventory
cu ft	cubic feet
d	tree or log diameter (at any specified point)
dbh	diameter breast height
dib	diameter inside bark
dob	diameter outside bark
f	frequency (statistical notation)
h	height
ha	hectare (10,000 m^2)
k	kilo, or thousand (used with SI units)
M	thousand (used with English units)
n	number of (statistical notation)
p	growth (increment) percent
RF	representative fraction
sp gr	specific gravity
v	volume

TREE DIAMETERS

4-2 Diameter at Breast Height   This is the most frequent tree measurement made by foresters. In the United States, dbh has been tradi-tionally defined as the stem diameter, outside bark, at a point 4.5 ft (1.37 m) above ground. In countries that use the metric system, dbh is taken 1.30 m above ground as measured from the uphill side of the stem. In this book, if dbh and ba are expressed in English units, they will represent measurements made at 4.5 ft above ground. If they are expressed in metric units, it should be assumed that measurements were made at 1.3 m above ground.

Dbh measurements are usually made with a diameter tape, tree caliper, or Biltmore stick (Fig. 4-1). Collectively, instruments employed in determining tree diameters are referred to as *dendrometers*. Where instrumentation permits, diameters are recorded in centimeters and tenths of centimeters. The most common dbh *classes* employed are those based on intervals of 2 and 4 cm.

With a diameter tape, tree circumference is the variable actually measured. The tape graduations, based on the relationship between the diameter and circumference of a circle, provide for direct readings of tree diameter. If a steel diameter tape is level and pulled taut, it is the most *consistent* method of measuring dbh. However, since tree cross sections are rarely circular, taped readings of noncircular trees will be positively biased. Thus the tape may be less accurate than caliper measurements when irregular stems are involved.

Wooden or steel tree calipers provide a quick and simple method of

Figure 4-1 Measurement of dbh with tree calipers and diameter tape.

directly measuring dbh. For ordinary cruising work, a single caliper measurement will usually suffice. Directional bias can be minimized by measuring all diameters from the tree face closest to a cruise plot center. If stem cross sections are decidedly noncircular, two caliper readings at right angles should be made and the average diameter recorded. When caliper arms are truly parallel and in correct adjustment, the instrument gives reliable measures of dbh, and it is ideal for measuring small trees. The diameter tape is preferred for bigger stems, because large calipers are bulky and awkward to handle in thick underbrush.

A modification of the conventional caliper is the diameter "fork," a two-pronged instrument that can be held in one hand while measuring small trees. One prong of the fork is movable and spring-loaded, resulting in an automatic adjustment to the sides of the stem. Diameters are read from a built-in arc-type scale on the fork (Fig. 4-2).

The Biltmore stick is a straight wooden stick specially graduated for direct readings of dbh. Based on a principle of similar triangles, the stick must be held horizontally against the tree dbh at a predetermined distance from the observer's eye. The cruiser's perspective view is compensated for by the dbh graduations; i.e., the scale units get progressively shorter as tree diameters increase. Graduations for the Biltmore stick may be computed by this formula:

$$\text{dbh graduation} = \sqrt{\frac{A d^2}{A + d}}$$

where A is the fixed distance from the eye to the stick in centimeters, and d is any selected tree diameter in centimeters.

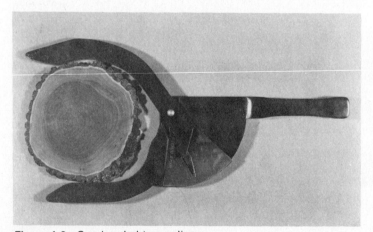

Figure 4-2 One-handed tree caliper.

Because of the difficulty of maintaining the proper distance from eye to tree, the Biltmore stick must be regarded as a rather crude measuring device. With care, diameters of small trees can be read to the nearest 2 or 3 cm, but accuracy tends to decrease for larger trees, because of the shortened intervals between graduations. The Biltmore stick is handy for occasional cruising work, but tree calipers or the diameter tape should be used for most measurements of individual trees.

4-3 Stem Diameters for Irregular Trees Whatever the type of dendrometer used, constant care must be exercised to measure trees exactly at breast height—or at a rational deviation from this point when irregular stems are encountered. For trees growing on slopes, for example, it is recommended that dbh be measured from the *uphill* side of the tree.

When swellings, bumps, depressions, or branches occur at dbh, tree diameters may be taken just above or below the irregularity at a point where it ceases to affect normal stem form. If a tree forks immediately above dbh, it is measured below the swell resulting from the double stem. Stems that fork below dbh are considered as two separate trees. Species with large buttresses are measured above the pronounced swell or "bottleneck"; such measurements are sometimes referred to as *normal diameters*.

When there is heavy snow cover on the ground or when diameters are measured under floodwater conditions, a pole should be used as a probe to locate true ground level; otherwise, the point of diameter measurement may be made too high up on the tree stem.

If successive diameter measurements are taken on the same trees (as on permanent sample plots), relative accuracy can be improved by marking the exact dbh point on each tree. And when calipers are used, measurements should be made *in the same direction* each time.

Measuring tree diameters at 3 to 5 m above ground would have some advantages over traditional dbh measurements because (1) stems are likely to have less taper or swell at such heights, and (2) cross sections are usually more nearly circular. Thus a "standard diameter" further up the tree might be more highly correlated with stem volume. For reasons of convention and ease of measurement, however, it appears likely that the concept of dbh may even outlast the board foot in the United States.

4-4 Diameters Inside Bark Although dbh measurements are made outside bark, a common objective for computing tree volume is the diameter inside bark. Reliable measures of bark thickness are essential, because the breast-height ratio of dib/dob is often applied to estimate inside-bark diameters for inaccessible points on the tree stem.

The standard measurement tool employed is called a *bark gauge* (Fig. 4-3). Since bark thickness tends to vary from one side of a tree to

Figure 4-3 Measurement of bark thickness at breast height.

another, a minimum of two readings—on opposite sides of the tree—should be taken. When dob is obtained with calipers, the two bark measurements should be made exactly where the caliper arms make contact with the tree stem. The two readings are added together and subtracted from dob to obtain dib.

Where dbh is determined with a diameter tape, bark thickness should be measured radially from the wood surface to the contour of the tape. Two or more thicknesses should be measured, depending on the eccentricity of the cross section. By this technique, bark thickness is regarded as the difference in diameters of two concentric circles, one defined by the bark surface, and the other by the interior wood surface (Mesavage, 1969).

When commercially manufactured bark gauges are not available, a fair substitute can be improvised by filing graduations on the steel bit of a sharpened screwdriver, or by using a carpenter's brace and auger bit.

4-5 Upper-Stem Diameters Out-of-reach diameters are frequently required in studies of tree form, taper, and volume. Although such diameters are best obtained by direct measurement, the use of ladders and climbing irons is time-consuming, awkward, and often hazardous. As a result, a number of diverse upper-stem dendrometers have been proposed. These include such items as calipers attached to a pole, binoculars with a mil scale in one eyepiece, telescopic stadia devices, and split-image rangefinders. A comprehensive investigation of optical dendrometers has been conducted by Grosenbaugh (1963).

Most upper-stem dendrometers are limited in usefulness because either they do not provide sufficient accuracy or they are prohibitively expensive. Some are also quite complex in operation. An ideal upper-stem dendrometer would be simple to use, portable, relatively inexpensive, accurate at tree heights of 20 to 40 m, and operable independently of distance from point of measurement. Although it may be unrealistic to expect all these attributes in a single instrument, several are incorporated in the pentaprism tree caliper (Wheeler, 1962).

In effect, the pentaprism caliper may be compared to an imaginary giant caliper that can be clamped on a tree stem at any point and from any distance without special calibration. Two pentaprisms, one fixed and the other movable, are mounted so that extended parallel lines of sight may be viewed simultaneously (Fig. 4-4). Prisms are oriented so that the right side of the tree stem is brought into coincidence with the left side, which is viewed directly. A scale is provided so that dob may be read through the fixed (left-hand) prism at the point of coincidence.

Tests of the Wheeler pentaprism caliper indicate that upper-stem diameters as high as 20 m above ground may be read to an accuracy of 0.5 to 1.0 cm. Greater accuracy may be feasible if an optical-lens system is used to replace the sighting tube on original models of the instrument.

Perhaps the most popular instrument for measuring upper-stem diameters is the Barr and Stroud optical dendrometer. Mounted on a tripod, this instrument is a split-image, coincident-type magnifying rangefinder for estimating inaccessible diameters, heights, and distances. According to the manufacturer, model FP 15 is designed to the following accuracy specifications:

Diameter: 2.5 mm for tree diameters of 3.8 to 25 cm, and 1 percent for diameters of 25 to 500 cm.
Height: 1.5 percent at all heights above 10° elevation.
Distance: 0.2 percent at 14 m, 0.6 percent at 27 m, 1.2 percent at 91 m, 2.2 percent at 183 m, and 6.8 percent at 610 m.

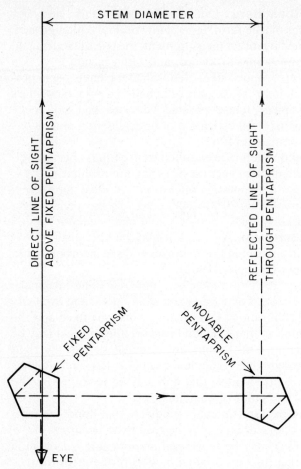

Figure 4-4 Schematic diagram of the Wheeler pentaprism tree caliper. (*Drawing by U.S. Forest Service.*)

The instrument readings are nonlinear for both distance and diameter; scale readings must therefore be transformed by using tables supplied by the manufacturer or by use of special computer programs. Such conversions can be tedious when a large number of readings are involved.

Field tests of this instrument have shown that the manufacturer's claims for accuracy can be substantiated under good sighting conditions. Extensive use of such optical dendrometers may provide the forester with a means of eliminating the conventional tree-volume table. With reliable dendrometer readings, volume growth for the upper stem may be determined on standing trees by repeated measurements at specified time intervals.

4-6 Tree-Crown Diameters Measurements of tree-crown diameters are of interest because, for many species, these measurements may be closely correlated with stem diameters. Such relationships have been verified for a number of conifers, notably those occurring in open-grown, even-aged stands. As a result, tree-volume tables based on crown diameter (in lieu of dbh) can be constructed for use with aerial photographs (Fig. 4-5).

Crown diameters may be measured either on the ground or on aerial photographs. The difference in perspective afforded by the two measurement techniques can lead to varying results, even for the same trees. If the crowns are imaged on small-scale photographs, for example, only that part of the diameter visible from above is measured; narrow, single branches and irregular crown perimeters may not be resolved by the photographic system. Therefore, photo-measured crown diameters are sometimes smaller than crown measurements made on the ground.

If an aerial volume table is based on photo measurements of tree crowns, the biases and/or errors of the interpreter are incorporated into the table. This will be acceptable, provided other interpreters with different biases do not have to use the same table. If ground measurements of crown diameters are used instead, each interpreter first measures a group of "test trees" to establish an individual photo/ground adjustment ratio. Such tables can then be utilized by large numbers of interpreters.

The assessment of crown diameter is a simple linear measure. On the ground, two persons with steel tape and plumb bobs align themselves at opposite edges of the tree crown by using a vertical sighting device such as a periscope. Two or more diameter measurements are taken for each tree. Very small individual branches and minor crown irregularities are usually ignored. The nearer the widest part of the crown is to ground

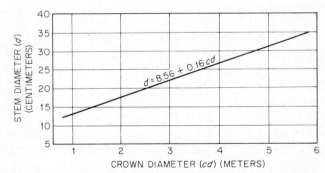

Figure 4-5 A simple linear regression illustrating the relationship between stem diameters and crown diameters for *Pinus radiata*. Based on measurements of 304 trees near Rotorua, New Zealand.

level, the more accurate the resulting measurement. As a rule, field-measured crown diameters should be recorded to 0.1 m.

Various linear scales, tube magnifiers, and "wedges" are available for measuring crown diameters on aerial photographs. Careful observers can measure within ±0.1 mm, and so accuracy is dependent on image scale, film resolution, and individual ability. Care must be exercised to avoid the inclusion of crown shadows as part of the measurement. It has been observed that most airphoto measurements tend to improve as one changes from paper prints to black-and-white film diapositives to color transparencies. Improvements are partially due to higher resolution, and with color transparencies because of better contrast between tree images and backgrounds.

TREE HEIGHTS

4-7 Height-Measurement Principles The heights of trees less than 10 to 15 m tall may be determined directly with lightweight, telescoping measuring poles. For taller trees, heights are usually estimated indirectly with instruments that are collectively known as *hypsometers*. Many types of height-measuring devices have been evolved, but only a few have gained wide acceptance by foresters. The trigonometric principle most frequently embodied in hypsometers is illustrated in Fig. 4-6. The observer locates himself at a fixed horizontal distance from the base of the tree, such as 30 m. Tangents of angles to the top and base of the tree are multiplied by horizontal distance to derive the height of each measured section of the stem. The Abney level and several

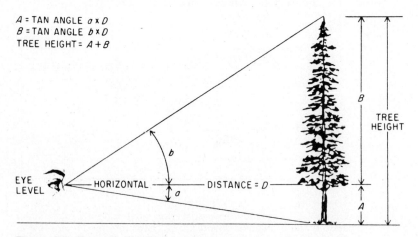

Figure 4-6 Principle of height measurement with the Abney level.

clinometers operate on this principle, yielding height readings directly in meters at fixed horizontal distances from the tree.

When an instrument such as the Abney level is used on gentle terrain, a level line of sight from the observer's eye will usually intercept the tree stem somewhere between stump height and the tree top. As a result, angular readings to the base and the top of the tree will appear on *opposite* sides of the zero point on the graduated instrument scale. In such instances, the two readings must be *added* together to obtain the desired height value.

In mountainous terrain, the observer's hypsometer position may be below the base of the tree or occasionally above the desired upper point of measurement. If a level line of sight from the observer fails to intercept the tree stem, both angular readings will then appear on the *same side* of the instrument zero point. Tree height is derived by taking the *difference* between the two readings. Heights are recorded in meters and tenths of meters.

The *Merritt hypsometer* embodies a different principle of height measurement. Based on similar triangles, this linear scale is often imprinted on one face of a Biltmore stick. It is commonly used for estimating merchantable rather than total heights, and graduations are based on log and half-log intervals. The hypsometer is positioned at a fixed distance from the eye, and the observer must stand a specified distance from the tree. In use, the Merritt hypsometer is held vertically, with the lower end of the stick on a line of sight to stump height. With the stick held firm, the observer then glances up to note the log height at the desired point on the upper stem. Improvised rules may be calibrated for any desired arm reach and specified distance by this relationship:

$$\frac{\text{Arm reach}}{\text{Distance from tree}} = \frac{\text{scale interval}}{\text{log height}}$$

The foregoing ratio is solved to determine the scale interval, and this distance is uniformly marked off on a straight rule to define the desired log-height spacings. The Merritt hypsometer is a useful aid for estimating tree heights by log intervals, but it is not reliable enough for precise work.

4-8 Total versus Merchantable Heights Total tree height is the linear distance from ground level to the upper tip of the tree crown. The tip of the crown is easily defined when trees have conical shapes, but it may not be readily discernible for deciduous trees having irregular or round-topped crowns. Thus the measurement of total height is more applicable to coniferous trees having *excurrent* branching characteristics than to broad-leaved deciduous trees with *deliquescent* branching patterns. Recording of total heights is preferred to merchantable lengths on permanent sample plots when tree-growth measurements are based on periodic remeasurements of the same trees. Here, measurement of the entire stem is likely to be more objective and less subject to errors of judgment than heights measured to an ocularly selected merchantable top. In regions where trees more than 50 m tall occur in dense stands, it may be virtually impossible to view both the crown tip and base of the tree from a single ground observation point. In such instances, tree tallies by merchantable lengths may provide the only practical alternative.

Merchantable tree height refers to the usable portion of the tree stem, i.e., the part for which volume is computed or the section expected to be utilized in a commercial logging operation. For smooth, straight stems, merchantable height may be simply defined as the length from an assumed stump height to an arbitrarily fixed upper-stem diameter. Exact location of the upper diameter limit may require considerable proficiency in ocular estimation, perhaps including occasional checks with an upper-stem dendrometer.

When upper limits of stem merchantability are not dictated by branches, crook, or defect, minimum top diameters may be chosen as a percentage of dbh. With sawtimber-sized trees, for example, minimum top diameters may be set at approximately 60 percent of dbh for small trees, 50 percent of dbh for medium-sized trees, and 40 percent of dbh for large trees. This procedure, more often applied to conifers than to hardwoods, rationally presumes that the larger the dbh, the rougher the upper stem of a tree. Thus top-log scaling diameters will be larger for mature or old-growth trees than for smaller, second-growth stems. When merchantable heights are tallied for inventory purposes, minimum top diameters must be selected in accordance with the particular volume table to be used. Failure to observe this precaution may result in inaccurate estimates of individual tree volume.

4-9 Accuracy of Height Measurements Accurate height measurements can be obtained only if the base and top of the tree are clearly discernible and if the tree does not lean more than 3 or 4°. As a rule, conifers with pyramidal tops are more accurately measured than round-topped trees that have an indefinite crown apex. In the latter case, the observer's line of sight is apt to follow along the side of the crown and result in a positive measurement error.

Systematic errors occur when measuring trees that lean toward or away from the observer; heights should therefore be measured at right angles to the direction of lean to minimize errors. For hypsometers that require a fixed horizontal measure from tree to observer, distances should be taped rather than paced. Most hypsometers yield best results when the observer stands at a distance equal to or greater than tree height. Few instruments are reliable for reading vertical angles that exceed 45°. Accidental errors made by the observer can be detected only by repeated measurements of the same trees.

In the hands of a careful observer, hypsometers such as the Abney level will provide readings within 2 to 5 percent of true heights for trees up to about 30 m tall. As an illustration, 304 radiata pines ranging from about 12 to 25 m tall were selected for a measurement test near Rotorua, New Zealand. Total tree heights were first determined by a land surveyor using a theodolite; these measurements were regarded as absolute values for purposes of the comparative test. Later, the same heights were independently measured by a forester using an Abney level.

In the tabulation that follows, plus-or-minus deviations from the theodolite readings are shown in units of 0.3 m. It can be seen that 75 percent of the Abney readings were within ±0.3 m of the theodolite values and over 90 percent were within ±0.6 m. Since 155 of the deviations were positive and 149 were negative, it would appear that no systematic biases accompanied the measurements.

Deviation (m)	Number of trees	% of total	Cumulative %
±0.0	103	34	33.9
±0.3	125	41	75.0
±0.6	55	18	93.1
±0.9	13	4	97.4
±1.2	5	2	99.0
±1.5	3	1	100.0
Total	304	100	

4-10 Tree Tallies It is essential that neat, concise, and accurate records be maintained when trees are measured and tallied in the field. Foresters have generally adopted the dot-dash system for indicating the number of trees tallied. The first four tallies are made by forming a small square with four pencil dots; the next four tallies are indicated by drawing successive lines between the dots to make a completed square, and the ninth and tenth tallies are denoted by diagonals placed within the square (Fig. 4-7).

Field tallies should always be made in pencil, because inked recordings tend to smear and become illegible when record sheets get wet.

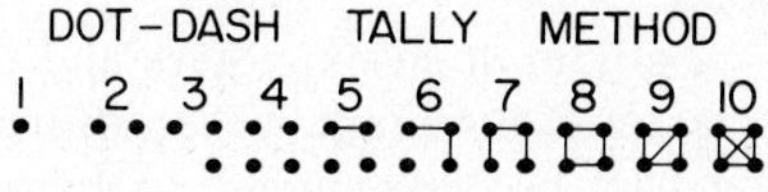

DOT–DASH   TALLY   METHOD

Figure 4-7 Dot-dash tally method.

Erasures can be avoided by circling erroneous tallies; partial erasures often result in confusion and lead to later errors in office computations, particularly when several different persons are required to decipher field tabulations. Tally sheets, including pertinent locational headings, should be filled out completely *in the field*—not several hours later back at headquarters. Organization is just as important in field record keeping as it is in office bookkeeping.

TREE FORM

4-11 Form Quotients Because trees taper, often irregularly, from stump to top, it is sometimes necessary to make an evaluation of stem form in the construction or application of tree-volume tables. The rate of tree taper varies not only by species but also by age, dbh, and tree height.

A *form quotient* is the ratio of some upper-stem diameter to dbh. The value is always less than unity and is usually expressed as a percentage. Higher form quotients indicate lower rates of stem taper and correspondingly greater tree volumes. For a given species, form quotients are lowest for open-grown trees with long live crowns and highest for forest-grown trees with relatively short crowns. Thus for given soil and site conditions, stand density has an indirect effect on tree-taper rates. The primary expression of form that has been used in the United States is known as *Girard form class*.

4-12 Girard Form Class This form quotient is computed as the ratio between stem diameter, *inside bark*, at the top of the first 5-m or 10-m (16- or 32-ft) log and dbh, *outside bark*. As an example, a tree with a first-log scaling diameter of 40 cm and a dbh of 50 cm has a Girard form class of 40/50 = 0.80, or 80 percent (Fig. 4-8).

Sawtimber-volume tables based on Girard form class assume that trees having the same diameter and merchantable height will have similar, though not necessarily identical, rates of taper in the sawlog portion *above the first log*. It is thereby implied that all volume differences in trees of the same diameter and merchantable height may be attributed largely to taper variations occurring *in the first log*. Girard form-class tables are *composite* volume tables; i.e., they are compiled independently of tree species and are applicable to both coniferous and broad-leaved trees.

Upper-stem diameters and bark thicknesses are best determined by direct measurement. When this is not feasible, dob at the top of the first log can be determined with an optical dendrometer, and the corre-

Figure 4-8 The points of diameter measurement for determining Girard form class are shown by tree bands at dbh and at the top of the first 16-ft (5-m) log. This ponderosa pine has a form class of 82 and a total height of 69 ft (21 m).

sponding dib computed from a breast-height ratio of dib/dob. Or, the form class can be ocularly estimated by using a simple sighting device such as that suggested by Wiant (1972). When applying Girard form-class values, the difference between one class and another (e.g., 79 versus 80) amounts to approximately 3 percent in terms of merchantable tree volume.

4-13   Taper Functions   If a series of diameter measurements is taken at intervals along the entire bole, average taper rates may be derived for groups of trees characterized by a particular shape or form category. Such tabulations are referred to as *taper tables*. These tables may be constructed by complete stem analyses of felled trees or from optical dendrometer readings of standing trees. With such information, taper curves may be defined for trees of any size, thus permitting the calculation of tree volumes for any degree of stem utilization.

A number of attempts have been made to derive rates of stem taper for various species by means of mathematical functions. Although no universal expression for taper curves has been adopted, Munro[1] has shown that for certain coniferous species, upper-stem diameters (dib) can be reliably predicted from this parabolic function:

$$\frac{(\text{dib})^2}{(\text{dbh})^2} = a + b\,\frac{h}{h_t} + c\,\frac{h^2}{h_t^2}$$

and

$$\text{dib} = \text{dbh}\,\sqrt{a + b\,\frac{h}{h_t} + c\,\frac{h^2}{h_t^2}}$$

where *dib* is estimated at any given height (h) above ground

h_t = total tree height

$a, b, c,$ = regression coefficients

By use of this function, it may be possible to estimate upper-stem dib within ± 2 to 4 cm.

TREE AGE

4-14   Definitions   The age of a tree is defined as the elapsed time since germination of the seed or the time since the budding of the sprout or cutting from which the tree developed. The age of a plantation is commonly taken from the year it was formed, i.e., exclusive of the age of the nursery stock that may have been planted.

The terms *even-aged* and *uneven-aged* are often applied to forest stands; therefore, it is appropriate to define these expressions. *Even-aged stands* are those in which tree ages do not differ by more than 10 to 20 years. In stands where the harvesting or rotation age is 100 years or more,

[1]Munro, D. D. 1968. Methods for describing distribution of soundwood in mature western hemlock trees. Univ. of British Columbia, Ph.D. thesis, 188 pp.

however, age differences up to 30 percent of the rotation age may be allowed (Society of American Foresters, 1971).

Uneven-aged stands are those where age differences exceed the stated limits or where three or more age classes are represented. *All-aged stands* are rarities that are virtually nonexistent. In theory, they include trees of all ages from minute seedlings to the harvest or rotation age.

The selection of sample trees for age and site index determinations in even-aged stands requires an evaluation of relative dominance or crown levels for various trees. Four crown classes are recognized:

1 *Dominant.* Trees with crowns extending above the general level of the crown cover and receiving full light from above and partly from the side; larger than the average trees in the stand, with crowns well developed but possibly somewhat crowded on the sides.

2 *Codominant.* Trees with crowns forming the general level of the crown cover and receiving full light from above, but comparatively little from the sides; usually with medium-sized crowns more or less crowded on the sides.

3 *Intermediate.* Trees shorter than those in the two preceding classes, but with crowns either below or extending into the crown cover formed by codominant and dominant trees, receiving little direct light from above and none from the sides; usually with small crowns considerably crowded on the sides.

4 *Overtopped.* Trees with crowns entirely below the general level of the crown cover, receiving no direct light either from above or from the sides.

4-15 Age from Annual Rings Many tree species found in northern temperate zones grow in diameter by adding a single and distinctive layer of wood each year. The formation of this layer starts at the beginning of the growing season and continues well through it. Earlywood (or springwood) is more porous and lighter in color than latewood (or summerwood). The combination of one springwood and one summerwood band comprises a year's growth. On a stem cross section, these bands appear as a series of concentric rings. Thus a count of the number of rings gives the age of a tree at the point where the count is made; a ring count made on the cross section at ground level provides the total age of the tree.

If the annual ring count is made on a stump cross section or higher up on the stem, the count provides the age of the tree from that point upward. It is therefore necessary to add the number of years required for the tree to attain the height of measurement to derive total tree age.

Although the most reliable ring counts are made on complete cross sections, it is obvious that except on logging operations, this method involves destructive sampling. Ages of standing trees are therefore determined by extracting a radial core of wood with an instrument called an *increment borer*. The hollow auger of the increment borer is pressed against the standing tree (usually at dbh) and turned until the screw bit reaches the center of the tree. A core of wood is forced into the hollow auger; the borer is then given a reverse turn to snap the core loose and permit its removal with a special extractor. The number of annual rings on the core gives the age of the tree from the point of the boring upward (Fig. 4-9).

The reliability of annual ring counts depends on the species and the environmental conditions under which a particular tree may be growing. Fast-growing coniferous species in northern temperate zones usually provide the easiest counts. Difficulties are encountered when there is little contrast between springwood and summerwood, as in the case of some diffuse-porous, deciduous broad-leaved species.

Trees growing under adverse environmental conditions may produce extremely narrow or almost nonexistent rings that are difficult to count except on sanded cores or cross sections. A catastrophe such as an extended drought or tree defoliation by insects, followed by favorable growth conditions, can lead to the formation of *false rings*. Such rings, which often display an incomplete circumference, may be distinguishable

Figure 4-9 Extraction of a core of wood with an increment borer (left) and measurement of the core (right). Annual rings are clearly discernible in the right-hand view. (*U.S. Forest Service photographs.*)

only when cross sections are available for analysis. Other anomalies in annual ring sequences are discussed in Chap. 15, Dendrochronology.

4-16 Age without Annual Rings In many forest regions of the world (e.g., Australia, New Zealand, and numerous other countries in tropical or southern temperate zones), tree growth is generally *not* characterized by annual rings. Annual rings are usually absent in tropical conifers and in diffuse-porous, evergreen broad-leaved species, unless they are growing in subalpine or alpine conditions. Therefore, except where plantations are established, it may only be possible to approximate individual tree ages.

For a limited number of species around the world, e.g., *Pinus strobus*, the age of young trees may be estimated from branch whorls. The seasonal height growth of the tree begins with the bursting of the terminal bud, which lengthens to form the leader. At the base of the leader, a circle of branchlets grow out at the same time, thus marking the height of the tree as it was before the season's growth started. The following year, the process is repeated, and so on. A count of these branch whorls will give the approximate age of the tree. For some species, 2 to 4 years must be added to account for the early growth years when no whorls were produced.

When neither annual rings nor branch whorls can be relied upon, age determination for trees in natural stands is extremely difficult. *Relative* tree age can be roughly gauged by the relative size of the tree, shape and vigor of the crown, and texture or color of the bark. Occasionally, the age of trees in naturally regenerated even-aged stands can be closely approximated from the year of the logging operation that resulted in the establishment of the stand. In similar fashion, trees whose germination followed a catastrophic event such as a fire or hurricane can also be dated. And in a few instances, counting the annual rings of "indicator species" may help to ascertain the ages of nearby trees that do not exhibit annual rings. For example, ring counts on certain scrub species have been used to assist in determining the age of associated eucalyptus trees in Tasmania (Carron, 1968).

PROBLEMS

4-1 Number 20 standing trees of varying diameters. Ocularly estimate each dbh within 2-cm-diameter classes. Then, in order, measure diameters with (*a*) a Biltmore stick, (*b*) a diameter tape, and (*c*) calipers. Tabulate all measurements according to tree number on a single tally sheet. Using the average of two caliper readings as a standard, obtain plus-or-minus deviations for the other three diameter estimates. Discuss your findings and preferences in a brief written report.

4-2   Design and construct a one-handed tree caliper of the "fork" type.

4-3   Design and construct a simple bark gauge with metric graduations.

4-4   Construct an upper-stem dendrometer based on twin prisms, a rangefinder, or the stadia principle. Test on 10 or more trees of known dimensions.

4-5   Design and construct an instrument for measuring tree crown diameters from the ground. Obtain average crown diameters for at least 10 trees and compare with airphoto measurements of the same crowns.

4-6   Number 20 standing trees of varying total or merchantable heights. In order, obtain heights by (*a*) ocular estimation, (*b*) Merritt hypsometer, (*c*) Abney level, and (*d*) any other available clinometer. Tabulate and analyze findings as in Problem 4-1, using Abney readings as the measurement standard.

4-7   Construct a Biltmore stick and Merritt hypsometer for your own arm reach. Graduate the rule by 2-cm-diameter classes and for height intervals most commonly used in your locality.

4-8   Number 5 to 10 standing trees (preferably mature conifers), and determine for each (*a*) Girard form class and (*b*) another expression of tree form suggested by your instructor. Use an upper-stem dendrometer for obtaining out-of-reach diameters. Which form expression is most easily derived in the field and which is most commonly used in your region?

4-9   Select 50 to 100 felled trees on a logging operation and obtain dib measurements at 1-m intervals from dbh to top. Construct a taper curve for the species, or summarize average values in a taper table.

4-10 Select several eccentric tree stumps at a recent harvesting site and obtain complete tree cross sections from each. Also obtain two increment cores from each stump—one across the longer radius and one across the shorter radius. Have several persons count the rings on the cores; then compare results with stump counts. For the species evaluated, how many years must be added to stump age to obtain total tree age? Can you detect any false rings on the cross sections? Does the eccentricity of cross sections tend to be predictable; i.e., is the long axis of cross sections aligned in a fairly constant compass direction? If so, can you give possible explanations for this growth pattern?

4-11 Attempt to determine the ages of several mature trees in natural stands by methods other than annual ring counts. Prepare a brief report on the favored estimation technique for a species in your locality.

REFERENCES

Anonymous
1973. Conversation in a mensuration lab. *J. Forestry* **71**:498-500.

Avery, T. E., and Canning, James
1973. Tree measurements on large-scale aerial photographs. *New Zealand J. Forestry* **18(2)**: 252-264, illus.

Brickell, James E.
1970. More on diameter tape and calipers. *J. Forestry* **68**:169-170.

Carron, L. T.
1968. *An outline of forest mensuration.* Australian National University Press, Canberra, A.C.T. 224 pp., illus.

Grosenbaugh, L. R.
1963. Optical dendrometers for out-of-reach diameters: A conspectus and some new theory. *Forest sci. Monograph* 4. 47 pp., illus.

International Union of Forestry Research Organizations
1959. The standardization of symbols in forest mensuration. Reprinted in 1965 as Tech. bul. 15, Univ. of Maine, Orono, ME. 32 pp.

Jackson, M. T., and Petty, R. O.
1973. A simple optical device for measuring vertical projection of tree crowns. *Forest Sci.* **19:**60-62, illus.

Kozlowski, T. T.
1971. *Growth and development of trees.* Vol. II: Cambial growth, root growth, and reproductive growth. Academic Press, Inc., New York. 514 pp., illus.

McGraw-Hill Book Company
1966. Technical composition standards. McGraw-Hill Book Company, New York. 48 pp.

Mesavage, Clement
1969. New Barr and Stroud dendrometer, model FP 15. *J. Forestry* **67:**40-41, illus.

1969. Measuring bark thickness. *J. Forestry* **67:**753-754, illus.

Roberts, Edward G.
1968. Standardization of symbols in forest mensuration. *J. Forestry* **66:**494.

Society of American Foresters
1971. *Terminology of forest science, technology, practice and products.* W. Heffer and Sons, Ltd., Cambridge, England. 349 pp., illus.

Wheeler, P. R.
1962. Penta prism caliper for upper-stem diameter measurements. *J. Forestry* **60:**877-878, illus.

Wiant, Harry V.
1972. Form class estimates — a simple guide. *J. Forestry* **70:**421-422, illus.

Chapter 5

Tree and Stand Volumes

5-1 Sectional and Basal Areas The determination of cross-sectional areas and volumes for geometric solids is basic to the derivation of tree volumes. Although trees are rarely circular in form, they are commonly *presumed* to be circular for purposes of computing sectional areas. Therefore, areas are derived as follows:

$$\text{Area} = \frac{\pi d^2}{4} = 0.7854 d^2$$

When d is measured in centimeters, the area will be in square centimeters. However, it is customary to express cross-sectional areas in square meters, even though diameters are measured in centimeters. Since there are $10,000 \text{ cm}^2/\text{m}^2$, the relationship is therefore modified to read:

$$\text{Area (m}^2) = 0.00007854 d^2$$

For a cross section having a diameter of 40 cm, the area would be

$0.00007854(40)^2 = 0.1257$ m². If this diameter were taken from a cylinder 10 m long, the cubic volume would be $0.1257(10) = 1.257$ m³. When tree cross-sectional areas are computed for dbh measurements, the resulting values are know as *basal areas*. The basal area for an entire stand of trees is usually expressed in square meters per hectare.

5-2 Sectional Volumes If tree stems were cylinders, cubic volumes would be derived by merely multiplying cross-sectional area times length. However, because of taper, only very short sections can be regarded as cylindrical. Still, there are several common geometric solids from which truncated sections can be extracted to approximate various portions of tree stems. Volumes of these solids of revolution are computed as follows:

Name of solid	Volume computation
Paraboloid	Area/2 × length
Conoid	Area/3 × length
Neiloid	Area/4 × length

As a rule, trees approximate the shape of truncated neiloids while the effects of butt swell are apparent. Logs from middle sections of tree stems are similar to truncated conoids, while upper logs approach the form of paraboloids. From the foregoing, it can be generalized that tree shape resembles (1) neiloid when taper tends to decrease, (2) a conoid when taper is relatively constant, and (3) a paraboloid when taper tends to increase.

Cubic volumes for all solids of revolution are computed from the product of their *average* cross-sectional area and length. Thus the principal problem is that of accurately determining the elusive average cross section. Three common formulas in use are

Huber's: Cubic volume $= B_{1/2}(L)$

Smalian's: Cubic volume $= \dfrac{(B + b)}{2}L$

Newton's: Cubic volume $= \dfrac{(B + 4B_{1/2} + b)}{6}L$

where $B_{1/2} =$ cross-sectional area at log midpoint
$B =$ cross-sectional area at large end of log
$b =$ cross-sectional area at small end of log
$L =$ log length

Areas and volumes are computed inside bark. Huber's formula assumes that the average cross-sectional area is found at the midpoint of the log; unfortunately, this is not always true. The formula is regarded as intermediate in accuracy, but its use is limited because (1) bark measurements or empirical bark deductions are required to obtain mid-diameters inside bark and (2) the midpoints of logs in piles or ricks are often inaccessible and cannot be measured.

Smalian's formula, though requiring measurements at both ends of the log, is the easiest and least expensive to apply. It also happens to be the least accurate of the three methods, especially for butt logs having flared ends. Excessive butt swell must be allowed for by ocularly projecting a normal taper line throughout the log or by cutting flared logs into short lengths to minimize the effect of unusual taper. Otherwise, log volumes may be overestimated by application of an average cross-sectional area that is too large. Because it has neither of the disadvantages cited for Huber's formula, Smalian's method of volume computation holds the greatest promise of the three for production log scaling.

Newton's formula necessitates the measurement of logs at the midpoint and at both ends. Although it is more accurate than the other two methods, the expense incurred in application limits its use to research, experimental techniques, and checks against other cubic volume determinations. It will be noted that for cylinders, all three formulas provide identical results.

5-3 Types of Volume Tables A volume table is a tabulation that provides the average contents of standing trees of various sizes and species. Volume units most commonly employed are cubic meters, although board feet, cubic feet, or cords may be used in the United States. Volumes may be listed for the merchantable sawlog portion of the stem only, for both sawlog and pulpwood top sections, or for the entire stem including the stump.

The principal variables ordinarily associated with standing tree volumes are dbh, stem length in terms of merchantable or total height, tree form or taper, species, and locality. Tree-volume tables that are based on the single variable of dbh are called *single-entry*, or *one-variable*, *volume tables*; those that require the user to also obtain estimates of tree height and possibly form or taper are referred to in this book as *multiple-entry tables*.

Volume tables may also be classified as *species tables* or *composite tables*. In the first instance, separate tables are constructed for each important timber species or groups of species that are similar in terms of tree form. On the other hand, composite tables are intended for application to diverse species, often including both conifers and hardwoods. To compensate for inherent differences in stem taper and volume between various species groups, provision is usually made for additionally measuring tree form, or correction factors are developed for various species. Otherwise, composite tables will overestimate volumes for some trees while significantly underestimating volumes of others.

The main disadvantage of species tables is the large number of species encountered in most regions. When it is not feasible to construct separate tables for each species, those of similar taper and shape must be grouped together within specified localities. To avoid such difficulties, composite tables utilizing some measurement of tree form in lieu of species differentiation have been adopted in several regions.

SINGLE-ENTRY VOLUME TABLES

5-4 Introduction Volume tables based on the single variable of dbh may be constructed from existing multiple-entry volume tables or from the scaled measure of felled trees. Such tables are particularly useful for quick timber inventories because height and form estimates are not required and trees can be tallied by species and dbh only. Elimination of height and form also tends to assure greater uniformity in volume estimates, particularly when two or more field parties are working in the same project area.

Volume tables based on dbh alone are sometimes compiled for inventories of relatively small areas, but this is not an essential condition; in some instances, these tables may be applicable over large regions. The exact number of sample measurements required depends upon characteristics of the tree species involved, variability of soil-site conditions, and the desired geographic area of application.

5-5 Construction from Felled-Tree Data This method often relies upon tree measurements obtained during a harvesting operation. Sample trees should be selected in a unbiased manner and a sufficient number of measurements made to span the desired range of dbh classes for each species involved. For each sample tree, direct measurements should be obtained of dbh, tree volume in desired units, and total tree height. The last item, though not actually needed for constructing the table, serves as a useful indication of the sites or geographic areas to which the table may be applied.

To determine the relationship between the variables, average tree volumes are plotted over average dbh, according to preselected diameter classes. Each plotted point is weighted by the number of trees represented, and a balanced freehand curve is fitted graphically to the points. The expected curve form for cubic-volume/dbh relationships is illustrated in Fig. 5-1. Tree volumes are then read from the curve for each desired dbh class and incorporated into a single-entry volume table; average total heights of sample trees may also be listed by dbh classes for information of the user.

This method of constructing a single-entry volume table works reasonably well when felled trees of representative sizes are available for measurement. However, some foresters have expressed the opinion that felled trees rarely make up a typical sample of standing trees because they represent a different population or have distinctive characteristics that influenced their volume and thus caused them to be cut. If this theory is correct and felled trees are nonrepresentative samples, volume tables derived from such data would be biased and unreliable. As an alternative, tables might be constructed from height/diameter relationships as described in the next section.

5-6   Construction from a Multiple-Entry Table   This method of deriving a volume table based on dbh presumes that a definitive height/diameter relationship exists for the species under consideration, i.e., that trees of a given diameter class tend to be of similar height and form. If this is true, all trees in a given dbh class can be logically assigned the same average volume. Height/diameter relationships can often be established for species that grow under uniform site conditions. When soils and topography are notably varied, it is usually necessary to construct tables for each broad site class encountered.

Field measurements of 50 to 100 merchantable or total heights, spanning the desired range of tree dbh classes, should be obtained from the selected project area. If the multiple-entry volume table to be used is

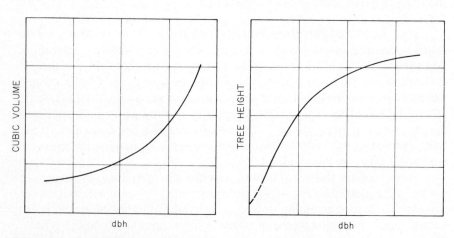

Figure 5-1 Expected curve forms for cubic-volume/dbh and height/dbh relationships.

based on merchantable heights, field measurements must be carefully taken to identical top diameters or merchantability limits.

Average tree height is computed for each diameter class; these averages are then plotted over the midpoints of the respective dbh classes. As in the preceding section, plotted points are weighted by the number of trees represented, and a freehand curve is fitted to the data. The curve should trend toward an intersection of the Y axis at a height of 1.3 m, since trees less than this height will have zero dbh. The expected curve form for height/dbh relationships is shown by Fig. 5-1.

After the balanced curve has been fitted, heights are read from the curve for each desired dbh class. These two variables are then used to interpolate average tree volumes from an appropriate multiple-entry table. The derived single-entry table consists merely of a listing of tree volumes by dbh classes. However, the average heights as read from the curve are sometimes included as an indication of the site conditions to which the table applies.

VOLUME-LINE FUNCTIONS

5-7   The Volume/Basal-Area Relationship   When tree volumes are plotted over measures of dbh, the relationship is represented by a curve, often parabolic in form. However, for many species growing in even-aged stands, this association can be transformed to a straight line by relating volumes to squared diameters or basal areas rather than to dbh values. The linear regression of individual tree volumes on their respective basal areas is termed a *volume line*. The line is established by a least-squares fit of the function $Y = a + b(X)$. In this instance, Y is the dependent variable of tree volume, and X is the independent variable of basal area. In the solution of the equation, the regression coefficient a (i.e., the Y intercept) is usually negative.

Although the volume-line concept is not strictly limited to even-aged stands, the linear function of volume on basal area is particularly suited to those stands that are characterized by relatively uniform tree heights within diameter classes. Once the volume line has been established for a particular stand, tree volumes can be estimated from their basal areas, and stand volumes can be derived as the sum of individual tree volumes. And, if desired, the independent variable of basal area can be transformed back to dbh equivalents for incorporation in a single-entry volume table, or tarif table.[1] Such a table is defined by a particular volume line and is referred to by an index called a *tarif number*.

[1]The term *tarif* is of Arabic origin and simply means tabulated information. Since the spelling is "tariff" in Great Britain and Australia, it is an unfortunate choice of words because (*a*) the term can be confused with schedules of import duties, and (*b*) "tarif table" is redundant. A preferred designation might be "volume-line table."

5-8 Preconstructed Volume Tables The slope of a volume line may vary by species, age, height, and other factors, but all lines that are based on the same upper limit of stem merchantability tend to converge at a common point. In terms of metric measurements, this point has been empirically determined at a volume of 0.005 m^3 for a basal area of 0.004 m^2 (merchantable top diameter of 7 cm, outside bark). This common point of convergence is relatively unaffected by species, tree age, or site differences.

With the lower end of the volume line defined by a fixed coordinate position, one additional point defines the slope of the line. This point may be specified as the volume corresponding to a basal area of 1.0 m^2. This volume is used to identify the line and is thus termed the tarif number. As shown by Fig. 5-2, a volume of 21 m^3 paired with a basal area of 1.0 m^2 is identified with the volume-line, or tarif, number of 21.

Lines covering any desired range of volume/basal-area relationships can be derived in advance, and each line can be converted to a preconstructed single-entry volume table (Table 5-1). "Comprehensive" tarif tables provide the added features of tree volumes in several units of measure and utilization limits, as well as volume/basal-area ratios and growth multipliers, all within a related system.

5-9 Determining the Tarif Number Selection of the appropriate tarif number requires a technique for relating field measurements of trees to the preconstructed single-entry tables. Gaining "access" to the proper table is easily accomplished if dbh and volume can be determined for several representative sample trees from the stands of interest. A knowledge of dbh and corresponding tree volume permits the use of the tarif tables themselves for assigning a tarif number to each sample tree. The various tarif numbers thus selected are then summed and divided by the number of sample trees to derive an average tarif number for a plot or stand.

Table 5-1 Example of a Tarif Table*

Dbh (cm)	Volume in cubic meters (over bark) for tarif numbers of:					
	10	15	20	25	30	35
25	0.15	0.22	0.29	0.36	0.43	0.50
30	0.21	0.32	0.42	0.53	0.63	0.74
35	0.29	0.44	0.58	0.73	0.87	1.02
40	0.38	0.58	0.77	0.96	1.15	1.34
45	0.49	0.73	0.98	1.22	1.47	1.71
50	0.60	0.91	1.21	1.51	1.82	2.12

*From Hamilton, 1973 (abridges). The original table covers a range of dbh classes from 7 to 100 cm and tarif numbers from 10 to 60.

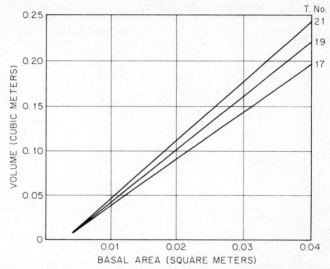

Figure 5-2 The volume/basal-area relationship. (*Adapted from Hamilton, 1973.*)

The dbh and volume for selected sample trees can be determined from felled-tree data, from existing multiple-entry volume tables (if available), or they may be derived from optical dendrometer measurements as outlined in a later section of this chapter.

Volume-line, or tarif, tables have two important advantages over single-entry tables constructed from volume/dbh or height/dbh curves. Since the method is based on a linear function, errors due to incorrect curve-fitting are minimized. And, since the average tarif number tends to be the same for all trees (regardless of dbh) in a given stand, sampling methods are simplified.

MULTIPLE-ENTRY VOLUME TABLES

5-10 Form-Class Tables Multiple-entry volume tables provide an estimate of individual tree volume based on dbh, height, and sometimes a measure of tree form. Tree form is a difficult variable to describe, and there is often a high degree of variability in form, both within and between species. Nevertheless, many form-class volume tables have been prepared, and those based on Girard form class are typical of the tables still in use.

The theory and measurement of Girard form class were discussed in the preceding chapter. Volume tables based on this concept of first-log taper have been among the most widely accepted tables in the United

Table 5-2   Multiple-Entry Volume Table, Girard Form Class 80*

Dbh (in.)	d(cm)†	Volumes‡ by 16.3-ft log intervals			
		1 log (5 m)	2 logs (10 m)	3 logs (15 m)	4 logs (20 m)
12	30.5	8.9	15.7	21.0	24.8
		0.252	0.444	0.595	0.702
16	40.6	15.9	28.2	38.2	46.2
		0.450	0.798	1.082	1.308
20	50.8	25.2	44.8	60.9	74.0
		0.714	1.268	1.724	2.095
24	61.0	37.0	65.6	89.6	108.7
		1.048	1.858	2.537	3.078
28	71.1	51.1	90.3	123.8	150.9
		1.447	2.557	3.506	4.273

*From Mesavage, 1947 (abridged).
†Metric equivalent of column 1.
‡First volumes listed are cubic feet, inside bark; volumes below are in cubic meters.

States (Table 5-2). The greatest disadvantages in using these tables are (1) the almost universal tendency toward rough estimates of form class rather than actual measurements and (2) the wide variations in upper-stem form that cannot be adequately accommodated by measuring butt-log taper only. Furthermore, it does not appear to be generally realized that the upper-log taper rates used to construct the tables were derived solely from *ocular estimates.*

Form-class tables have enjoyed a long and useful life, but sizable volume errors can occur when the upper-stem taper for a particular species differs appreciably from rigidly assumed taper rates. Thus there is a general trend away from the use of form-class tables toward the computation of tree volumes from mathematical functions.

5-11   Tree Volumes from Mathematical Functions   The preferred method for constructing multiple-entry tree-volume tables is by regression analysis. By this approach, a number of independent variables can be analyzed to determine their relative value in predicting the dependent variable of tree volume. And regression equations involving several independent variables and hundreds of sample observations can be efficiently solved by use of electronic computers.

Although many independent variables have been incorporated into regression equations for predicting tree volume, measurements of stem diameter and height tend to account for the greatest proportion of the variability in cubic volume. Thus, tree volumes for a given species and site class may be predicted from the "combined variable" method described by Spurr (1952):

$$v = a + b(d^2h)$$

This formula is, of course, identical to the equation $Y = a + b(X)$. We have merely substituted the combined variable of "diameter squared times height" for the quantity "X" in the basic equation for a straight-line relationship. Solution of the equation is by the method of least squares.

The diameters, heights, and volumes required to develop the volume function are ideally obtained by direct stem measurements of felled trees. In intensively managed plantations, it is sometimes feasible to cut down randomly selected sample trees for this purpose, irrespective of harvesting schedules. If felled trees are not available, volumes may be computed from optical dendrometer measurements of standing trees. By this approach, diameter readings are made at intervals along the stem, and sectional volumes are computed by Smalian's or another suitable formula. These sectional volumes are then summed to produce an estimate of total stem volume.

Although form is not included as an independent variable in this volume function, differences in tree taper tend to be accounted for by the employment of separate prediction equations for each species and for each age or site class. The combined variable method has been used to predict tree volumes in loblolly pine plantations, and the resulting equations accounted for 96 percent or more of the variation in observed volume (Bailey and Clutter, 1970).

AERIAL VOLUME TABLES

5-12 Individual Tree Volumes Multiple-entry tree-volume tables based on dbh and total height can be converted to aerial volume tables when correlations can be established between crown diameters and stem diameters (Chap. 4). Photo determinations of crown diameter are substituted for the usual ground measures of dbh, and total heights are measured on stereoscopic pairs of photographs by the parallax method.

The preferred method of constructing aerial tree-volume tables, however, is by regression analysis. If a strong relationship exists between crown diameters and stem diameters, tree volumes may be predicted by use of the combined variable equation as described in the preceding section:

$$v = a + b(CD^2h)$$

where CD is tree-crown diameter, and other symbols are as previously described.

Volume estimates based on this, or similar, prediction equations will generally have a lower precision (i.e., greater standard error) than those estimates based on dbh and height because tree volumes are more closely correlated with dbh than with crown diameter. And, of course, dbh can be measured with greater precision. Nevertheless, aerial tree-volume tables have proven to be cost efficient for many inventories, particularly for coniferous species growing in relatively inaccessible regions.

As an example, the Forest Management Institute of Ottawa, Canada, has successfully used large-scale aerial photography to inventory a forest of approximately 2,700 km^2 in the Mackenzie River Delta, Northwest Territories. An equation was developed to estimate tree volumes (largely white spruce) on the delta; it was applied to all trees on selected photo sample plots to provide plot-volume estimates. An inventory objective was to estimate total timber volume within ±20 percent at a probability level of 0.95. The airphoto approach proved to be the most cost-efficient means of achieving this objective.

Large-scale, high-quality aerial photography is essential for obtaining reliable crown-diameter and height measurements of individual trees. Furthermore, image resolution must be sufficient to permit reliable *stem counts* so that tree volumes can be expanded to an area basis. Black-and-white film diapositives or color transparencies at a scale of 1:5,000 or larger are recommended for consistent photographic interpretation results.

5-13 A Single-Entry Aerial Volume Table Since more time and effort is required for measuring tree heights than crown diameters on aerial photographs, several attempts have been made to reduce interpretation time by constructing single-entry tables based on crown diameter alone. One method that has been successfully employed is the derivation of aerial volume tables from existing tarif tables. Table 5-3 was formulated from tarif tables by this procedure:

   1 A tree-volume equation was produced from optical dendrometer measurements of 58 standing trees; on the basis of this data, a tarif access table was derived.
   2 An existing tarif table was selected for the area from which sample trees were drawn.
   3 A crown-diameter/stem-diameter relationship, based on 600 tree measurements, was established for the sample area.
   4 The crown-diameter/stem-diameter relationship was used to convert the selected tarif table to a single-entry aerial volume table based on crown diameter.

Although Table 5-3 is applicable only to a limited area in northern

Table 5-3 Single-Entry Aerial Tree-Volume Table for Young-Growth Ponderosa Pine*

Crown diameter (m)	Merchantable volume (m^3, to 10-cm top)
2.5	0.0453
3.0	0.0821
3.5	0.1246
4.0	0.1813
4.5	0.2492
5.0	0.3086
5.5	0.3823
6.0	0.4673
6.5	0.5523
7.0	0.6457
7.5	0.7562
8.0	0.8638
8.5	0.9771

*Hitchcock, Harry C. III. 1973. Constructing an aerial volume table from existing tarif tables. Northern Arizona Univ., M.S. thesis.

Arizona, the *method* of constructing the single-entry table may be useful in other areas where crown and stem diameters are closely correlated.

5-14 Aerial Stand-Volume Tables Where only small-scale aerial photographs are available to interpreters, emphasis is on measurement of *stand variables* rather than individual tree variables. Aerial stand volume tables are multiple-entry tables that are usually based on assessments of two or three photographic characteristics of the dominant-codominant crown canopy: average stand height, average crown diameter, and percent of crown closure. These tables may be derived by multiple regression analysis; photographic measurements of the independent variables are made by several skilled interpreters to develop a volume prediction equation.

5-15 Crown Closure Photographic and ground measurements of tree heights and crown diameters have been previously described. *Crown closure*, also referred to as *crown cover* and *canopy closure*, is defined by photo interpreters as the percent of a forest area occupied by the vertical projections of tree crowns. The concept is primarily applied to even-aged stands or to the dominant-codominant canopy level of uneven-aged stands. When used in this context, the maximum value possible is 100 percent.

In theory, crown closure contributes to the prediction of stand volume because such estimates are approximate indicators of stand density, e.g., number of stems per hectare. Since basal areas and numbers of trees cannot be determined directly from small-scale photography, crown closure is sometimes substituted for these variables in volume prediction equations. Photographic estimates of crown closure are normally used because reliable ground evaluations are much more difficult to obtain.

At photo scales of 1:15,000 and smaller, crown-closure estimates are usually made by ocular judgment, and stands are grouped into 10 percent classes. Ocular estimates are easiest in stands of low density, but they become progressively more difficult as closure percentages increase. Minor stand openings are difficult to see on small-scale photographs, and they are often shrouded by tree shadows. These factors can lead to overestimates of crown closure, particularly in dense stands. And, if ocular estimates are erratic, the variable of crown closure may contribute very little to the prediction of stand volume.

With high-resolution photographs at scales of 1:5,000 to 1:15,000 it may be feasible to derive crown-closure estimates with the aid of finely subdivided dot grids. Here, the proportion of the total number of dots that fall on tree crowns provides the estimate of crown closure. This estimation technique has the virtue of producing a reasonable degree of consistency among various photo interpreters; it is therefore recommended wherever applicable.

5-16 Stand-Volume Estimates Once an appropriate aerial stand-volume table has been selected (or constructed), there are several procedures that can be employed to derive stand volumes. One approach is as follows:

1 Outline tract boundaries on the photographs, utilizing the effective area of every other print in each flight line. This assures stereoscopic coverage of the area on a minimum number of photographs and avoids duplication of measurements by the interpreter.

2 Delineate important forest types. Except where type lines define stands of relatively uniform density and total height, they should be further broken down into homogeneous units so that measures of height, crown closure, and crown diameter will apply to the entire unit. Generally, it is unnecessary to recognize stands smaller than 2 to 5 ha.

3 Determine the area of each condition class with dot grids or a planimeter. This determination can sometimes be made on contact prints.

4 By stereoscopic examination, measure the variables for entering the aerial stand-volume table. From the table, obtain the average volume per hectare for each condition class.

5 Multiply volumes per hectare from the table by condition class areas to determine gross volume for each class.

6 Add class volumes for the total gross volume on the tract.

5-17 Adjusting Photo Volumes by Field Checks Aerial volume tables are not generally reliable enough for purely photographic estimates, and some allowance must be made for differences between gross volume estimates and actual net volumes on the ground. Therefore, a portion of the stands (or condition classes) that are interpreted should be checked in the field. If field volumes average 60 m³/ha as compared with 80 m³/ha for the photo estimates, the adjustment ratio would be 60/80, or 0.75. When the field checks are representative of the total area interpreted, the ratio can be applied to photo volume estimates to determine adjusted net volume. It is desirable to compute such ratios by forest types, because deciduous, broad-leaved trees are likely to require larger adjustments than conifers.

The accuracy of aerial volume estimates depends not only upon the volume tables used, but also on the ability of interpreters who make the essential photographic assessments. Since subjective photo estimates often vary widely among individuals, it is advisable to have two or more interpreters assess each of the essential variables.

TREE-WEIGHT TABLES

5-18 Field Tallies by Weight The continued emphasis upon weight scaling as a basis of payment for pulpwood and sawlogs will eventually result in field tallies based on tree weights rather than on various units of volume. It is only logical that standing trees should be measured in terms of the same units as those on which log purchases and sales are transacted.

An example of a tree-weight table for standing timber is shown by Table 5-4. For each dbh and total height class, merchantable tree weights

Table 5-4 Tree-Weight Table for Planted Slash Pines*

Dbh (in.)	d (cm)†	Tree weights‡ for total heights of:			
		40 ft (12.2 m)	50 ft (15.2 m)	60 ft (18.3 m)	70 ft (21.3 m)
6	15.2	146	199	252	
		66	*90*	*114*	
8	20.3	311	405	499	593
		141	*184*	*226*	*269*
10	25.4	522	669	816	963
		237	*303*	*370*	*437*
12	30.5	781	992	1,204	1,416
		354	*450*	*546*	*642*

*From McGee, 1959 (abridged). Merchantable weights shown include bark and wood to a 4-in. (10-cm) top diameter.
†Metric equivalent of column 1.
‡First weights listed are in pounds; those listed below are in kilograms.

of bark and wood are given in pounds and kilograms. Any ordinary volume table can be converted to a weight basis if weight/volume equivalents can be reliably established.

5-19 Dry-Wood Weight Yields The primary concern of the pulp and paper industry is that of determining *dry-wood* weight yields, exclusive of bark. To predict such yields requires reliable determinations of average specific gravity and moisture content for entire tree stems so that wood densities can be computed in terms of kilograms per cubic meter (Fig. 5-3). The product of wood density and tree volume provides an estimate of tree weight.

For some coniferous species, the average specific gravity of merchantable tree stems is highly correlated with the specific gravity as determined from increment cores taken at dbh. Such a relationship has been established for loblolly pine stands in South Carolina and used to construct a dry-weight yield table for natural stands (Zobel et al., 1969). In this particular study, differences in site quality and stand density had little effect on the specific gravity of the average tree; however, there was a close cor-

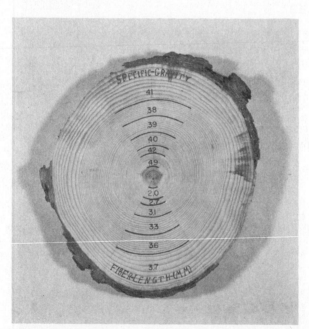

Figure 5-3 Variations in specific gravity and fiber length in a cross section of ponderosa pine. These changes in specific gravity are due largely to varying proportions of springwood and summerwood in annual rings.

relation between stand age and specific gravity. Of course, all three of these factors may affect the *volume* of wood produced and thus the dry weight of wood per hectare.

Adoption of the metric system will likely result in additional applications of tree-weight relationships in the United States.

PROBLEMS

5-1 From your instructor or from a logging operation, obtain dimensions of three merchantable logs cut from the same tree. Determine cubic volumes of each by Huber's, Smalian's, and Newton's formulas. Tabulate results and explain reasons for differences noted.

5-2 Construct a single-entry tree-volume table based on either felled-tree measurements or a height/dbh relationship.

5-3 Determine the appropriate tarif number for an even-aged stand of trees in your locality.

5-4 Obtain 50 to 100 paired measurements of dbh and crown diameter for a coniferous species. If the variables appear to be linearly correlated, fit a simple linear regression to the data by the method of least squares. Then use the relationship to convert a single-entry tree-volume table into an aerial volume table.

5-5 Convert an existing tree-volume table into a tree-weight table.

5-6 By regression analysis, determine whether the specific gravity for entire tree stems is closely correlated with specific gravity at dbh for a selected species.

REFERENCES

Avery, T. E.
1958. Composite aerial volume table for southern pines and hardwoods. *J. Forestry* **56**:741-745. illus.
———— **and Meyer, Merle P.**
1959. Volume tables for aerial timber estimating in northern Minnesota. *U.S. Forest Serv., Lake States Forest Expt. Sta. Paper* 78. 21 pp., illus.
Bailey, Robert L., and Clutter, Jerome L.
1970. Volume tables for old-field loblolly pine plantations in the Georgia Piedmont. *Georgia Forest Res. Council Report* 22, *Series* 2. 4 pp.
Burkhart, Harold E., and Clutter, Jerome L.
1971. Green and dry weight for old-field loblolly pine plantations in the Georgia Piedmont. *Georgia Forest Res. Council Report* 22, *Series* 4. 11 pp.
Bryan, M.B., and McClure, Joe P.
1962. Board-foot and cubic-foot volume computing equations for southeastern tree species. *U.S. Forest Serv., Southeast. Forest Expt. Sta. Paper* 145. 10 pp., illus.
Hamilton, G.J.
1973. Timber measurement for standing trees using tariff tables. *British*

Forest Commission Booklet 36, Her Majesty's Stationery Office, London, England. 31 pp.

Hazard, John W., and Berger, John M.
1972. Volume tables vs. dendrometers for forest surveys. *J. Forestry* **70**:216-219, illus.

Honer, T.G.
1965. A new total cubic foot volume function. *Forestry Chron.* **41**:476-493, illus.

McGee, C.E.
1959. Weight of merchantable wood with bark from planted slash pine in the Carolina Sandhills. *U.S. Forest Serv., Southeast. Forest Expt. Sta. Note* 128. 2 pp.

Mesavage, Clement
1947. Tables for estimating cubic-foot volume of timber. *U.S. Forest Serv., Southern Forest Expt. Sta., Occas. Paper* 111. 70 pp.

Minor, C.O.
1951. Stem-crown diameter relations in southern pine. *J. Forestry* **49**:490-493, illus.

Moessner, Karl E.
1957. Preliminary aerial volume tables for conifer stands in the rocky mountains. *U.S. Forest Serv., Intermount. Forest and Range Expt. Sta. Res. Paper* 41. 17 pp., illus.

Myers, Clifford A.
1963. Volume, taper, and related tables for southwestern ponderosa pine. *U.S. Forest Serv., Rocky Mt. Forest and Range Expt. Sta. Res. Paper* RM-2. 24 pp., illus.

Pope, Robert B.
1962. Constructing aerial photo volume tables. *U.S. Forest Serv., Pacific Northwest Forest and Range Expt. Sta. Res. Paper* 49. 25 pp., illus.

Spurr, Stephen H.
1952. *Forest inventory.* The Ronald Press Company, New York. 476 pp., illus.

Turnbull, K.J., Little, G.R., and Hoyer, G.E.
1972. *Comprehensive tree-volume tarif tables.* State of Washington, Department of Natural Resources, Olympia. 23 pages plus appendix, illus.

—— **and Hoyer, G.E.**
1965. Construction and analysis of comprehensive tree-volume tarif tables. State of Washington, Department of Natural Resources, Olympia. Report No. 8, 63 pp., illus.

Zobel, Bruce, Roberds, James H., and Ralston, James
1969. Dry wood weight yields of loblolly pine. *J. Forestry* **67**:822-824, illus.

Chapter 6

Site, Stocking, Density, and Growth

6-1 Introduction As defined by the Society of American Foresters (1971), *site* refers to "an area considered in terms of its environment, particularly as this determines the type and quality of the vegetation the area can carry." If required, site may be classified qualitatively into site *types*, by their climate, soil, and vegetation, or quantitatively into site *classes*, by their potential to produce primary wood products.

Insofar as foresters are concerned, the primary purposes of site measurement are (1) to identify the productivity of forest stands, both present and future, and (2) to provide a frame of reference for land management diagnosis and prescription. In the United States, most attention has been given to the first purpose, while little attention has specifically been directed toward the second (Jones, 1969).

Theoretically, it should be possible to measure site directly by analyzing the many factors affecting the productivity of forests, such as soil nutrients and moisture, temperature regimes, available light, topography, and so on. Although attempts at direct measurement of site have been made, such an approach may not be of immediate value to the practicing forester; consequently, indirect estimates of site are frequently employed.

6-2 Evaluations of Site Foresters are often concerned with timber as an end product. Thus, the volume of desired primary wood products (cubic meters of sawtimber, etc.) might seem to be a useful measure of site. However, the volume of timber on an area may be affected by factors other than site. For instance, varying density levels, past cutting practices, or species composition tend to limit the usefulness of volume as a measure of site.

Basic to site quality is soil, a medium that is relatively stable and which has a controlling influence on the productivity of forest stands. Soil attributes that can be important from the standpoint of forest production include characteristics which are comparatively permanent (thickness and texture of the A horizon, permeability, and parent material) and characteristics which are subject to change (quantity of humus, nitrogen content, structure of surface layers, etc.). Site cannot be completely measured in terms of soil, however. The principal advantage of using soil characteristics in measuring site is that such assessments are independent of the forest stand; therefore, such measures may be applied not only where well-developed forest stands occur but also where they are absent, as on deforested or nonforested areas.

Under undisturbed, natural conditions, some indicator plants comprising the lesser vegetation may be associated with site. The practicing forester should be aware of these relationships, since this information can provide a quick appraisal of the productivity of forest stands. The principal drawbacks to the use of plant indicators are that (1) the method permits site evaluation only in relative or qualitative terms, and (2) a sound background in plant ecology is a prerequisite for reliable classifications.

Of all the commonly applied indirect measures of site, tree height in relation to tree age has been found the most practical, consistent, and useful indicator. Theoretically, height growth is sensitive to differences in site quality, little affected by varying density levels and species compositions, and strongly correlated with volume. This measure of site is termed *site index*. Site index is the most widely accepted quantitative measure of site in the United States.

As generally applied, site index is measured by determining the average total height of dominant and codominant trees in well-stocked, even-aged stands at specified index ages, such as 25, 50, or 100 years. When these two variables (total height and age) have been ascertained for a given species, they are used as coordinates for interpolating site index from a specially prepared set of curves. For example, if the average total height of a stand of young-growth Arizona ponderosa pine is 20 m at an age of 75 years, the site index would be read as 25 from Fig. 6-1. This means that the expected stand height for this site is 25 m at the index age of 100 years.

In preparing site-index curves for various species, either age at breast height or total age may be used as the independent variable. Age at breast height is preferable, because this is a standard point of tree-diameter measurement and a convenient height for making increment borings. When total age is used, it is necessary to estimate the number of years required for the tree to grow from seed to the height where an increment boring is made; this number is then added to the annual ring count to obtain total age. Use of age at breast height in lieu of total age eliminates the need for such arbitrary correction factors.

Many recent studies have shown that in the absence of a forest stand, site index can be evaluated by interpretation of topography and soil factors that are related to tree growth. For example, the site index for white and black oaks in Indiana can be predicted from such factors as depth of surface soil, distance from ridgetop, slope steepness, and stone, silt, and clay content (Hannah, 1968). Similar relations exist in other regions.

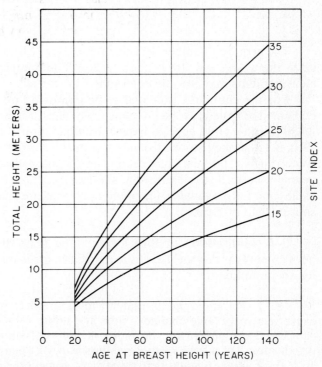

Figure 6-1 Site-index relationships for young-growth ponderosa pine. The index age is 100 years at breast height. (*Adapted from Minor, 1964.*)

6-3 Field Measurement of Site Index To determine the site index of a forest stand, average total height and age are determined from measurements obtained from *site trees*. Site trees should meet certain specifications, such as being dominant or codominant and even-aged, showing no evidence of crown damage, disease, sweep, crook, forking, or prolonged suppression.

Measurements of total height are commonly made with a hypsometer, while age may be determined by extracting an increment core. The number of trees measured depends upon the variability of total heights and ages in the stand being evaluated. The number of sample units required to estimate total height and age for a given confidence interval and probability level can be determined by application of the formula for computing sampling intensity (Chap. 2). As an example, if the average total height is to be measured with ± 1.25 m at a confidence probability of 90 percent, and a preliminary sample of five total height measurements indicates a standard deviation of ± 1.9 m, the required number of height measurements may be determined by

$$n = \left[\frac{(2.132)\,(1.9)}{1.25} \right]^2 = (3.24)^2 = 10.5, \text{ or } 11, \text{ measurements}$$

The required number of measurements will be slightly less than 11, since there are now 10 *df* (Sec. 2-20). The sampling intensity of age measurements may also be determined by similar computations.

For the site-index potential to be expressed on a standard basis, a definite stand age must be presumed. For most regions, the period in the life of the stand that approximates the culmination of mean annual growth (Sec. 6-15) in well-stocked stands has been selected as the indexing age. Accordingly, 100 years has been used for most western species and 50 years for eastern species. Special site-index curves based on an index age of 25 years are available for plantations that are managed on rotations shorter than 50 years.

6-4 Limitations of Site Index The main drawbacks that have been cited regarding the use of site index as a measure of forest productivity are as follows:

1 Exact stand age is difficult to determine, and small errors can cause relatively large changes in the site-index value.
2 The concept of site index is not well suited for uneven-aged stands, areas of mixed species composition, or open lands.
3 Effects of stand density are not considered except by arbitrary selection of site trees in well-stocked stands that have been unaffected by past suppression. Other variables associated with stand volume (that is,

dbh and stem form) are not directly taken into account. As a result, an index based on total height and age alone may not provide a valid estimate of the growing capacity for a particular site.

4   Site index is not a constant; instead, it may change periodically due to environmental and climatic variations.

5   Except in limited instances, the site-index value for one species cannot be translated into a usable index for a different species on the same site (Doolittle, 1958).

In spite of the foregoing limitations, site index is a useful tool because it provides a simple numerical value that is easily measured and understood by the practicing forester. Its use will apparently be continued until the day when the varied factors affecting the productivity of forests can be reduced to an equally simple and quantitative measurement.

STOCKING AND STAND DENSITY

6-5   Definitions   Stocking and stand density have often been used interchangeably, but the two terms are not synonymous. *Stocking* is a qualitative expression that compares the existing number of trees in a stand to the number desired for optimum growth and volume. Accordingly, stands may be referred to as understocked, fully stocked (the theoretical ideal), or overstocked. Stands that deviate from full stocking may also be described in relative terms, such as 30 percent stocked or 110 percent stocked.

In contrast to the comparative nature of stocking, *stand density* is a quantitative term describing the degree of stem crowding within a stocked area. Density is usually expressed as some combination of stem diameter, basal area, height, form, or number of trees per hectare (Fig. 6-2).

6-6   Measures of Stocking   The main difficulty arising from the application of stocking concepts is that of deciding just what should constitute full stocking for a particular species on a given site. As outlined by Bickford (1957), "the stocking that results in maximum yield is the ideal that every forest manager would like to have if he only knew what it was and could recognize it if he saw it." Although stocking can also be specified in terms of the capacity of an area to support trees, most foresters think of stocking in terms of "best growth" rather than as a measure of site occupation.

Stocking levels are of prime concern to the forest manager because controlled changes in these levels may allow the forester to shorten or lengthen his rotation, favor desired species, and maximize the yield of selected timber products. Although the extremes of stocking can be easily recognized, full stocking can only be defined as a closed canopy stand

Figure 6-2 Relative stocking and stand density may be approximated at various points in a stand by use of canopy photographs. (*U.S. Forest Service photograph.*)

that represents the "average best" to be found. Understocked stands are characterized by trees of rough form, excessive taper, and a high live-crown ratio. Overstocked stands may represent a stagnated condition, with trees exhibiting a low live-crown ratio and numerous dead stems. In both instances, the result is a reduction in net volume increment from the "fully stocked" ideal.

6-7 Measures of Stand Density In essence, stand density quantifies stocking. Ideally, density expressions are correlated with stand growth and volume and are unrelated to the age of the stand and the quality of the site. Although many different expressions of density exist, those selected for use by the practicing forester should be clearly understood, consistent, objective, and easy to apply.

One of the more widely used expressions of stand density is *basal area* on an area basis. While basal area may not be indicative of tree size-class distribution patterns (particularly in uneven-aged stands), it is an objective measure of density. Furthermore, basal area is easily determined in the field and readily converted to stand density expressions. Many multiple-use relations have been developed with basal area as an independent variable.

The percentage of a forest area covered by the vertical projections of tree crowns is referred to as *crown closure* (Chap. 5). Strictly speaking, this is a measure of area occupation rather than stand density. In even-aged stands, crown closure may be proportional to basal area per hectare. This relationship has led to the development of indices between estimates of crown closure obtained from aerial photographs and basal area (Moessner, 1964).

The surface area of the main stem of trees in a stand, termed *bole area*, is an expression of stand density that measures the actual growing surface, or cambium area, which produces merchantable wood. Therefore, bole area was originally proposed as an expression of growing stock density for silvicultural purposes (Lexen, 1943). Bole area measures also describe a surface that absorbs short-wave radiation from the atmosphere and re-radiates long-wave radiation onto surrounding areas. Thus the measure may have special utility in quantifying stand densities for ecological purposes.

Perhaps the most logical measure of stand density is simply the *number of trees* occurring on an area. Unfortunately, unless coupled with some indication of tree size, spacing, or distribution, this expression of density may have little value. Variations of this density expression include the number of trees in relation to diameter, height, or tree form. Use of all three factors together leads to a measure of density based on volume.

The most obvious expression of stand density is *volume of trees* on an area. Ultimately, density must be expressed in terms of volume for purposes of economic evaluation in the development of forest management plans. Volumes should be in terms of cubic meters for flexibility in the interpretation of multiple primary wood products. Cubic meters will give the closest approximation to the multiple product potential for trees of any diameter, height, and form class. Furthermore, cubic meters may be converted into other specific product measurement units if desired.

GROWTH FORMS

6-8 Introduction The assessment of growth of individual trees and forest stands (an aggregation of individual trees) is an important consideration for the practicing forester. All living organisms, including trees, exhibit characteristic patterns of growth, or *growth forms*. Growth forms may be studied in detail by ecologists, and the forest manager should possess some appreciation of these concepts to better understand the growth patterns of trees, stands, and associated organisms within the forest community.

Essentially, two basic patterns of growth may be recognized: the *J-shaped*, or *exponential*, growth form, and the *S-shaped*, or *sigmoid*, growth form. These two patterns may be combined or modified in many ways according to the distinctive growth properties of different organisms and their relationship with environments.

6-9 The J-shaped Growth Form With the J-shaped form, the growth of individual organisms and the number of organisms occupying an area increases rapidly and then stops abruptly as environmental resistance (food, space, or seasonal factors) comes into play. When the upper limit of growth is reached, the organism may remain at this level for a time or begin to decline. The J-shaped growth form may be considered an incomplete S-shaped form, particularly in situations where a sudden limiting effect is brought to bear prior to the self-limiting effects within the population itself.

Many forest insect populations follow a J-shaped growth trend, with individuals and densities increasing throughout a life span which ends with the first frost of the season. Also, annual plants comprising the lesser vegetation of a forest may be characterized by J-shaped growth forms.

6-10 The S-shaped Growth Form With the S-shaped form, the growth of individual organisms and the number of organisms on an area are slow during an establishment phase, become rapid (as in the J-shaped form) during a midlife phase, and finally slow down in a late-life phase as environmental resistance increases. A more-or-less equilibrium state is reached and maintained in this latter phase, in contrast to the abrupt stop in the J-shaped form. The upper limit of growth increase, which may be described as an upper asymptote of the S-shaped curve, is called the *carrying capacity* (Odum, 1971). Growth beyond the carrying capacity will theoretically cause a deterioration of site quality.

Individual tree and stand growth, two aspects that foresters are concerned with, can be represented by the S-shaped form. Generally, the growth of a tree is relatively slow during establishment. Then, following establishment, growth is quite rapid during midlife, eventually slowing down in late life (Fig. 6-3). Since a forest stand is an aggregation of trees, the composite growth pattern of a stand can also be considered to approximate the S-shaped form. The growth of many livestock (cattle, sheep, and goats) and wildlife (deer, elk, and upland game) that utilize various foods produced in a forest may also be characterized by the S-shaped curve form.

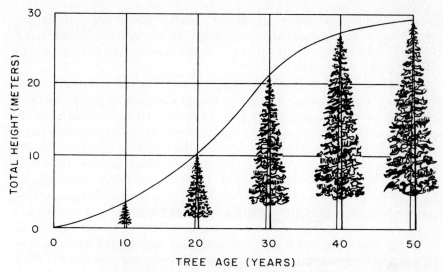

Figure 6-3 The S-shaped curve form characterized the growth pattern for many organisms. The J-shaped growth form is approximated by the lower half of this curve.

TREE GROWTH

6-11 Introduction The physiology and morphology of tree growth involves an elongation and thickening of roots, stems, and branches. Initial linear growth of all tree parts is attributed to the original growing tissue, or primary meristem. Subsequent radial growth takes place as the result of division and enlargement of the secondary meristem (cambium), which produces new wood and bark between the previously formed wood and bark. Generally, diameter and height increases are the elements of tree growth that are of most interest to foresters, since volume growth may be determined from these elements. Root and branch growth are often of lesser importance.

6-12 Increases in Diameter Tree growth is an intermittent process characterized by changes in stem form and dimension over a period of time. In northern temperate forests, a growing tree adds an annual layer of wood just under the bark, from ground level to tip and all around the stem. These layers appear as annual rings in cross section (Chap. 4). Accordingly, tree age can be determined by counting the annual rings, and the volume of each ring is a measure of the wood added to the central stem in a particular year.

Annual rings tend to be wider during the early life of a tree. As age increases, the ring width gradually decreases, resulting in a reduction of annual diameter growth. In addition to age, the rate of diameter growth is dependent on soil moisture availability and the amount of leaf surface functioning in the photosynthetic process. Wider spacing among trees results in more root-growing space and larger crowns which, in turn, lead to faster diameter growth.

Where annual ring growth is determined from the measurement of increment cores, special care must be taken to avoid bias caused by non-circular cross sections and elliptical ring patterns. Under certain environmental conditions, trees may grow faster in one compass direction (e.g., on the northern or eastern side of the stem) than in other directions. When this occurs, the slowest diameter growth rates (most narrow rings) will often occur on the side of the stem that is opposite the fastest growing sector. Thus it may be necessary to obtain two or more increment cores to determine realistic *average ring widths* for such trees (Fig. 6-4).

6-13 Increases in Height   Changes in tree height are of prime concern for predicting future stand composition and for selecting the ideal crop trees in pure stands. The typical course of height growth is exemplified by the S-shaped growth form. Height growth proceeds slowly until the seedling is well established; this is followed by a period of rapid growth during midlife, the length of which depends on the species and site involved. As a tree begins to attain maturity, height growth gradually

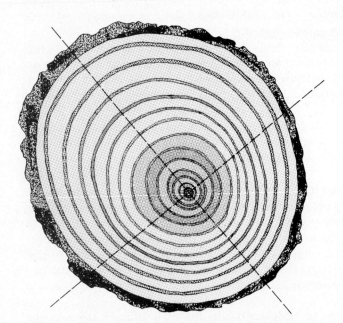

Figure 6-4   Eccentric tree cross section illustrating varying annual ring widths. Measurements of past growth on such trees will differ according to the radii selected for increment borings.

tapers off but never completely ceases as long as the tree is living and healthy.

The rate of height growth over a given span of time is dependent on many of the same factors that affect diameter growth, e.g., age, stand density, and climate.

6-14 Increases in Volume Volume growth of a tree can be considered a reflection of the composite effects of diameter and height growth. Even though the *width* of annual rings normally decreases as the tree becomes older, this thinner wood layer is added over a larger stem diameter or bole surface. Therefore, the *volume* of wood added annually may be equal to or greater than that of previous years (Gessel et al., 1960). To fully quantify volume growth, changes in the rate of height growth during the life of a tree must also be evaluated.

The S-shaped growth curve follows the same general configuration for most elements of tree growth—whether this be diameter, height, or volume. Although the exact form of the cumulative growth curve will differ with the variable used and the climatic fluctuations involved, the elongated S-shaped pattern is a characteristic that can be invariably expected. From the foregoing, it can be seen that wood production in the central stem of a tree can be predicted by measuring past rates of diameter and height growth. Indeed, the primary objective of most tree-growth studies is the reliable prediction of future wood yields.

6-15 Current, Periodic, and Mean Annual Growth There are different ways of expressing the growth of a tree or a forest stand. Regardless of the expression selected, the growth must be quantified by an indication of the time during which the increment occurred, e.g., whether daily, monthly, annually, or over a period of years.

The increase in tree volume for 1 year is referred to as the *current annual growth*. However, because current growth is difficult to measure for a single year, the average annual growth over a period of 5 to 10 years is commonly substituted instead. The differences in tree volume between the start and the end of a growing period, divided by the number of years involved, is properly termed *periodic annual growth*. By contrast, the *mean annual growth* is derived by dividing total tree volume at any point in time by total age at that time.

Current or periodic annual growth, whether based on volume or tree-size characteristics, increases rapidly, reaches a crest, and then drops off rapidly. In comparison, mean annual growth increases more slowly, attains a maximum at a later age, and falls more gradually. When curves of current (or periodic) and mean annual growth are plotted over tree age, they intersect at the peak of the latter (Fig. 6-5). This "culmination point" for mean annual growth is regarded as the ideal harvesting or rotation age

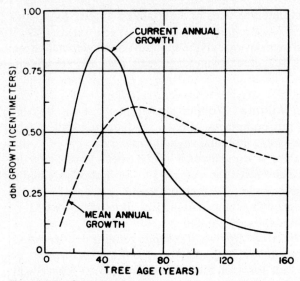

Figure 6-5 Graphic comparison of the current annual and mean annual growth curves of a tree. (*Adapted from Bruce and Schumacher, 1950.*)

in terms of most efficient volume production. The rotation age actually selected, however, is also dependent on trends in stumpage values, tree-size specifications for various products, and other management considerations.

6-16 Past Growth from Permanently Marked Trees One of the most reliable methods of estimating the growth of standing timber is from periodic measurements of diameter and height on permanently marked trees. Such measurements can easily be converted to volumes at the start and the end of a growth period. Then, periodic annual growth (pag) may be determined by

$$\text{pag} = \frac{v_2 - v_1}{n}$$

where v_2 = volume at end of growth period
v_1 = volume at start of growth period
n = number of years in growth period

For example, if v_2 is 1.89 m³, v_1 is 1.16 m³, and the growth period is 10 years, periodic annual growth of the tree may be computed as

$$\text{pag} = \frac{1.89 - 1.16}{10} = 0.073 \text{ m}^3/\text{year}$$

Although estimates of tree growth derived from measurements of permanently marked trees are statistically reliable in the sense that sampling errors are eliminated (all measurements are repeated on the same trees), a drawback to this method is the long "wait-out" period. Since trees grow at relatively slow rates, it normally takes 3 to 10 years to detect and measure a growth element. Thus, an investment in time is necessary in applying this method.

6-17 Tree Growth as a Percentage Value The calculation of tree growth in percentage terms is an expression of the average rate of change in size or volume over a given period. Because each year's annual ring is added over the cumulative size of the tree stem, tree growth has been most frequently regarded as a compound interest relationship. Depite the apparent logic of the compound interest theory, however, observations of actual volumes in uncut timber stands at three or more points in time indicate that tree growth is sometimes best described by *simple interest rates* (Grosenbaugh, 1958).

Actually, the argument of compound versus simple interest is largely an academic question, because growth percent alone has little practical value in management decision making. A large number of growth percent formulas have been proposed in previous years, many of which are misleading because of the inherent nature of tree growth itself. Because the base dimensions of a tree are constantly increasing, a uniform annual-ring width results in a progressively lower and lower annual interest rate as the tree gets larger. Thus when the absolute increment remains constant, interest rates can appear astounding for small trees but strictly mediocre for larger ones.

Compound interest formulas are readily available in standard texts on forest finance and valuation. In terms of simple interest, the growth percentage in volume at any age is the current (periodic) annual growth divided by the "base volume" at the beginning of the growth period. Expressed as a formula, annual simple interest rates may be computed by

$$\text{Growth percent } (p) = \frac{v_2 - v_1}{n \times v_1}(100)$$

It will be recognized that this formula is merely a modification of the relationship presented in the preceding section. By substituting the values from Sec. 6-16, the annual simple interest rate would be

$$p = \frac{1.89 - 1.16}{10(1.16)}(100) = 6.3 \text{ percent}$$

6-18 Past Growth from Stem Analysis   The most accurate method of determining accumulated tree-volume growth is by complete stem analysis. Although it is possible to obtain needed measurements and annual-ring counts by climbing and boring standing trees, the usual technique requires that sample trees be felled and cut into sections at the end of a designated growth period. Diameter inside bark at the beginning of the growth period is derived by counting annual rings back to the desired year. The total starting volume of all tree sections is subtracted from current volume to obtain cubic-meter growth.

The exact method followed in making a complete stem analysis, including points of stem measurement and intervals between sections, varies according to tree form and desired precision. Therefore, the procedures outlined in Table 6-1 are intended merely to serve as an *illustra-*

Table 6-1   Stem-Analysis Computations for a Tree-Growth Period of 8 Years

Section height above ground (m)	Average diameter (cm)	Basal area (m²)	Average basal area (m²)		Section length (m)	Section volume (m³)
0.3	37.1	0.1080	(Stump)	0.1080	0.3	0.0324
3.3	32.5	0.0829	(Section 1)	0.0954	3.0	0.2862
6.3	26.7	0.0558	(Section 2)	0.0694	3.0	0.2082
9.3	22.1	0.0384	(Section 3)	0.0471	3.0	0.1413
12.3	13.2	0.0137	(Section 4)	0.0260	3.0	0.0780
15.0	0.0	(Conoid)	(Top)	0.0046	2.7	0.0124

Present total height: 15 m   Present cubic volume: 0.7585 m³

Section height above ground (m)	Average diameter (cm)	Basal area (m²)	Average basal area (m²)		Section length (m)	Section volume (m³)
0.3	30.7	0.0740	(Stump)	0.0740	0.3	0.0222
3.3	27.2	0.0581	(Section 1)	0.0660	3.0	0.1980
6.3	22.9	0.0412	(Section 2)	0.0496	3.0	0.1488
9.3	19.0	0.0283	(Section 3)	0.0348	3.0	0.1044
12.3	10.9	0.0093	(Section 4)	0.0188	3.0	0.0564
14.1	0.0	(Conoid)	(Top)	0.0031	1.8	0.0056

Previous total height: 14.1 m   Previous cubic volume: 0.5354 m³
Gross growth: 0.2231 m³
Periodic annual growth: 0.2231/8 = 0.0279 m³/year

tion of the computations involved. In this example, an 8-year growth period is presumed for a coniferous tree having a total height of 15 m at the time of felling.

The tree is severed 0.3 m above ground to minimize effects of butt swell; it is then cut into uniform 3-m lengths, excepting the final 2.7-m top section. Present dib is obtained at each cutting point; for elliptical cross sections, this is derived by averaging minimum and maximum diameters. Next, average cross-section diameters are converted to basal area in square meters, followed by computations of present cubic volume for each section.

In Table 6-1, stump content is computed as the volume of a cylinder; i.e., taper in the first 0.3-m section is ignored. *Present* volumes of the four 3-m sections are derived from Smalian's formula, and content of the top 2.7-m section is computed as the volume of a conoid.

To obtain *previous* stem volume, diameters are measured by counting back eight annual rings (the number of years in the growth period) from the present. Cubic volumes for stump and lower stem sections are calculated as before. For the top section, however, previous length must be determined by making several trial-and-error cuts from the tip downward—until the first annual ring preceding the growth period is located. Once the previous top length has been measured, its cubic content is again computed as the volume of a conoid (or other suitable geometric solid).

The difference in stem volume between the beginning and end of the specified growth period represent gross growth. When this value is divided by the number of years in the growth period (8 in this example), the result is a measure of periodic annual growth.

Some stem analyses require that sectional cuts be made at both stump and dbh levels, depending on the objectives. In such cases, the stem section below dbh is usually regarded as a cylinder for purposes of deriving cubic volume. Cutting intervals above dbh may also be shortened to 1 m or less when greater precision is desired. To facilitate analysis during inclement weather, stem sections about 2.5 cm thick can be extracted at desired intervals and the actual analysis performed indoors.

6-19 Past Growth from Volume/Age Associations Knowledge of diameter, height, and age relationships can provide a readily available means of estimating tree growth. Since these relationships may often be generated from well-planned forest inventories, estimates of tree growth can be derived with little additional effort.

Essentially, graphical representations of diameter/age and height/age relationships are used to develop a curve to illustrate the association between volume and age (Fig. 6-6). Then, for any arbitrarily selected growth period, volumes are read from the curve to represent (1) volume at start of

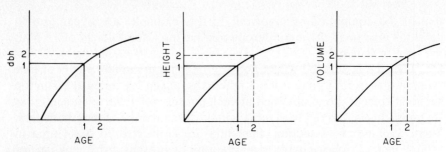

Figure 6-6 Dbh/age, height/age, and volume/age relationships used to estimate periodic annual tree growth.

growth period and (2) volume at end of growth period. With this information, periodic annual growth may be determined by following the procedure described in Sec. 6-16.

6-20 Interpreting Growth Trends The principal reason for analyzing the past growth of trees is to establish a pattern for predicting future growth. From the standpoint of practical forest management, growth prediction is usually approached from a *stand* basis rather than in terms of individual trees. However, because tree growth is the integral component of stand growth, the trends of tree-size increases have been considered first.

Because the rate of tree growth in diameter, height, form, and volume is heavily dependent on relative age, as indicated by the S-shaped growth form, predictions of future yields from past growth should be limited to short periods of time—usually not more than 5 to 10 years. Otherwise, large errors will result from the assumption that future growth will be equivalent to or similar to past growth. As a rule, growth predictions are most reliable during the midlife of a tree, i.e., when size increases can be characterized by the central (near-linear) portion of the S-shaped curve. When growth curves are available for the desired species, future growth for short time periods can be approximated by ocular extension of such trends. Curves of periodic or mean annual growth can be utilized in like fashion, but the hazards of this procedure for extended time periods are readily apparent.

STAND GROWTH

6-21 Introduction By definition (Society of American Foresters, 1971), a *forest stand* is a community of trees possessing sufficient uniformity as regards composition, age, spatial arrangement, or condition to be distinguishable from adjacent communities. Theoretically, the growth of a stand is the summation of the growth rates of all the individual trees comprising the stand. Actually, the summation of individual tree growth rates will not necessarily equal the growth of a stand because of natural mortality and harvested production.

Two additional definitions are also appropriate here. A *stand table* is a tabulation of the total *number of stems* (or average number of stems per unit area) in a stand or compartment, by species and dbh classes. A *stock table* lists the total *volume* of trees (or average volume per unit area) in a stand, by species and dbh classes. Since stock tables are usually derived from stand tables, the two listings are sometimes combined in a single tabulation.

6-22 Components of Stand Growth The basic elements of stand growth are accretion, mortality, and ingrowth (Gilbert, 1954). *Accretion* is the growth on all trees that were measured at the beginning of the growth period. It includes the growth on trees that were cut during the period plus those trees that died and were utilized. *Mortality* is the volume of trees initially measured that died during a growth period and were not utilized. The volume of those trees that grew into the lowest inventoried diameter class during the growth period is termed *ingrowth*.

The growth elements of accretion, mortality, and ingrowth may be conveniently designated by the letters A, M, and I, respectively. Expressions of gross growth GG, net growth NG, and volume increase or production P for a given area may then be derived as follows:

$$\text{Gross growth } GG = A + I$$
$$\text{Net growth } NG = A - M \quad \text{(ingrowth excluded)}$$
$$\text{Production } P = A - M + I$$

Gross growth is a measure of the change in total volume for a given stand. In any given diameter class, it is the change in volume, plus mortality, during the growth period.

Net growth represents the stand-volume increment based on the initial trees after mortality has been deducted. When ingrowth is added to net growth, the result is volume increase or *production*, i.e., a measure of the net change in volume during a specified growth period. If certain trees were harvested during a growth period, yield volume Y must also be considered in computing production values. The preceding formula thus becomes

$$P = A - M + I + Y$$

For those foresters who wish to determine how much timber they can cut during a growth period, volume increase or production P provides the best estimate. However, it should be remembered that ingrowth is often a large and variable component of production. When ingrowth volume fluctates widely from one growth period to another, it may be difficult to maintain production at preconceived levels.

Accretion is regarded as the best measure for comparing volume yields from two or more different methods of forest management or cutting. Because some cutting methods make more efficient use of the growing stock than others, accretion provides a useful index to the effects of a given treatment on the growth of trees initially present in the stand (Gilbert, 1954). Net-growth estimates are primarily valuable on large areas where mortality rates can be readily determined. Net-growth values for small tracts may be unreliable because the loss of one large tree can offset the growth on several hectares of land.

To evaluate growth trends by diameter classes, average annual-diameter increments should be used. Such increments are the basis for the stand table projection method of predicting stand growth.

6-23 Past Growth from Permanent Plots   From a statistical viewpoint, the most reliable method of estimating stand growth is from repeated measurements of marked trees on permanent sample plots. Information derived by this method may be used to formulate expressions of gross growth, net growth, and volume increase or production for a given stand. Furthermore, knowledge of ingrowth, mortality, and yield that is obtained from permanent plots may also be used in the application of yield tables and in the stand-table projection method of estimating growth.

The size and number of permanent sample plots established to provide estimates of stand growth are dependent on the species composition, variability in density, costs of implementation, and level of sampling precision. Such considerations are taken into account in planning a forest inventory for any specified objective.

A drawback to assessing growth from marked trees on permanent sample plots is the long "wait-out" period. However, the investment in time may be acceptable to the practicing forester if reliable estimates of ingrowth, mortality, and yield can be obtained.

6-24 Growth Predictions from Yield Tables   A *yield table* is a tabular presentation of the growth pattern for a managed, even-aged stand. In essence, a yield table presents volume and possibly other stand characteristics per unit area for even-aged stands by age, site, and other specified conditions. Generally, yield tables are used in forestry to regulate cuttings, determine rotation age, and derive estimates of stand growth. Only the latter use will be considered here.

Yield tables for even-aged stands are of several types, depending on the independent variables employed. *Normal yield tables* show relationships between volume and other stand parameters and two independent variables: stand age and site index. These tables are based on the concept of "normal stocking," a holdover from European forestry practices. Normal or full stocking describes a stand that (theoretically) completely occupies a site and makes full use of its growth potential. A normal forest would be comprised of a normal distribution of age classes, normal growing stock, and consequently, a normal increment. In such a hypothetical forest, tree crowns are fitted together so that no sunlight is wasted, and each crown is matched with a root system that fully utilizes the soil (Bickford, 1957).

Unfortunately, stand densities defined as normal may represent severe overstocking. For example, in interior ponderosa pine stands, full stocking is better indicated by root closure than by the space occupied by tree crowns (Myers, 1966). Normal stocking is so often in excess of that necesary to meet management goals that in some instances recommendations have been made to accept 50 to 70 percent of normal yield table values as standards. Although normal yield tables may have been useful in the early years of American forestry, their shortcomings are widely recognized (Curtis, 1972).

Empirical yield tables, similar to normal yield tables except for the concept of normality, are based on actual "average stands" rather than full stocking. Therefore, the problem of selecting fully stocked stands as a developmental basis is eliminated. However, empirical yield tables may not be an improvement over normal yield tables (Myers, 1966). Stand densities that are sampled to represent actual average stocking may differ from desired management objectives, particularly in the case of uncut or conservatively cut stands.

Variable-density yield tables, which generally show relationships between volume and independent variables such as stand age, site index, and stand density are rapidly replacing the outmoded concept of normal yield tables. Including stand density as an independent variable seems a more reasonable approach since the degree of normal stocking need not be identified. Furthermore, variable-density yield tables describe volumes across the full range of important stand characteristics.

Variable-density yield tables are replacing the other types of yield tables in forestry practice. Consequently, while the general procedures followed in developing estimates of stand growth are essentially similar for all types of tables, a variable-density yield table will be used to illustrate the application of yield tables for growth determination.

The yield (or volume) of black spruce in Minnesota for each of three site-index classes by combinations of stand age and density (basal area) is presented in Table 6-2. For a given site index and basal area, volume can

Table 6-2   Yield in Cubic Feet per Acre for Black Spruce on Organic Soils in Minnesota*

	Site Index 45							
Stand age (years)	**Stand basal area (square feet per acre)**							
	40	60	80	100	120	140	160	180
	Cubic feet per acre†							
60	919	1,361	1,798	2,232	2,663	3,092		
80	956	1,416	1,870	2,322	2,770	3,216	3,660	4,103
100	979	1,449	1,915	2,377	2,836	3,293	3,748	4,201
120	994	1,472	1,946	2,415	2,881	3,346	3,807	4,268
140	1,005	1,489	1,968	2,442	2,914	3,383	3,850	4,316
160	1,014	1,502	1,984	2,463	2,939	3,412	3,883	4,352
180	1,021	1,512	1,997	2,479	2,958	3,434	3,909	4,381
200	1,026	1,520	2,008	2,492	2,974	3,452	3,929	4,404
	Site Index 35							
60	788	1,167	1,542	1,914	2,283	2,651		
80	819	1,214	1,604	1,990	2,375	2,757	3,138	
100	839	1,242	1,642	2,038	2,432	2,823	3,213	3,601
120	852	1,262	1,668	2,070	2,470	2,868	3,264	3,658
140	862	1,276	1,687	2,094	2,498	2,900	3,301	3,700
160	869	1,287	1,701	2,112	2,519	2,925	3,329	3,731
180	875	1,296	1,712	2,125	2,536	2,944	3,351	3,756
200	880	1,303	1,721	2,137	2,549	2,960	3,368	3,776

*From Perala, 1971 (abridged).
†Gross peeled volume (entire stem) for trees 3.6 in. (9.15 cm) and larger. Blocks indicate extent of basic data.

be read directly at the desired stand age.[1] For example, it may be assumed that a stand of black spruce has a basal area of 18.4 m²/ha (80 sq ft per acre) on an area where the site index is 10.7 m (35 ft) at 80 years. The expected yield at age 80 is read from the table as 112.2 m³/ha (1,604 cu ft per acre). To determine the expected yield at a future time, such as age 120, it is necessary to estimate basal-area growth for the period from 80 to 120 years. According to Table 6-3, which gives net basal-area growth by initial age and basal-area density, total basal-area growth for this period is 13.7 m²/ha (31.5 + 28.2, or 59.7 sq ft per acre). Thus projected basal area of the stand at age 120 is 32.1 m²/ha (140 sq ft per acre). At age 120, then, the expected yield is 200.7 m³/ha (2,868 cu ft per acre). The predicted periodic annual growth is (200.7 − 112.2)/20, or 4.4, m³/ha for this particular stand.

[1] Since yield tables were not available in metric units, values for the example cited are described in both English and metric units.

Table 6-3 Ten-Year Net Basal Growth in Square Feet per Acre for Black Spruce on Organic Soils in Minnesota*

Stand age (years)	Stand basal area (square feet per acre)†							
	40	60	80	100	120	140	160	180
60	37.0	39.9	36.5	28.6	17.5	4.1	−11.1	
80	28.2	32.2	31.5	27.0	19.5	9.7	− 2.1	
100	23.1	27.5	28.2	25.8	20.8	13.7	4.7	− 5.9
120	19.8	24.3	25.9	24.9	21.7	16.6	9.8	1.5
140	17.4	22.0	24.2	24.3	22.4	18.9	13.8	7.3
160	15.7	20.3	22.9	23.7	22.9	20.6	17.7	12.1
180	14.4	19.0	21.9	23.3	23.3	22.1	19.7	16.1

*From Perala, 1971.
†For trees 3.6 in. (9.15 cm) and larger. Block indicates extent of basic data.

Even though the variables of site index, stand age, and density are carefully determined, there are likely to be some errors resulting from this method of stand-growth prediction. The effect of unusual climatic cycles during a short prediction period may result in erratic growth patterns that cannot be accommodated by the "average conditions" implicit in a yield table. Another factor that may contribute to growth prediction errors is the actual amount of mortality occurring in the stands under consideration. Although yield tables are customarily constructed in terms of *net* yield, a specific mortality rate has been necessarily presumed. When the actual mortality differs appreciably from the assumed "standard," adjustments of tabular yields are required before reliable growth predictions can be expected.

Many variable-density yield tables include specific relationships between stand growth and age, site index, and density. Generally, these relationships are computed simply as the differences between initial yield and final yield by site-index classes for combinations of stand age and density.

STAND-TABLE PROJECTION

6-25 Characteristics of Stand Projection   This method of growth prediction recognizes the structure of a stand, and growth projections are made according to dbh classes. The method is best suited to uneven-aged, low-density, and immature timber stands. In dense or overmature forests where mortality rates are high, stand-table projection may be of questionable value for providing reliable information on net stand growth.

The procedure ordinarily followed in the stand-table-projection method of growth prediction may be briefly summarized as follows:

1 A present stand table showing the number of trees in each dbh class is developed from a conventional inventory.

2 Past periodic growth, by dbh classes, is determined from increment borings or from remeasurements of permanent sample plots. When increment borings are used, growth values must be converted from an inside-bark basis to outside-bark readings

3 Past diameter-growth rates are applied to the present stand table to derive a future stand table showing the predicted number of trees in each dbh class at the end of the growth period. Numbers of trees in each class must then be corrected for expected mortality and predicted ingrowth.

4 Both present and future stand tables are converted to stock tables by use of an appropriate single-entry volume table. Thus for short growth periods, the expected changes in tree height during the growth period are inherently accommodated by diameter increases.

5 Periodic stand growth is obtained as the difference between the total volume of the present stand and that of the future stand.

6-26 Diameter Growth Rates of diameter growth outside bark are best obtained from repeated measurements of permanent sample plots. Consecutive inventories of the same trees provide a direct evaluation of combined wood and bark increment at dbh. As a result, many of the problems encountered in estimating stem growth from increment borings can be avoided.

When diameter growth is not available in the foregoing form, it is customary to rely on increment borings at dbh instead. Assuming we wish to estimate diameter growth (outside bark) for the last 10 years, estimates for each dbh class might be handled according to the following step-by-step procedure:

1 Measure present dbh to the nearest 0.1 cm and subtract diameter bark thickness to obtain present dib at breast height.

2 From an increment boring, obtain the 10-year wood growth in diameter and subtract from present dib to derive dib at breast height 10 years ago.

3 For each diameter class recognized, plot present diameter bark thickness over present dib at breast height. Draw a smooth, balanced curve through the plotted points. Read off appropriate bark thicknesses for each dib 10 years ago (step 2) and add these values together to arrive at an estimate of dbh (outside bark) 10 years ago.

4 Subtract dbh (outside bark) 10 years ago from present dbh to derive the estimated growth in diameter during the stated time period. If future growth is presumed to equal past growth, this information may be applied directly in a stand-table projection.

6-27   Stand Mortality and Ingrowth   The reliability of stand-table projections leans heavily on the derivation of realistic estimates of mortality and ingrowth. As with diameter increment, such information is preferably obtained from consecutive inventories of permanent sample plots; in reality, there is no other sound procedure for making these predictions. Mortality rates are desired for each dbh recognized in the stand table because the natural demise of smaller stems is usually much greater than for large diameters. Only when growth predictions are made for very short time periods (perhaps 3 years or less) can mortality be regarded as a negligible factor.

For growth predictions of 5 to 10 years, ingrowth is usually accounted for by having the present stand table include several diameter classes below the minimum dbh desired in the future stand table. As an illustration, if 10-year growth predictions are planned for trees 24 cm dbh and larger, the initial stand table might include all stems that might logically grow into the 24 cm dbh class during the interim, e.g., those stems presently 16 cm or more in diameter.

6-28   A Sample Stand Projection   A present stand table, expected mortality, and 10-year diameter growth rates for an 8-ha stand of southern pines are presented in Table 6-4. To illustrate the application of stand-table projection, it will be assumed that a 10-year volume-growth prediction is desired for stems in the 24-cm-dbh class and larger. Present and future volumes are to be derived from a single-entry volume table. The 16-cm and 20-cm trees are included in the present stand table to accommodate ingrowth into larger diameter classes.

Table 6-4   Present Stand Table, Mortality, and Expected 10-Year Diameter Growth for an 8-ha Stand of Southern Pines

Dbh class (cm)	Present stand (No. of stems)	Expected mortality (%)	Expected survival (No. of stems)	10-year dbh growth* (cm)
16	522	40	313	5.6
20	352	35	229	5.8
24	179	25	134	6.1
28	88	20	70	5.6
32	40	15	34	6.1
36	11	10	10	6.6
40	10	10	9	5.3
44	8	20	6	4.6
Total	1,210		805	

*From Judson, 1965.

Because mortality has been deducted from the present stand in Table 6-4, the next step is the application of diameter growth rates in deriving a future stand table. The method used here was proposed by Chapman and Meyer (1949). The upward movement of trees into larger dbh classes is proportional to the ratio of growth to the chosen diameter class interval. Using the 16-cm-dbh class as an example,

$$\text{Growth-index ratio} = \frac{\text{growth rate (cm)}}{\text{dbh interval (cm)}} = \frac{5.6}{4.0} = 1.40$$

The interpretation of a growth-index ratio of 1.40 is that 100 percent of the trees move up one dbh class, and 0.40, or 40 percent, of these advance two classes. Thus, of the 313 trees expected to survive in the 16-cm-dbh class, 60 percent (188 trees) move up to the 20-cm class and 40 percent (125 trees) move all the way to the 24-cm class. None of the trees will remain in the 16-cm class in this instance. However, if the growth-index ratio had been less than unity, for example 0.80, 80 percent of the trees would move up one class interval, and 20 percent would remain in the present dbh class. For the dbh classes under consideration, growth-index ratios and the future-stand table are shown in Table 6-5.

Once the future-stand table has been derived, present and future volumes (stock tables) can be obtained from an appropriate single-entry volume table as illustrated in Table 6-6. Volume production is computed for each dbh class as the difference between present and future volumes. For this hypothetical stand, the predicted net-volume growth for the 10-year

Table 6-5   Application of Growth-Index Ratios in Deriving a Future Stand Table for an 8-ha Stand of Southern Pines

Dbh class (cm)	Present stand surviving (No. of stems)	Growth-index ratio	No. of stems moving up (by dbh classes)			Future stand table (no. of stems)
			No change	1 class	2 classes	
16	313	1.40	0	188	125	0
20	229	1.45	0	126	103	188
24	134	1.52	0	64	70	251
28	70	1.40	0	42	28	167
32	34	1.52	0	16	18	112
36	10	1.65	0	4	6	44
40	9	1.32	0	6	3	22
44	6	1.15	0	5	1	12
48	0	—	—	—	—	8
52	0	—	—	—	—	1
Total	805		0	451	354	805

Table 6-6 Predicted 10-Year Volume Production of an 8-ha Stand of Southern Pines

Dbh class (cm)	Present stand table (No. of stems)	Future stand table (No. of stems)	Volume per tree (m³)	Present stock table (m³)	Future stock table (m³)	Volume production (m³)
16	313	0				
20	229	188				
24	134	251	0.25	33.5	62.8	29.3
28	70	167	0.40	28.0	66.8	38.8
32	34	112	0.61	20.7	68.3	47.6
36	10	44	0.86	8.6	37.8	29.2
40	9	22	1.20	1.1	26.4	25.3
44	6	12	1.50	0.9	18.0	17.1
48	0	8	1.90	0	15.2	15.2
52	0	1	2.40	0	2.4	2.4
Total	805	805		92.8	297.7	204.9

period is 204.9 m³, or 25.6 m³/ha. On an *annual basis* (periodic annual growth), the predicted growth per hectare is 25.6/10, or 2.56, m³.

PROBLEMS

6-1 Prepare a brief report on (*a*) the use of soil characteristics to measure site quality in your locality or (*b*) the possibilities of using indicator plants comprising lesser vegetation as a measure of site in your locality.

6-2 Assess the site quality of a forest stand in your locality by determining the site index, using an appropriate site-index relationship.

6-3 Determine site-index values of different species growing in mixture on the same area. What would be the expected difference in cubic volume per unit area for the two species at the index age, assuming that average stem diameter (dbh) is about the same for both species?

6-4 On recent aerial photographs of your locality, locate 10 to 30 circular sample plots that represent a wide density range in terms of crown closure. Then, visit each plot and obtain ground estimates of basal area per unit area for the dominant-codominant stems that were visible on the photographs. On graph paper, plot basal-area values over crown closure. If a definite trend is evident, fit a balanced curve to the plotted points. Explain possible reasons for the pattern of plotted points obtained.

6-5 Prepare curves of periodic and mean annual growth for an important timber species growing in your locality. Does the culmination of mean annual growth roughly coincide with the accepted rotation age for that species? Give reasons for differences, if any.

6-6 Using simple interest rates, compute the growth percent of an even-aged stand in your locality. Explain possible reasons why simple interest rates may give erroneous estimates of growth percent in uneven-aged stands.

6-7 Make a complete stem analysis of a tree that is 20 to 40 years old. Using a growth period of 5 to 10 years, compute (*a*) present cubic volume, (*b*) periodic annual growth, and (*c*) predicted future volume 5 to 10 years hence.

6-8 If data are available from remeasured permanent plots in your locality, compute stand accretion, gross growth, net growth, and production for several plots representing similar stand conditions.

6-9 Using an appropriate variable-density yield table, estimate 10-year periodic annual growth of an even-aged stand for an important timber species in your locality. Select the 10-year growth period to represent the midlife of the stand.

6-10 Predict periodic annual growth of an uneven-aged stand in your locality by applying the stand-table-projection method.

REFERENCES

Bickford, C. Allen, et al.
 1957. Stocking, normality, and measurement of stand density. *J. Forestry* **55**:99-104.

Brickell, James E.
 1968. A method for constructing site index curves from measurements of tree age and height — its application to inland Douglas-fir. *U.S. Forest Serv., Intermount. Forest and Range Expt. Sta. Res. Paper* INT-47. 23 pp., illus.

Brown, Harry E., and Worley, David P.
 1965. The canopy camera in forestry. *J. Forestry* **63**:674-680, illus.

Bruce, Donald, and Schumacher, Francis X.
 1950. *Forest mensuration*, 3d ed. McGraw-Hill Book Company, New York. 483 pp., illus

Chapman, H.H., and Meyer, W.H.
 1949. *Forest mensuration.* McGraw-Hill Book Company, New York. 522 pp., illus.

Clutter, Jerome L.
 1963. Compatible growth and yield models for loblolly pine. *Forest Sci.* **9**:354-371.

Curtis, Robert O.
 1970. Stand density measures: An interpretation. *Forest Sci.* **16**:403-414.

———
 1972. Yield tables past and present. *J. Forestry* **70**:28-32.

Ffolliott, Peter F.
 1965. Determining growth of ponderosa pine in Arizona by stand projection. *U.S. Forest Serv., Rocky Mt. Forest and Range Expt. Sta. Res. Note* RM-52. 4 pp., illus

Doolittle, Warren T.
 1958. Forest soil-site relationships and species comparisons in the Southern Appalachians. *Soil Sci. Soc. Am. Proc.* **22**:455-458.

Gessel, Stanley P., Turnbull, Kenneth J., and Tremblay, F. Todd
 1960. How to fertilize trees and measure response. National Plant Food Institute, Washington, D.C. 67 pp., illus.

Gilbert, Adrian M.
1954. What is this thing called growth? *U.S. Forest Serv., Northeast. Forest Expt. Sta. Paper* 71. 5 pp.

Gingrich, Samuel F.
1967. Measuring and evaluating stocking and stand density in upland hardwood forests in the central states. *Forest Sci.* **13**:38-53.

Grosenbaugh, L.R.
1958. Allowable cut as a new function of growth and diagnostic tallies. *J. Forestry* **56**:727-730.

Hall, O.F.
1959. The contribution of remeasured sample plots to the precision of growth estimates. *J. Forestry* **57**:801-811.

Hannah, Peter R.
1968. Topography and soil relations for white and black oak in southern Indiana. *U.S. Forest Serv., North Central Forest Expt. Sta. Res. Paper* NC-25. 7 pp., illus.

Heilberg, Svend O., and White, Donald P.
1956. A site evaluation concept. *J. Forestry* **54**:7-10.

Jones, John R.
1969. Review and comparison of site evaluation methods. *U.S. Forest Serv., Rocky Mt. Forest and Range Expt. Sta. Res. Paper* RM-51. 27 pp., illus.

Judson, George M.
1965. Tree diameter growth in Alabama. *U.S. Forest Serv., Res. Note* SO-17. 3 pp.

Lexen, Bert
1943. Bole area as an expression of growing stock. *J. Forestry* **41**:883-885.

Minor, Charles O.
1964. Site index curves for young-growth ponderosa pine in northern Arizona. *U.S. Forest Serv., Rocky Mt. Forest and Range Expt. Sta., Res. Note* RM-37. 8 pp., illus.

Moessner, Karl E.
1964. Two aerial photo basal area tables. *U.S. Forest Serv., Intermount. Forest and Range Expt. Sta.* 7 pp.

Myers, Clifford A.
1966. Yield tables for managed stands with special reference to the Black Hills. *U.S. Forest Serv., Rocky Mt. Forest and Range Expt. Sta. Res. Paper* RM-21. 20 pp., illus.

Odum, Eugene P.
1971. *Fundamentals of ecology*, 3d ed. W. B. Saunders Company, Philadelphia. 574 pp., illus.

Perala, Donald A.
1971. Growth and yield of black spruce on organic soils in Minnesota. *U.S. Forest Serv., North Central Forest Expt. Sta. Res. Paper* NC-56. 16 pp., illus.

Roe, Arthur L.
1967. Productivity indicators in western larch forests. *U.S. Forest Serv., Intermount. Forest and Range Expt. Sta. Res Note* INT-59. 4 pp.

Chapter 7

Primary Wood Products

7-1 Introduction This chapter describes techniques for measuring stacked roundwood, storage piles of wood chips or residues, and individual logs. Because of the continued use of such units as the cord and the board foot, some of the measurement techniques are described in both English and metric terms.

When trees are cut into lengths of 2.4 m (8 ft) or more, the sections are referred to as *logs*. By contrast, shorter pieces are called sticks or *bolts*. The process of measuring volumes of individual logs is termed *scaling*. Logs may be scaled in terms of board feet, cubic feet, cubic meters, or weight. Stacks of roundwood bolts are commonly measured in cords, cubic feet, cubic meters, or weight, Pulpwood chips and related sawmill residues (bark, sawdust, etc.) may be assessed in terms of cubic volume or weight. In many parts of the United States, these materials are measured in "units" of 2,400 lb (1,089 kg) of ovendry weight.

The ideal measurement unit for primary wood products would be one that is absolute, unambiguous, accurate, simple, and inexpensive to apply (Ker, 1962). As illustrated by the discussions that follow, however, the ideal unit has yet to be discovered. Among the more promising techniques are weight-scaling methods and autoscanning devices for measuring sawlogs and veneer logs.

STACKED WOOD AND CHIPS

7-2   The Cord and The Cubic Meter   Stacked ricks of wood are measured in cords or cubic meters. A standard cord of wood is a rick that measures $4 \times 4 \times 8$ ft and contains 128 cu ft. Inasmuch as this space includes wood, bark, and sizable voids, the cord is more of an indication of space occupied than actual wood measure. Of course, cordwood is not necessarily cut into 4-ft lengths, and it is rarely stacked in rectangular ricks having 32 sq ft of surface area. Any stacked rick of roundwood may be converted to standard cords by this relationship:

$$\frac{\text{Width (ft)} \times \text{height (ft)} \times \text{bolt length (ft)}}{128}$$

When cordwood is cut into lengths shorter than 4 ft (e.g., firewood), a rick having 32 sq ft of surface area may be referred to as a *short cord*. If a similar rick is made up of bolts longer than 4 ft, it may be termed a *long cord or unit*. In the United States, pulpwood is commonly cut into lengths of 5, 5.25, and 8.33 ft. When these stick lengths are multiplied by a cord surface area of 32 sq ft, the resulting units occupy 160, 168, and 266.6 cu ft of space, respectively.

Where the metric system is employed, stacked wood is measured in cubic meters; 1 m^3 is equivalent to 35.3 cu ft (Fig. 7-1). A stacked rick of wood is converted to cubic meters by simply measuring all three dimensions of the rick in meters and obtaining the product of these dimensions:

$$m^3 = \text{width (m)} \times \text{height (m)} \times \text{bolt length (m)}$$

7-3   Solid Contents of Stacked Wood   Purchasers of stacked roundwood are primarily interested in the amount of solid-wood volume contained in various ricks rather than in the total space occupied. The solid-wood content is affected by bark thickness, diameter and length of bolts, straightness, freedom from protruding knots, and closeness of stacking. Smooth, straight bolts of large diameter tend to have the highest solid-wood contents; the proportion of solid wood to total rick space may range from about 0.50 to 0.75. Therefore, mills purchasing stacked wood have traditionally developed their own cubic-volume conversions based

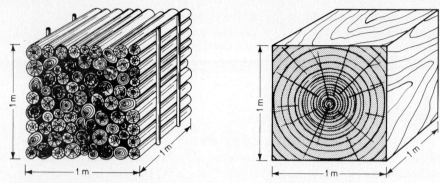

Figure 7-1 Stacked cubic meter (left) and solid cubic meter (right)
of roundwood.

on the size and quality of wood being delivered; there is no single proportion that is considered reliable over large forest regions.

Estimates of solid-wood content can be easily made with a steel tape
graduated into 100 equal parts. The tape is stretched diagonally across the
ends of the stacked bolts, and the number or graduations falling on wood
(as opposed to bark and voids) provides the desired proportion. Several
observations should be made for each rick to obtain reliable estimates.

7-4 Inventories of Chip Piles Large stockpiles of pulpwood
chips, bark, or sawdust may be periodically measured for inventory and
cost-accounting purposes. In the past, such inventories have been made
by plane-table surveys or by ground surveys designed for computing
stockpile cross sections. Today, cubic volumes of materials up to 30 m
high and covering 20 ha of land or more may be estimated efficiently by
photogrammetric methods.

By this approach, stockpiles are first imaged on stereoscopic pairs of
large-scale aerial photographs (e.g., 1:500). The stockpiles are then contoured at intervals of 0.3 m (1 ft) by using a stereoscopic plotting instrument based on the floating-dot (parallax) principle as described in
Chap. 3. After contours have been determined, the area of each contoured layer, or "slice," is determined by planimetry and the cubic volume of the pile computed, layer-by-layer.

If the stockpile consists of wood chips, the calculated cubic volume
may be converted to weight units by periodic sampling of the chips to establish local weight/volume ratios. It has been determined, for example,
that green southern pine chips weigh approximately 288 to 384 kg/m³ (18
to 24 lb per cu ft). Local corrections should be made for variations in density in different piles of the same materials because settling and compac-
tion will result in significant changes in weight/volume ratios.

A photogrammetric assessment has the advantage of permitting an easy cut-off time for inventories since all photographs can be obtained on a single date. It provides a permanent record of the stockpile size at a specific date and time, and volume can be rechecked at any later time if questions arise as to the accuracy of the estimate.

BOARD-FOOT LOG-SCALING

7-5 The Board-Foot Anomaly The board foot is equivalent to a plank 1 in. thick and 12 in. (1 ft) square; it contains 144 cu in. of wood. Although the board foot has been a useful and fairly definitive standard for the measure of sawed lumber, it is an ambiguous and inconsistent unit for log-scaling.

A *log rule* is a table or formula showing estimated volumes, usually in board feet, for various log diameters and lengths. During the past century, at least 100 board-foot log rules have been devised, and several have been widely adopted. However, none of these rules can accurately predict the mill output of boards, except when near-cylindrical logs are sawed according to rigid assumptions on which the rules are based. Although the scaler might employ any of several rules that indicate different log volumes, there is only one correct measure of the boards produced. Thus the terms *board-feet log scale* and *board feet of lumber* are rarely, if ever, synonymous.

The formula commonly used for determing the board-foot content of sawed lumber is

$$\text{bd ft} = \frac{\text{thickness (in.)} \times \text{width (in.)} \times \text{length (ft)}}{12}$$

Accordingly, a 1 in. $\times$ 12 in. $\times$ 12-ft plank contains 12 bd ft, and a 2 in. $\times$ 8 in. $\times$ 24-ft plank includes 32 bd ft. This method of computation is not entirely correct even for sawed lumber because of accepted dimensional differences between rough green boards versus finished (seasoned and planed) lumber. A green "two-by-four" may be originally cut to the nominal size of 2 $\times$ 4 in., but it can be acceptable in finished form and sold as a two-by-four if it measures only 1 1/2 $\times$ 3 1/2 in. The purchaser of 1,000 bd ft of finished lumber is therefore likely to receive considerably less than the volume implied by rigid adherence to the formula cited.

7-6 General Features of Board-Foot Log Rules To be considered equitable to both buyer and seller, a log rule must be *consistent*; i.e., volumes should be directly correlated with log sizes over the entire range of dimensions encountered. Few log rules currently in use can meet this simple requirement. Most of the differences between board-foot log scale and the sawed lumber tally can be attributed to the inflexible assumptions that necessarily underlie such rules:

1 Logs are considered to be cylinders, and volumes are derived from the small ends of logs. Volume outside the scaling cylinder, resulting from log taper, is generally ignored. In a few instances, a fixed rate of taper is presumed to somewhat compensate for this volume loss.

2 It is assumed that all logs will be sawed into boards of a certain thickness (usually 1 in.) with a saw of a specified thickness or "kerf."

3 A fixed procedure for sawing the log and allowing for slabs is postulated (Fig. 7-2).

4 There is a tacit implication that all sawmills operate at a uniform level of efficiency which provides equal lumber yields from similar logs. The fact that some mills may be able to cut and market shorter or narrower boards than others is disregarded.

As a corollary to the foregoing, the terms *minimum board width* and *maximum scaling length* are worthy of definition. Minimum board width refers to the narrowest board for which volume would be computed by a

Figure 7-2 One method of sawing a ponderosa pine log. Losses due to saw kerf and shrinkage are apparent. Log diameter is 38 cm (15 in.).

given log rule. For most rules, the minimum board width is not smaller than 4 in. or larger than 8 in. Maximum scaling length indicates the longest tree section that may be scaled as a single log. Such a limitation is essential where log rules include no taper allowance; otherwise an entire tree might be scaled from the top end as a 6-in. log. Local scaling practices usually limit the maximum scaling length to 16 ft, though 32 ft may be acceptable in a few regions.

Log rules have been constructed from empirical rules of thumb, sawmill lumber tallies, ratios of board feet to cubic feet, diagrams, mathematical formulas, and by combinations of these techniques. The three most commonly used log rules in the United States are the Scribner, Doyle, and International 1/4-in. All three are included in the Appendix.

There is always some disparity between log scale and lumber yield. If the lumber output is greater, the excess difference is called *overrun*. When log scale values are larger than sawed output, an *underrun* occurs. Overrun and underrun are expressed as a percent of log scale by this relationship:

$$\text{Percent overrun or underrun} = \frac{\text{mill tally} - \text{log scale}}{\text{log scale}} \times 100$$

When log sizes and sawmilling practices are equal, the amount of overrun or underrun is primarily dependent on the log rule used for scaling.

7-7 Scribner Log Rule Developed by J. M. Scribner around 1846, this rule was derived from diagrams of 1-in. boards drawn to scale within cylinders of various sizes. A saw kerf of 1/4 in. is presumed. The exact minimum board width allowed is not definitely known, although it appears to have been 4 in. for at least some log diameters. No taper allowance was included, so the rule ignores all volume outside scaling cylinders projected from small ends of logs. Therefore, this rule will normally underscale logs unless the maximum scaling length is held to about 16 ft. When the volumes of 16-ft logs are desired, the rule-of-thumb formula $0.8 (d - 1)^2 - d/2$ provides a close approximation of the Scribner log rule (Grosenbaugh, 1952).

In general, the Scribner rule is considered to be intermediate in accuracy, although it does not provide board-foot volumes that are entirely consistent with changing log diameters. A slight modification of the rule is the Scribner Decimal C log rule. Here, the original Scribner volumes are rounded off to the nearest 10 bd ft, and the last zero is dropped. This innovation is presumably an aid to the scaler who must record and total volumes for large numbers of logs. The Scribner Decimal C is the official rule of the U.S. Forest Service in Western United States. For eastern national forests, the International 1/4-in. rule is generally used.

7-8 Doyle Log Rule This rule, devised by Edward Doyle about 1825, is based on a mathematical formula

$$\text{bd ft} = \left(\frac{d-4}{4}\right)^2 l$$

where d is the log diameter in inches, and l is the log length in feet.

For 16-ft logs, the formula may be reduced to merely $(d-4)^2$. Despite the fact that the formula is algebraically incorrect, use of the rule has persisted in southern and eastern United States. It was originally intended that the rule provide for a slabbing allowance of 4 in. and a saw kerf of 5/16 in., or 25 percent. The 4-in. slab deduction is more than twice the amount ordinarily needed, and the kerf deduction is actually only about 4.5 percent. The net result is a highly inaccurate and inconsistent log rule that greatly underscales small logs because of the excessive slab deduction. Conversely, large logs are overscaled, for the insufficient kerf deduction is no longer absorbed by the heavy slab deduction.

The biggest fault of the Doyle rule lies in its inconsistency rather than its basic inaccuracy. The fact that volumes increase erratically with changing log diameters prohibits uniform adjustments in log prices to compensate for the abortive scale values. The rule can thus be considered a fair basis for transactions only when both buyers and sellers of logs are fully aware of its deficiencies. To provide a slight concession to the seller of small logs, some purchasers may either allow the inclusion of one bark thickness in measuring log diameters, or record a scale equal to the log length when Doyle values are less than that amount. However, such local rules of thumb do little to alleviate the inherent inequalities of this anomalous rule.

7-9 International Log Rule This rule, based on a reasonably accurate mathematical formula, is the only one in common use that makes an allowance for log taper. Devised in 1906 by Judson Clark, the International rule includes a fixed taper allowance of 1/2 in. per 4 ft of log length. Thus scale values for a 16-ft log are derived by totaling board-foot volumes of four 4-ft cylinders, each 1/2 in. larger in diameter than the previous one. In addition to the allowance for taper, the rule also provides rational deductions for slabbing and saw kerf. The original International 1/8-in. rule assumed a 1/8-in. saw kerf, plus 1/16 in. allowance for board shrinkage, giving a total deduction of 3/16 in. The International 1/4-in rule, devised from the original, provides for a 1/4-in. saw kerf plus 1/16 in.

for shrinkage or total kerf deduction of 5/16 in. Slabs are deducted in the form of an imaginary plank 2.12 in. thick and having a width equal to log diameter. It is assumed that all logs are cut into boards 1 in. thick.

The International 1/8-in. rule for a 4-ft log section is

$$\text{bd ft} = 0.22d^2 - 0.71d$$

Some years after the International 1/8-in. rule was published, it was modified to make it applicable for sawmills employing a 1/4-in. kerf (total kerf and shrinkage allowance of 5/16 in.). Instead of all scale values being recomputed by the process described here, the 1/8-in. rule was reduced by the converting factor of 0.905. Thus, for 4-ft sections, the formula for the 1/4-in. rule may be expressed as $0.905(0.22d^2 - 0.71d)$. For 16-ft log lengths, a simpler formula, $0.8(d - 1)^2$, will provide approximate volumes for the International 1/4-in. rule (Grosenbaugh, 1952).

Of the three principal log rules described here, the International is undoubtedly the most consistent, and it becomes quite accurate for mills producing mainly 1-in. boards with a 1/4-in. saw thickness. The International 1/4-in. rule has been officially adopted by several states and is widely used on the U.S. Forest Survey. In spite of its relative virtues, however, it has never gained the favor accorded such rules as the Scribner and even the Doyle for scaling work. Unrealistic as it may seem, many foresters are required to derive forest inventory data with the International rule and then handle log sales based on Scribner or Doyle volumes.

7-10 Scaling Straight, Sound Logs The scaling of a straight and sound log is simply a matter of determining its length and average dib at the small end. Lengths may be estimated or measured with a tape. Diameters are commonly determined with a *scale stick*, i.e., a rule graduated in inches and imprinted with log rule volumes for varying lengths. The "average" log diameter to be scaled is ocularly selected in most cases. However, on unusually elliptical logs the two extreme diameters may be measured for computing an average value.

Depending on local scaling practices, the minimum scaling diameter is ordinarily set at 6 to 8 in. Smaller logs are given zero scale (*culled*), i.e., disregarded and eliminated from the scale record. When log diameters fall exactly halfway between scale-stick graduations (such as 12.5 in.), it is customary to drop back to the lower value—12 in. in this instance. Scaling diameters definitely above the halfway mark are raised to the next largest graduation; thus a 12.6-in. log would be scaled as 13 in.

Log lengths are usually taken at 2-ft intervals, although 1-ft intervals may be allowed for certain species. All logs should have a trim allowance of 2 to 6 in. When logs are cut "scant" (without sufficient trim allowance) or in odd lengths, the scale is ordinarily based on the next shortest acceptable length. When long logs or tree-length sections are being scaled, the locally adopted maximum scaling length should be observed to avoid loss of volume due to excessive taper.

7-11 Log Defects If a log is straight and free from defects, the gross scale (as read from the scale stick) is also the *net* or *sound* scale. From the standpoint of log scaling, defects include only those imperfections that will result in losses of wood *volume* in sawing the log. By contrast, those imperfections affecting log *quality* or *grade* only are not regarded as scaling defects. Thus scale deductions are made for such items as rot, wormholes, ring shake, checks, splits, and crook but not for sound knots, coarse grain, light sap stain, or small pitch pockets.

Making scale deductions for log defects is basically a matter of determining (1) the type and extent of the defect and (2) computing the board-foot volume that will be lost as a result. When the defect volume is subtracted from gross log scale, the usable volume remaining is the net or sound scale. Although certain guides or rules can be developed to somewhat standardize deduction techniques, the extent of many interior log defects can be learned only by working with experienced scalers and seeing defective logs sawed into boards on the mill carriage.

A point worthy of mention is that no deductions are made for defects outside the scaling cylinder or for those that penetrate 1 in. or less into the scaling cylinder. Defects outside the scaling cylinder are disregarded because this volume is ordinarily excluded from the original log scale (except for the International rule). Defects that penetrate the scaling cylinder 1 in. or less may be ignored because this portion of the log is normally lost in slabbing anyhow. If, for example, an exterior defect penetrates 3 in. into the cylinder of a log scaled by the Scribner rule, only the last 2 in. of penetration would be considered in making a scale deduction.

The principal forms of quantitative log defects encountered are

1 Interior defects, such as heartrot or decay, hollow logs, and ring shake (mechanical separation of annual rings)
2 Exterior or peripheral defects, such as sap rot, seasoning checks, wormholes, catface, and fire or lightning scars
3 Crook defects, such as excessive sweep, crook, and forked or "crotched" logs
4 Operating defects, such as breakage, splits, and end brooming

7-12 Board-Foot Deduction Methods Defect deductions can be accomplished by at least three approaches, viz., by reducing log diameters, by reducing log lengths, or by diagraming defects for mathematical computations. Exterior or peripheral defects (checks, sap rot) are best handled by diameter reductions. Butt rot and many crook defects are accommodated by reducing log lengths. For internal and partially hidden defects, the diagram-formula method is suitable. By this method, interior defects are enclosed by an imaginary solid and the board-foot contents computed for subtraction from gross log scale. Deductions are made as 1-in. boards, and that part of the defective section that would normally be lost as saw kerf is not deductible. For the Scribner and other cylinder log rules assuming 1-in. boards and a 1/4-in. kerf, the standard deduction formula is

$$\text{bd ft loss} = \frac{w \times t \times l}{15}$$

where w = width of defect enclosure, in.

$\quad t$ = thickness of defect enclosure, in.

$\quad l$ = length of defect enclosure, ft

One inch is usually added to both the width and thickness of the defect in calculating the deduction. For defects that run from one end of a log to the other, measurements are taken at the larger defect exposure. It will be recognized that this is the basic board-foot formula for lumber except that the denominator has been changed from 12 to 15. This reduction to 80 percent of the solid board-foot content effectively removes the 20 percent deduction due to a 1/4-in. saw kerf, because this portion would be lost anyway. For the International 1/4-in. rule, where the kerf-shrinkage allowance is actually 5/16 in., a denominator of 16 rather than 15 has been suggested for the formula. Several common log defects are illustrated in Fig. 7-3. Detailed techniques for scaling defective logs are given in the *National forest log scaling handbook* (USDA, 1964).

7-13 Veneer Logs Illogical as it may appear, veneer logs are ordinarily measured and purchased in terms of board-feet log scale. To compensate for the fact that size and quality standards are more stringent than for most sawlogs, a premium price is paid for logs of veneer quality. This price may sometimes amount to two or three times the price paid for logs that are sawed into yard lumber. Although grading specifications for veneer logs vary widely, quality requirements are based largely on species, log diameter, and freedom from defects such as crook, knots, bird peck, worm holes, ring shake, stains, and center rot.

For most hardwood species, veneer logs must have a minimum scaling diameter of 14 in.; preferred lengths range from 6 to 16 ft, plus trim allowance. Sellers can expect top prices for veneer logs only when wood is freshly cut and free from sap stains or discolorations that result from prolonged exposure.

Instead of scaling veneer logs in terms of board feet, it would be more

Figure 7-3 Ponderosa pine logs at a sawmill yard. Several logs have interior defects or fire scars (note arrows).

realistic to compute their contents in cubic feet or calculate expected yield in terms of veneer sheets of a given thickness. For rotary-cut veneers obtained from sound logs, output can be closely estimated from the difference between two cylinders—one based on the dib of the veneer bolt at the small end and the other based on a presumed core diameter. Thus the maximum surface area of rotary-cut veneer to be expected from a sound wood cylinder may be computed by

$$\text{Veneer yield in square feet} = \frac{B - b}{t}\, w$$

where B = cross-sectional area of log at small end, sq ft
      b = cross-sectional area of residual core, sq ft
      t = veneer thickness, thousandths of a foot
      w = sheet width (log length), ft

For excessively tapered logs, actual yields may be greater than that indicated, because some veneer is obtained from material outside the presumed cylinder. On the other hand, yields may be less for logs having interior defects. Nevertheless, for sound logs the formula will provide predictions that are much more reliable and realistic than scale methods based on board feet. The relationship can also be easily adapted to metric units.

CUBIC-METER LOG-SCALING

7-14 Derivation of Cubic Volumes The cubic volume of a log is determined from the product of average cross-sectional area (inside bark) and log length. From a practical viewpoint, the primary problem is that of locating or calculating the average cross-sectional area (Sec. 5-2). Where logs have little taper or where the volume outside a "scaling cylinder" can be ignored, cross-sectional areas can be computed from small-end diameters. However, such an approach is generally suitable only for short logs or low-value species, unless a fixed rate of log taper is included in volume calculations.

For commercial log-scaling, cubic volumes are usually computed by use of Smalian's or Huber's formula. In British Columbia, for example, the official "B.C. firmwood cubic scale," based on Smalian's formula, is the only log scale in official use in the province (Dobie, 1972). In practice, the scaler records the log length twice, once under the top diameter and again under the butt diameter. The values are then "cubed" by compiling the full-length cylinder volumes for each scaled diameter and the resultant volumes cumulated and the total divded by two (Ker, 1966). The B.C. firmwood scale permits scaling deductions *only* for pathological defects, charred wood, and catface. Sweep, crook, shake, check, and split are *not* deductible defects.

In the United Kingdom and certain other British Commonwealth nations, Huber's formula is used to calculate log cubic volumes. Mid-diameters of logs are measured to the nearest centimeter, log lengths are recorded to the nearest 0.1 m, and volumes are tabulated in cubic meters (Table 7-1). The problems associated with the use of Smalian's and Huber's formulas have been outlined in Chap. 5; the choice of one versus the other depends largely on whether log ends or midpoints are more accessible for measurement.

The *xylometer*, or water-immersion, method has also been considered for determining cubic volumes, but few equipment models have progressed beyond the experimental stage. By this technique, volume of wood is derived through application of Archimedes' principle; i.e., the measured volume of water displaced is equivalent to the cubic volume of wood immersed.

7-15 Defect Deduction Methods Where logs are scaled in terms of cubic volume, a logical approach is to estimate the defect volume as a *proportion* of total log volume. Five formulas for handling common log

Table 7-1   Metric Log Rule*

Log dia. (cm)	Volumes in cubic meters for lengths of:				
	2 m	4 m	6 m	8 m	10 m
10	0.016	0.031	0.047	0.063	0.079
12	0.023	0.045	0.068	0.090	0.113
14	0.031	0.062	0.092	0.123	0.154
16	0.040	0.080	0.121	0.161	0.201
18	0.051	0.102	0.153	0.204	0.254
20	0.063	0.126	0.188	0.251	0.314
22	0.076	0.152	0.228	0.304	0.380
24	0.090	0.181	0.271	0.362	0.452
26	0.106	0.212	0.319	0.425	0.531
28	0.123	0.246	0.369	0.493	0.616
30	0.141	0.283	0.424	0.565	0.707
32	0.161	0.322	0.483	0.643	0.804
34	0.182	0.363	0.545	0.726	0.908
36	0.204	0.407	0.611	0.814	1.018
38	0.227	0.454	0.680	0.907	1.134
40	0.251	0.503	0.754	1.005	1.257

*Based on cylinder volumes ($0.00007854d^2/l$)

defects have been devised by Grosenbaugh (1952). In all cases, d refers to average log diameter in centimeters at the small end, l is log length in meters, and P is the proportion lost due to the defect. The relationships have been slightly modified to convert them from English to metric units.

Rule 1.   Proportion lost when defect affects entire section:

$$P = \frac{\text{length of defective section}}{l}$$

Rule 2.   Proportion lost when defect affects wedge-shaped sector:

$$P = \frac{\text{length of defective section}}{l} \times \frac{\text{central angle of defect}}{360°}$$

Rule 3.   Proportion lost when log sweeps (or when its curved central axis departs more than 5 cm from an imaginary chord connecting the centers of its end-areas; ignore sweep less than 5 cm):

$$P = \frac{\text{maximum departure} - 5\text{ cm}}{d}$$

Rule 4.   Proportion lost when log crooks (or when a relatively short section deflects abruptly from straight axis of longer portion of log):

$$P = \frac{\text{length of deflecting section}}{l} \times \frac{\text{maximum deflection}}{d}$$

Rule 5. Proportion lost when average cross section of interior defect is enclosed in ellipse (or circle) with major and minor diameters measurable in centimeters:

$$P = \frac{(\text{major})(\text{minor})}{(d - 2 \text{ cm})^2} \times \frac{\text{length of defect}}{l}$$

When rule 5 is applied, defects in the peripheral ring of the log (slab collar) can be ignored, but the ellipse should enclose a band of sound wood at least 1 cm thick. When the cubic scale for products other than sawlogs is being used, sweep ordinarily is not considered to cause loss, and $(d + 2 \text{ cm})^2$ is used instead of $(d - 2 \text{ cm})^2$ as a divisor for interior-defect deduction.

7-16 Merchantable Logs and Scaling Records Logs are considered merchantable (valuable enough for utilization) if they can be profitably converted into a salable product such as lumber. Nonmerchantable logs are referred to as *culls*. If minimum dimensional requirements are met, the distinction between merchantable and cull logs is usually determined by the amount of defect encountered. In many localities, logs are considered merchantable only if they are at least 50 percent sound. The exact percentage applied, of course, is dependent on log size and species. A high-value, black walnut veneer log might be acceptable if only 30 percent sound, but a yellow pine log having a comparable defect would probably be culled. Thus merchantability limits vary with locality, kind of log, and changing economic conditions.

Log-scaling data are recorded on specially printed forms or in scale books. A complete scaling record includes the individual log number, species, diameter, length, gross scale, type and amount of defect, and net scale. When few log defects are encountered, the essential tally may occasionally be limited to species, log length, and gross scale. Log diameters are normally needed only for calculating defect deductions.

To conserve writing space and time, the type of defect can be indicated by locally accepted letter codes. Suggested designations are rot, R; sweep, S; wormholes, W; crack, C; catface or fire scar, F; and so on. The completed scaling record should show additionally the location or name of purchaser, scaler's initials, date, and log rule used.

Standardized scaling records are essential when such tallies are the basis for log sales and purchases. When complete records of log dimensions and defects are required, scalers are more likely to make all measurements carefully. Furthermore, "check scaling" by supervisory personnel is most effective when specific data for each log are clearly noted in scale books.

7-17 Automated Log-scaling While log-scaling may continue to be a responsibility of foresters in the field, there have been promising developments in the design and application of automated scaling devices at large industrial sites. For example, the "autoscaler" illustrated in Fig. 7-4 measures the average diameter and length of each log (at each end) on a conveyor. At regular intervals, the processing unit prints a log inventory, by diameter/length classes, that summarizes such items as piece count, linear measure, and volumes by selected log rules. A similar installation near Longview, Washington, has indicated that diameters are reliably measured within ±0.25 in. (0.6 cm) and lengths within ±1 in. (2.5 cm).

MEASURING WOOD BY WEIGHT

7-18 Weight-scaling of Pulpwood The appeal of weight-scaling in the pulpwood industry may be largely attributed to changes in the locale of measurement and purchases. Whereas wood was formerly scaled in the forest, measurements are now made at concentration yards or at the mill. In recent years, a large segment of the pulp and paper in-

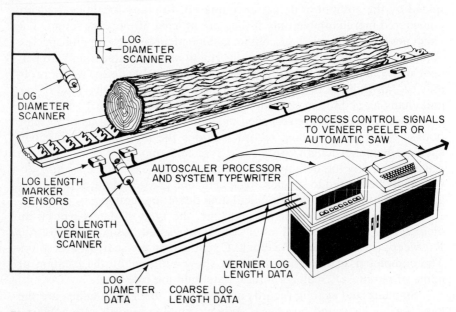

Figure 7-4 The LC-310 Autoscaler log-scaling system. (*Courtesy Atmospheric Sciences, Inc.*)

Figure 7-5 Weight-scaling of pine pulpwood. (*Courtesy Union-Camp Corporation.*)

dustry has adopted weight-scaling in lieu of linear measurements for stacked pulpwood (Fig. 7-5).

Weight/price equivalents are usually based on studies of freshly cut wood. It is thus implicit that mills favor green wood with a high moisture content or that purchasers be prepared to assume the cost of carrying large wood inventories for seasoning purposes. Since green wood is often preferred, there is some incentive for the producer to deliver his wood immediately after cutting. While there are indications that many species lose very little moisture during the first 4 to 8 weeks in storage, the widespread belief that pulpwood seasons and loses weight rapidly works in favor of mills that desire freshly cut material. From the mill inventory viewpoint, the greener the wood delivered, the longer it can be stored on the yard without deterioration—an important consideration in warm and humid regions.

Most mills utilizing weight-scaling have developed their own local conversions by making paired weighings and cordwood measurements of thousands of purchases. Weight equivalents may vary by species, mill localities, and points of wood origin.

The principal factors contributing to weight variations for a given species are wood volume, moisture content, and density or weight per cubic foot (or per cubic meter). Variations in wood volume, or the actual amount of solid wood in a cord, are caused by differences in bolt diameter, length, quality, and bark thickness. Moisture content varies within species for heartwood versus sapwood. Wood density is affected by percent of summerwood, growth rate, and position in the tree; i.e., density tends to decrease from the lower to the top portion of the stem.

7-19 Wood Density and Weight Ratios From a knowledge of moisture content and specific gravity (based on ovendry weight and green volume), the weight per cubic foot of any species may be computed by this relationship:

$$\text{Density} = \text{sp gr} \times 62.4 \left(1 + \frac{\%\ \text{moisture content}}{100} \right)$$

As an example, a weight/cord equivalent might be desired for a species having a specific gravity of 0.46, moisture content of 110 percent, solid wood volume per cord of 72 cu ft, and an estimated bark weight of 700 lb per cord. Substituting in the formula, we have:

$$\text{Density} = 0.46 \times 62.4 \left(1 + \frac{110}{100} \right) = 60.3\ \text{lb per cu ft}$$

Since there are 72 cu ft of wood per cord, the weight of solid wood per cord is 72×60.3, or 4,342, lb. By adding the bark weight of 700 lb, the total weight is found to be 5,042 lb per cord.

The foregoing technique of computing weight/cord ratios is valid only when both specific gravity and moisture content are accurately determined because small variations in these factors can result in large weight changes. For each 0.02 change in specific gravity at a level of 100 percent moisture content, the weight of wood will change about 2.5 lb per cu ft. At the same level, a moisture content difference of 5 percent can cause a weight change of 1 to 2 lb per cu ft.

Table 7-2 was derived by solving the wood-density formula for a wide range of specific gravities and wood-moisture contents. It may therefore be applied in developing approximate weight factors for a variety of tree species. For those who wish to compute wood densities directly in metric units, the preceding relationship is modified to this form:

$$\text{Density} = \text{sp gr} \times 1,000 \left(1 + \frac{\%\ \text{moisture content}}{100} \right)$$

The validity of this relationship can be verified from the earlier ex-

Table 7-2 Weight in Pounds per Cubic Foot of Green Wood at Various Values of Specific Gravity and Moisture Content

Moisture content of wood (%)	Weight in pounds per cubic foot for specific gravities* of:										
	0.30	0.34	0.38	0.42	0.46	0.50	0.54	0.58	0.62	0.66	0.70
30	24.3	27.6	30.8	34.1	37.3	40.6	43.8	47.0	50.3	53.5	56.8
40	26.2	29.7	33.2	36.7	40.2	43.7	47.2	50.7	54.2	57.7	61.2
50	28.1	31.8	35.6	39.3	43.1	46.8	50.5	54.3	58.0	61.8	65.5
60	30.0	33.9	37.9	41.9	45.9	49.9	53.9	57.9	61.9	65.9	69.9
70	31.8	36.1	40.3	44.6	48.8	53.0	57.3	61.5	65.8	70.0	74.3
80	33.7	38.2	42.7	47.2	51.7	56.2	60.7	65.1	69.6	74.1	78.6
90	35.6	40.3	45.1	49.8	54.5	59.3	64.0	68.8	73.5	78.2	83.0
100	37.4	42.4	47.4	52.4	57.4	62.4	67.4	72.4	77.4	82.4	87.4
110	39.3	44.6	49.8	55.0	60.3	65.5	70.8	76.0	81.2	86.5	91.7
120	41.2	46.7	52.2	57.7	63.1	68.6	74.1	79.6	85.1	90.6	96.1
130	43.1	48.8	54.5	60.3	66.0	71.8	77.5	83.2	89.0	94.7	100.5
140	44.9	50.9	56.9	62.9	68.9	74.9	80.9	86.9	92.9	98.8	104.8
150	46.8	53.0	59.3	65.5	71.8	78.0	84.2	90.5	96.7	103.0	109.2

*Based on weight when ovendry and volume when green. Values may be converted to kilograms per cubic meter by multiplying by 16.0185.
Source: "Wood Handbook," USDA, 1955.

ample. The previous result of 60.3 lb per cu ft multiplied by a conversion factor of 16.0185 is equivalent to 965.92 kg/m³. From the modified formula, we have:

$$\text{Density} = 0.46 \times 1{,}000 \left(1 + \frac{110}{100}\right) = 966 \text{ kg/m}^3$$

7-20 Weight-scaling of Sawlogs In general, the advantages of weight-scaling of pulpwood apply equally well to transactions involving sawlogs. The chief difference is that price adjustments must be made in weight-scaling of sawlogs to take care of variations in log quality and size. Without such adjustments, crooked or defective logs might command the same price as straight, clear logs, and small-diameter logs (yielding less lumber per ton) could bring as much as larger logs.

Circumstances most favorable to weight-scaling of sawlogs exist when truckloads are made up of a single species and when there is a relatively narrow range of log diameters present on any given load. It is therefore not surprising that numerous experiments in sawlog weight-scaling have been conducted with southern pine logs. Such logs are fairly uniform in size and quality, with few defect deductions being required. On the other hand, mixed hardwood logs of varying quality, degree of soundness and log size present certain obstacles to effective weight/scaling.

Because of the ingrained custom of using board-foot log rules, volume/weight conversions have been previously based on predicted log scales rather than on expected lumber yields. A series of 50 to 100 paired weighings and stick-scaled truckloads provides a basis for determining the weight per thousand board feet, according to a particular log rule. When log sizes encompass a wide diameter range, the number of logs per load should also be determined. Because diameter is a fair indication of log quality, the log count per ton is useful as a rough grading index or as a basis for premium payments.

Ideally, weight/volume relationships for sawlogs would either be derived on the basis of an expected mill tally of lumber or be computed independently of *any* presumed product. Except for custom and apathy, there is no reason why roundwood materials cannot be purchased and sold strictly on the basis of weight—without an implied conversion back to cords or board feet. Such a changeover might well be initiated when the United States adopts the metric system for measuring primary wood products.

7-21 Advantages of Weight-scaling The technique of weight-scaling roundwood materials continues to gain in popularity because of these and other reasons:

1   It encourages delivery of freshly cut wood to the mill.
2   The method is fast, requires no special handling, and saves time for both buyer and seller. A greater volume of wood can be measured in a shorter time period and with fewer personnel.
3   Weight-scaling is more objective than manual-scaling, and positive records of all transactions are provided by automatically stamped weight tickets.
4   Incentive is provided for better piling of wood on trucks; this tends to increase the volume handled by the supplier.
5   Woodyard inventories are more easily maintained because of greater uniformity in record-keeping

PROBLEMS

7-1   Determine the proportion of solid wood per cubic meter (or per cord) for a railroad car of roundwood in your locality. How does your estimate compare with the proportion used by nearby purchasers of stacked wood?
7-2   Visit a sawmill in your locality, and conduct a simple study of mill overrun based on two different log rules. Prepare a written report on your findings.

7-3 Prepare a written report of 1,000 to 2,500 words on either (*a*) advantages of cubic measure for log-scaling or (*b*) reasons why the concept of cubic measure is unacceptable to log purchasers and wood industries.

7-4 Construct a working model of a xylometer. Use the model to determine the cubic volumes of 10 small pieces of roundwood. Compare with volumes computed by Smalian's and Huber's formulas for the same pieces. Explain reasons for the differences.

7-5 Construct a display board of tree cross sections illustrating changes in wood specific gravity from stump to tree top. Use cross sections extracted at intervals of 1 m for an important timber species in your locality.

7-6 Review articles in foreign journals and summarize studies of weight/volume relationships in a country that has adopted the metric system.

REFERENCES

Anonymous

1970. Metric volume ready reckoner for round timber. *British Forest Commission Booklet* 26, Her Majesty's Stationery Office, London, England. 80 pp.

_____

1972. System scales logs automatically; uses infrared scan, digital control. *Forest Industries* (Sept.). 4 pp., illus.

Avery, T. E. and Herrick, A. M.

1963. *Field projects and classroom exercises in basic forest measurements.* Univ. of Georgia Press, Athens, GA. 151 pp., illus.

Dilworth, J. R.

1961. *Log scaling and timber cruising.* O.S.U. Cooperative Association, Corvallis, OR. 386 pp., illus.

Dobie, James

1972. Firmwood cubic scaling and conversion factors in British Columbia. Canadian Forestry Service, Vancouver, B.C. 14 pp.

Freese, Frank

1973. A collection of log rules. *U.S. Dept. Agr., Forest Service, Forest Prod. Lab. Gen. Tech. Rep.* FPL 1. 65 pp.

Grosenbaugh, L. R.

1952. Shortcuts for cruisers and scales. *U.S. Forest Serv., Southern Forest Expt. Sta. Occas. Paper* 126. 24 pp., illus.

Ker, J. W.

1966. The measurement of forest products in Canada: past, present and future historical and legislative background. *Forestry Chron.* **42**:29-38.

_____

1962. The theory and practice of estimating the cubic content of logs. *Forestry Chron.* **38**:168-172.

Mann, Charles N., and Lysons, Hilton H.

1972. A method of estimating log weights. *U.S. Forest Serv., Pacific Northwest Forest and Range Expt. Sta. Res. Paper* PNW-138. 75 pp., illus.

Serry, Victor
    1970. *Metrication in the timber and allied building trades*. Ernest Benn, Ltd., London, England. 188 pp., illus.
U.S. Department of Agriculture
    1964. *National forest log scaling handbook*. U.S. Forest Service, Government Printing Office, Washington, D.C. 193 pp., illus.

Chapter 8

Timber Inventory Systems

8-1 Introduction The usual purpose of a timber inventory is to determine, as precisely as available time and money will permit, the volume (or value) of standing trees in a given area. To attain this objective requires (1) a reliable estimate of the forest area and (2) measurement of all or an unbiased sample of trees within this area. No reliable timber inventory can be planned until the forester knows the location of all tract corners and boundary lines; recent aerial photographs and maps are therefore genuine assets for working in unfamiliar terrain.

The choice of a particular inventory system, often made at the forester's discretion, is governed by relative costs, size and density of timber, area to be covered, precision desired, number of people available for fieldwork, and the length of time allowed for the estimate. Other things being equal, the intensity of sampling tends to increase as the size of the tract decreases and as the value of the timber increases.

8-2 Classes of Timber Surveys The organization, intensity, and precision required in a timber inventory are logically based on the planned use of information collected. Therefore, no work should be initiated until inventory objectives have been clearly outlined and the exact format of summary forms to be compiled is known.

Depending on primary objectives, timber surveys may be conveniently classified as (1) land acquisition inventories, (2) inventories for logging or timber sales, (3) management plan inventories or continuous forest inventory systems, and (4) special surveys designed for evaluating conditions such as stand improvement needs, plantable areas, insect and disease infestations, or timber trespass.

For land acquisition or timber sales, the principal information desired is net volume and value of merchantable trees growing in operable areas. In simple terms, a stand is usually classed as "operable" when merchantable trees can be logged at a profit. Notations on timber quality, by species, are commonly required. For land acquisition surveys, additional information is needed on soil or site quality, presence of nonmerchantable growing stock, and proximity of the tract to mills or primary markets. Where timber values are relatively high, acquisition or sale inventories should be of an intensity that will produce estimates of mean volume within ±10 percent or less.

Management plan cruises, designed for providing information on timber growth, yield, and allowable cut, are no longer considered essential in all regions. In many instances, such cruises have been replaced by systems that make use of permanent sample plots (Chap. 9). As a rule, both types of cruises are of low intensity, and the information collected is primarily intended for management decisions and long-range planning. As a result, inventory data are summarized by large administrative units rather than by cutting compartments or logging units.

Special surveys are so diversified that few general rules can be stipulated. For locating spot insect or disease infestations, a survey might merely consist of an accurate forest type map with "trouble areas" located visually from aerial observations. Similarly, understocked stands in need of planting might be mapped from existing aerial photographs. In other instances, a 100 percent tree tally might be made for determining the number and volume of trees suitable for poles, piling, or veneer logs. Special surveys are also required in timber trespass cases. The estimation of timber volumes removed from cutover areas is discussed in a later section of this chapter.

SPECIAL INVENTORY CONSIDERATIONS

8-3 Methods of Tallying Timber In accordance with the tree-volume or tree-weight tables to be used, standing trees may be tallied by simple counts, by dbh and species only, or by various combinations of dbh, species, merchantable height, total height, form, individual tree-quality classes, and so on. The dot-dash tally method, merchantable height limitations, and tree form expressions have been described in Chap. 4.

Neophyte foresters should be particularly careful in estimating tree heights; upper limits of stem merchantability often change from one species or locality to another. When ocular estimates of tree heights are permitted, the conscientious forester will nevertheless "check his eye" by *measuring* every tenth or twentieth tree. Proficiency and consistency in inventory work are dependent on constant checks of estimation techniques.

Although tree diameters may be measured to the nearest 0.1 cm, it is often expedient to group such measurements into *dbh classes*; 2-cm and 4-cm classes are commonly employed. When 2-cm tree-diameter classes are used, the 18-cm-class boundaries commonly range from 17.000 to 18.999 + cm; the 20-cm class spans from 19.000 to 20.999 + , and so on. With 4-cm tree-diameter classes, the 20-cm class spans from 18.000 to 21.999+, and the 24-cm class ranges from 22.000 to 25.999+.

8-4 Tree-Defect Estimation The ability to make proper allowance for defective trees encountered on timber inventories requires experience that can be gained only by (1) repeated practice in estimating standing tree defects and (2) observing the sawing and utilization of defective logs at various mills.

When entire trees are classed as culls, they are either omitted from the field tally or recorded by species and dbh in a separate column of the tally sheet. For merchantable trees with evidence of interior defects, deductions for unsound portions of the stem may be handled by one of the following techniques:

1 For *visible defects*, dimensions of tallied trees are reduced in proportion to the estimated amount of defect. Thus a 40-cm-dbh three-log tree might be recorded as a 30-cm-dbh tree with three logs or possibly as a 40-cm-dbh tree with 2 1/2 logs. Refinements may be made in this technique by applying the defect-deduction formulas for log volumes as suggested by Grosenbaugh (Sec. 7-15).

2 For *hidden defects*, all trees are tallied in the field as sound. After gross volumes have been computed, a percentage is deducted in proportion to the total amount of timber presumed to be defective. Although this method will usually produce more consistent results than individual tree allowances, the drawback is the difficulty of deciding on the amount of the deduction to be applied to various species.

A promising technique has been developed by Aho (1966). From a detailed stem analysis of more than 1,600 felled trees, defect-deduction percentages have been derived through multiple regression analysis for four western conifers. These regression estimators are based on tree species, dbh, age, exterior indicators of decay, and infection courts. It is probable that similar regression equations can be developed for other timber species of commercial importance.

8-5 The Complete Tree Tally Under limited circumstances when scattered, high-value trees occur on small tracts, a complete or 100 percent tree tally may be feasible. Every tree of the desired species and size class may be measured, or the tally may be comprised of a 100 percent *count* of all stems plus a subsample (every *n*th tree) of actual measurements. The choice of methods depends on the stumpage value of trees inventoried, allowable costs, and desired precision.

Advantages of the complete tree tally are as follows:

1 More accurate estimates of total volume are possible, because every tree can be tallied by species, dbh, height, and quality class,

2 Deductions for defect can be accurately assessed, because cull percentages can be applied to individual trees as they are tallied.

3 It is not necessary to determine the exact area of the tract. Once boundaries have been located, the total estimate can be made without regard to area.

Disadvantages of the complete tree tally are:

1 High costs. Because of expense and time required, the 100 percent inventory is usually limited to small tracts or to individual trees of extra high stumpage value.

2 Trees must often be marked as they are recorded to avoid omissions or duplications in the field tally. This requires additional time and/or added personnel.

8-6 Organizing the Complete Tree Tally For dense stands of timber with large numbers of trees, it is desirable to have three persons in the field party. Two carry tree calipers for quick dbh measurements, while the third serves as recorder. If the area exceeds 5 ha in size, it is helpful to first lay out rectangles of about 50 × 200 m by using stout cord or twine. Then, depending on topography and underbrush, parallel strips 10 to 25 m wide can be traversed through each rectangle.

Fieldwork in dense stands proceeds most efficiently when it is feasible to merely count merchantable trees and restrict actual measurements to every tenth or twentieth stem. For pure stands that require little or no cull deductions, an alternative procedure might employ caliper measurements of dbh only for all stems, with volumes derived from single-entry volume tables or cumulative tally sheets. To ensure that no trees are overlooked or tallied twice, each stem should be marked at eye level on the side facing the unmeasured portion of the stand. In deciduous forests, complete stem tallies are preferably made during the dormant season when trees are leafless.

8-7 Timber Inventories as a Sampling Process Except for those circumstances where a complete tree tally is justified, the conduct of a timber inventory, or "cruise," is a sampling process. Among the considerations involved in developing an efficient sampling scheme are sample size, plot size and shape, and the sampling design, e.g., whether systematic, simple random, stratified random, etc. Many of these considerations are discussed in Chap. 2.

Regardless of inventory objectives, the method of selecting sample trees for measurement is based on some concept of sampling probability. The two concepts of concern here are (1) probability proportional to frequency and (2) probability proportional to size.[1]

Under the theory of *probability proportional to frequency*, the likelihood of selecting trees of a given size for measurement is dependent on the *frequency* with which that tree size occurs in the stand. This theory of sampling probability is implemented in the field by *plot sampling*, i.e., employment of field samples of fixed area. Within a plot's defined area, individual trees are tallied in terms of the characteristics to be assessed, such as species, dbh, height, or age. Then, the sample plot tallies are expanded to a per-unit-area basis by applying an appropriate expansion factor.

According to the theory of *probability proportional to size*, the chances of selecting a given tree for measurement are dependent on its *size*, e.g., diameter. Thus larger trees are more likely to be chosen for evaluation than smaller trees. This method of sample tree selection is exemplified by *point-sampling* or the Bitterlich system of inventory.

When the inventory sample unit is defined as a field plot of fixed area, it is often feasible to also define a finite population size N in terms of such sample units. However, when a point sample comprises the sample unit, the population size N can only be roughly approximated.

PLOT-SAMPLING

8-8 Defining Plot Sizes and Shapes The sizes of sample field plots are commonly determined on the basis of custom, tradition, and experience. However, the most efficient plot is the smallest size in relation to the variability produced (Sec. 2-23). There is a gradual trend toward

---

[1]Because of the introductory level of this book, the concept of probability proportional to prediction is not included.

the use of smaller sample plots by foresters in the United States; where 0.25-acre plots were formerly used extensively, plots of 0.10 acre and smaller are now more popular. Such changes are due partially to the fact that second-growth timber can be adequately sampled with small plots because such stands tend to be more homogeneous (less variable) than old-growth timber.

Plot shape is essentially a matter of personal preference. Circular plots have been popular for many years in the United States, but square or rectangular plots are more commonly used in other countries. In Tasmania (Australia), for example, the following rectangular plot sizes have been recommended:

Size and dimensions (English)		Size and dimensions (metric)	
0.20 acre	1 × 2 chains	0.08 ha	20 × 40 m
0.25 acre	1 × 2.5 chains	0.10 ha	20 × 50 m
0.50 acre	1 × 5 chains	0.20 ha	20 × 100 m

It may be argued that circular plots are more easily established on the ground, since the center point defines the sample area (Fig. 8-1). And

Figure 8-1 Measurement of a circular sample plot. Note center stake and plot radius tape. (*U.S. Forest Service photograph.*)

Figure 8-2 Measurement of a square sample plot; dimensions are 15 m on each side.

circular plots have less boundary per unit of area than any other plot shape. Nevertheless, circular-plot radii can be difficult to estimate in the field, especially in stands having a dense undergrowth. When the field crew is composed of two or more persons, square or rectangular plots are therefore recommended. The added time requires to establish four corner stakes is likely to provide dividends in the form of more reliable tree tallies (Fig. 8-2). Of even greater importance is the fact that the *sampling frame* can be more readily defined with square or rectangular plots than with circular plots (Sec. 2-24).

For inventories of planted stands, rectangular sample plots may be defined on the basis of original tree spacings. Several suggested plot sizes for planted stands are presented in Table 8-1, and plot sizes for natural stands are listed in Table 8-2. Where sample strips are used for timber inventories, they should be merely regarded as elongated, rectangular plots.

8-9 Sampling Intensity and Design Once the sample unit (i.e., plot size and shape) has been defined, the next step is to determine the *sampling intensity*; i.e., *how many* plots will be needed for a reliable timber estimate?

The intensity of plot-sampling is governed by the variability of the stand, allowable inventory costs, and desired standards of precision. The

Table 8-1   Rectangular Plot Sizes for Planted Stands*

Average spacing between rows (ft) (m)		3 rows wide	4 rows wide	6 rows wide	9 rows wide
		Distance in meters along the rows for plot sizes of:			
		0.005 ha	0.01 ha	0.02 ha	0.05 ha	0.10 ha
4	1.2	13.5	27.5	41	68.5	91
4.5	1.4	12	24.5	36.5	61	81
5	1.5	11	22	33	54.5	73
5.5	1.7	10	20	30	49.5	66.5
6	1.8	9	18	27.5	45.5	61
6.5	2.0	8.5	17	25	42	56
7	2.1	8	15.5	23.5	39	52

*From Bradley, 1971.

coefficient of variation in volume per unit area should first be estimated, either on the basis of existing stand records or by measuring a preliminary field sample of, perhaps, 10 to 30 plots. Then the proper sampling intensity can be calculated by the procedures outlined in Secs. 2-20 and 2-21.

The trend is away from the concept of fixed cruising percentages, for it is not the sampling fraction that is important, it is the number of sample units (of a specified kind) needed to produce estimates with a specified precision. In the final analysis, the best endorsement for a given plot size and sampling intensity is an unbiased estimate of stand volume that is bracketed by acceptable confidence limits.

After the sampling intensity has been determined, it is then necessary to decide on the *sampling design*, i.e., the method of selecting the nonoverlapping plots for field measurement. If sample plots are square or rectangular, the *sampling frame* is defined as a listing of all possible plots that may be drawn from the specified (finite) population or tract of land (Sec. 2-24). The sample plots to be visited on the ground can be drawn from such a listing by use of a table of random numbers (Secs. 2-26 and 2-27).

In spite of the statistical difficulties associated with systematic sampling designs, such cruises are still employed frequently. If used in combination with a fixed cruising percentage, systematic designs can

Table 8-2   Circular and Square Plot Sizes*

Shape of plot		Length in meters for plot sizes of:				
		0.005 ha	0.01 ha	0.02 ha	0.05 ha	0.10 ha
Circular:	*radius*	4.0	5.6	8.0	12.6	17.8
Square:	*sides*	7.1	10.0	14.1	22.4	31.6

*From Bradley, 1971.

rarely be expected to be cost efficient. On the other hand, where estimates of sampling precision are regarded as unnecessary, systematic sampling may provide a useful alternative to random sampling methods (Sec. 2-25).

8-10 Field Technique Circular-plot inventories are often handled by one person, but two or three persons can be used efficiently when square or rectangular plots are employed. Field directions are established with a hand or staff compass, and intervals between sample plots may be either taped or paced. When "check cruises" are to be made, plot centers or corners should be marked with stakes, cairns, or by reference to scribed trees. When a sample plot happens to fall at a transition line that divides two different types, stand sizes, or area conditions (e.g., forest versus open land), a question arises as to whether the sample location should be shifted. If the cruise estimate is to be summarized by types and expansion factors for each type (including nonforest areas) are determined, the plot should be moved until it falls *entirely* within the type indicated by its original center location.

In contrast to the foregoing, plots should not be shifted if a single area expansion factor is to be used for deriving total tract volumes. Under these conditions, edge effects, type transition zones, and stand openings are typically part of the population; therefore a representative sample would be *expected* to result in occasional plots that are part sawtimber and part seedlings—or half-timbered and half-cutover land. To arbitrarily move these plot locations would result in a biased sample.

With square or rectangular plots, the four corner stakes make it a simple matter to determine which trees are inside the plot boundaries. However, with circular plots, inaccurate estimation of the plot radii is a common source of error. As a minimum, four radii should be paced or measured to establish the sample perimeter. If an ordinary chaining pin is carried to denote plot centers, a steel tape can be tied to the pin for one-man checks of plot radii. When trees appear to be borderline, the center of the stem (pith) determines whether they are "in" or "out."

Separate tally sheets are recommended for each plot location and species; descriptive plot data can be handwritten or designated by special numerical codes. In some instances, field tallies are recorded directly on mark-sensed or prescored punch cards. It is usually most efficient to begin the tally at a natural stand opening (or due north) and record trees in a clockwise sweep around the plot. When the tally is completed, a quick stem count made from the opposite direction provides a valuable check on the number of trees sampled.

8-11 Inventory Summaries Although total stand volume is a major objective of most forest inventories, such information is most useful when it is summarized by tree sizes and species groups. It is important to know that a given stand contains 100,000 m³ of timber, but it is more valuable to know how this volume is *distributed* among various species groups and diameter classes. Thus the compilation of stand and stock tables is often a prime requisite in summarizing inventory results (Sec. 6-21).

Before plot data can be expanded to tract totals, it is necessary to obtain an estimate of stand areas or total forest area. For example, if fifty 0.1-ha plots are located in a stand of 80 ha, the stand area divided by the total area of sample plots provides the appropriate inventory-expansion factor. In this instance, the expansion factor would be computed as 80/5 = 16.

Where sample-based estimates of stand areas are accompanied by standard errors, the expansion of sample-plot volumes to tract totals should be handled as described in Sec. 2-22.

8-12   Timber Volumes from Stump Diameters   In timber trespass cases, it may be necessary to determine the volume of trees illegally removed during a clandestine logging operation. Since stem diameters cannot be measured at breast height, they must be estimated, by species or species groups, from available stump diameters. The conversion may be estimated by use of regression equations, or ratios may be derived "on location" from sample measurements of trees left standing.

As an example, correlations between stump diameter (inside bark) and dbh have been established for southwestern ponderosa pine by measurements of 1,483 felled trees (Myers, 1963). The linear regression for pines with stump diameters of 10 to 28 cm (4 to 11 in.) is

$$\text{dbh} = 0.23 + 1.05 \text{ (stump dia.)}$$

For stump diameters of 30 to 102 cm (12 to 40 in.) the equation is

$$\text{dbh} = 1.32 + 0.96 \text{ (stump dia.)}$$

The coefficient of determination (Sec. 2-34) is 0.99 for both relationships, and the standard error of estimate is ±0.30 cm (0.12 in.) for the first equation and ±0.53 cm (0.21 in.) for the second equation.

Once each dbh has been ascertained, volumes may be determined from single-entry volume tables. Or, if tree tops have not been scattered, lengths of removed merchantable stems may be obtained by measuring distances between paired stumps and tops. With this additional information, volumes can be derived from multiple-entry tables. When the cutover area is too large for a 100 percent stump tally, partial estimates based on sample plots may be used as in conventional inventories. The final volume summary should be accompanied by an appraisal of the stumpage value of timber removed, along with notes and photographs documenting damage to real property or to residual standing trees.

POINT-SAMPLING

8-13 The Concept of Point-sampling Point-sampling is a method of selecting trees to be tallied on the basis of their *sizes* rather than by their frequency of occurrence. Sample points, somewhat analogous to plot centers, are located within a forested tract, and a simple prism or angle gauge that subtends a fixed angle of view is used to "sight in" each tree dbh. Tree boles close enough to the observation point to completely fill the fixed sighting angle are tallied; stems too small or too far away are ignored. The resulting tree tally may be used to compute basal areas, volumes, or numbers of trees per unit area.

The probability of tallying a given tree depends on its cross-sectional area, its distance from the sample point, and the sighting angle used. The smaller the angle, the more stems will be included in the sample.

Point-sampling does not require direct measurements of either plot areas or tree diameters. A predetermined basal-area factor (baf) is established in advance of sampling, and resulting tree tallies can be easily converted to basal area per unit area. And the relationship between basal area and tree volume makes it feasible to use point-sampling for obtaining conventional timber inventory data when "counted" trees are recorded by merchantable or total height classes. Point sampling was developed in 1948 by Walter Bitterlich, a forest engineer of Salzburg, Austria. The introduction and adoption of the method in North America were largely due to the efforts of Lewis R. Grosenbaugh.

8-14 Sighting Angles Conversion of tree tallies to basal area is dependent on the selected sighting angle, or "critical angle." The sighting angle chosen, in turn, is based on the average size and distribution of trees to be sampled. Furthermore, from the standpoint of subsequent volume computations, it is desirable to select a sighting angle having a baf that can be expressed as a whole number rather than as a fractional number.

Any number of varied sighting angles may be selected. An angle of 104.18 min (baf of 10 sq ft per acre) is commonly used in second-growth sawtimber or dense pole-timber stands. Critical angles of 73.66 min (baf 5) and 147.34 min (baf 20) are employed for light-density pole stands and for large, old-growth sawtimber, respectively. In countries that have adopted the metric system, an angle of 70 min is often specified; this angle has a baf of 1 m^2/ha.

To illustrate the relationship between tree sizes and distances from the sample point, two sighting angles may be compared. The angle of 104.18 min (baf of 10 sq ft per acre) can be defined by placing a 1-in. horizontal intercept on a sighting base of 33 in. Thus, all trees located no farther than 33 times their diameter from the sample point will be tallied. Accordingly, a 1-in.-dbh tree must be within 33 in. of the point, a 12-in.-dbh tree will be tallied up to 396 in. (33.0 ft) away, and a 24-in. or 2-ft-dbh tree will be recorded up to a distance of 66 ft.

The sighting angle of 70 min (1 m²/ha) is defined on the basis of a 1:50 ratio, e.g., a 2-cm intercept on a sighting base of 1 m. With this relationship, trees within 50 times their diameter of the sample point will be tallied. Therefore, 8-cm trees will be tallied up to 4 m away, 16-cm trees can be 8 m distant, and so on (Fig. 8-3).

8-15 Developing Basal-Area Factors   The two sighting angles described in the preceding section will again be used for illustrative purposes. With the 1:33 ratio, a 2-ft-dbh tree will exactly cover the sighting intercept at a distance of 66 ft from the observer. The basal area of the tree (in square feet) is $\pi(1)^2$. If a circle with a radius of 66 ft encloses the sample point, its area can be computed as $\pi(66)^2$. And the ratio of the tree basal area to the encircled point is

$$\frac{\pi(1)^2}{\pi(66)^2} = \frac{1}{4,356} \qquad \text{or 1 sq ft of basal area per 4,356 sq ft}$$

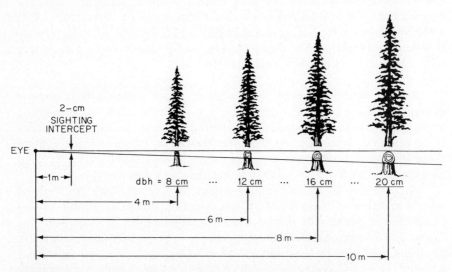

Figure 8-3 Tree sizes and limiting distances for a 1:50 angle gauge.

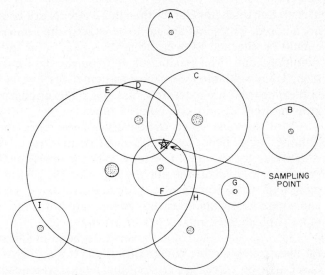

Figure 8-4 Imaginary zones proportional to stem diameter and encircling each tree determine which trees will be tallied at a given point. (*Adapted from Hovind and Rieck, 1970.*)

This relationship is the equivalent of 10 sq ft of basal area per acre; i.e., any tree completely covering the sighting intercept represents 10 sq ft of basal area *per acre* in trees of its size (Fig. 8-4).

With the 1:50 ratio, an 8-cm-dbh tree will exactly cover the sighting intercept at a distance of 4 m (400 cm) from the observer. The basal area of the tree is $\pi(4)^2$. If a circle with a radius of 400 cm encloses the sample point, its area can be computed as $\pi(400)^2$. And the ratio of tree basal area to the encircled point is

$$\frac{\pi(4)^2}{\pi(400)^2} = \frac{16}{160,000} = \frac{1}{10,000}$$

This relationship is equivalent to 1 cm² of basal area per 10,000 cm², or 1 m² of basal area per hectare. Thus any tree covering the sighting intercept represents 1 m² of basal area *per hectare* in trees of its size. If 18 trees are found to cover the sighting intercept at a sample point, the basal-area estimate at that point would be 18 m²/ha.

8-16 Instruments for Point-sampling A simple *angle gauge* may consist of a wooden rod with a peep sight at one end and a calibrated horizontal intercept at the other, e.g., a 1-m rod with a 2-cm intercept. In use, all tree diameters larger than the intercept are counted; those smaller are ignored. Trees that appear to be exactly the same size as the intercept should be checked by measuring their exact dbh and distance from the sampling point. The product of dbh and the appropriate "radius factor" (e.g., 1:33, 1:50, etc.) determines whether the tree is to be tallied. Truly borderline trees are extremely rare, since this circumstance can occur for growing trees at only one point in time.

With an angle gauge, the observer's eye represents the vertex of the sighting angle; hence the gauge must be pivoted or revolved about this exact point for a correct tree tally. When properly calibrated for use by a particular individual, the angle gauge may be just as accurate as other more expensive point-sampling devices. In dense sapling or pole stands and where heavy underbrush is encountered, it is often easier to use than more sophisticated relascopes or prisms.

The *Spiegel relascope* is a versatile, hand-held instrument developed for point-sampling by Walter Bitterlich. It may be used for determining basal area per acre, upper-stem diameters, tree heights, horizontal distances with correction for slope, and measurement of slope. Sighting angles are provided for four basal-area factors, and the instrument automatically corrects each angle for slope. The base has a tripod socket for use when especially precise measurements are desired.

Establishment of sighting angles with the Spiegel relascope is somewhat analogous to measuring distances with a transit and stadia rod; the principal difference is that the relascope subtends a horizontal angle, whereas the transit and stadia system is based on a vertically projected angle. The Spiegel relascope is complex in design but relatively simple to use. Its principal disadvantages are that it is relatively expensive, and it lacks the optical qualities for good sighting visibility on dark and rainy days.

The *wedge prism* is a tapered wedge of glass that deflects light rays at a specific offset angle. When a tree stem is viewed through such a wedge, the bole appears to be displaced, as if seen through a camera rangefinder. The amount of offset or displacement is controlled by the prism strength, measured in diopters; one prism diopter is equal to a right-angle displacement of one unit per 100 units of distance.

Field use of the prism requires that it be held precisely over the sample point at all times, for this point and *not the observer's eye* is the pivot from which the stand is "swept" by a 360° circle. All tree stems not completely offset when viewed through the wedge are counted; others are not tallied (Fig. 8-5). Trees that appear to be borderline should be measured and checked with the appropriate radius factor.

The prism may be held at any convenient distance from the eye, provided it is always positioned directly over the sample point. Proper orientation also requires that the prism be held in a vertical position and at

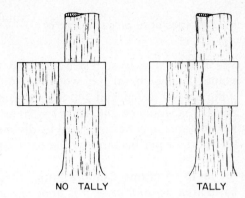

Figure 8-5 Use of the wedge prism for point-sampling.

NO TALLY   TALLY

right angles to the line of sight; otherwise, large errors in the tree tally may result (Fig. 8-6).

The wedge prism is simple, relatively inexpensive, portable, and can be as accurate as other angle gauges when properly calibrated and used. Some sighting difficulties are found in dense stands where displaced bole sections offset into one another, and corrections must be applied, as with the angle gauge, on slopes of 15 percent and more. Under such conditions, the Spiegel relascope is recommended over other devices since it incorporates automatic corrections for slope.

8-17   Basal-Area Calculations   As previously described, each tree tallied in point sampling, *regardless of its diameter*, represents the same basal area per unit area. The value is computed by the relationship:

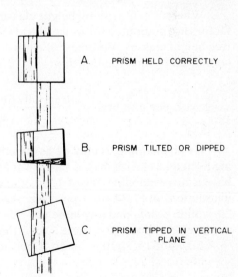

A.   PRISM HELD CORRECTLY

B.   PRISM TILTED OR DIPPED

Figure 8-6 Correct and incorrect methods of holding the wedge prism. (*Adapted from Hovind and Rieck, 1970.*)

C.   PRISM TIPPED IN VERTICAL PLANE

$$\text{ba (per acre or per hectare)} = \frac{\text{total no. of trees tallied}}{\text{no. of sample points}} \times \text{baf}$$

If the baf is 10 sq ft per acre, and 160 trees are tallied at 20 sample points, average basal area would be $160/20 \times 10 = 80$ sq ft per acre. Or, if the baf is 1 m²/ha, and 240 trees are tallied at 12 sample points, average basal area would be $240/12 \times 1 = 20$ m²/ha. The average number of trees per unit area may be computed by dividing average basal area of the stand (per acre or per hectare) by the basal area of the mean tree.

8-18 Volume Calculations Since all sizes of trees have the *same* basal area *per unit area*, it is unnecessary to measure dbh for computing total volumes. The field tally can be reduced to a simple stem count by *height* classes, with average volume per unit area computed from expansion factors for each dbh class.

With a baf of 10 sq ft per acre, for example, the expansion factor for the 12-in.-dbh class is derived by

$$\frac{\text{baf}}{\text{ba per tree}} = \frac{10}{0.785} = 12.74 \text{ trees per acre}$$

Or, for a baf of 1 m²/ha, the expansion factor for the 40-cm-dbh class would be

$$\frac{\text{baf}}{\text{ba per tree}} = \frac{1}{0.1257} = 7.96 \text{ trees per hectare}$$

Where a field tally by height classes alone is desired, such expansion factors are computed for those dbh classes that correspond to the selected tree height classes. Volumes for each designated height/dbh class are then computed by this relationship:

$$\text{Avg. vol. per unit area} = \frac{(\text{tree tally})(\text{expansion factor})(\text{vol. per tree})}{\text{no. of sample points}}$$

As an example, it may be assumed that field tallies are made according to height classes based on 16.3-ft (5-m) log intervals. If two-log trees have a corresponding dbh of 12 in., the expansion factor, from the preceding section, is 12.74 trees per acre. Assuming a tally of six such trees on 20 sample points and a volume per tree of 15.7 cu ft (from Table 5-2), the average volume per acre for this height/dbh class would be $(6 \times 12.74 \times 15.7)/20 = 60$ cu ft per acre.

A similar example may be illustrated in metric terms. If three-log (15-m) trees have a corresponding dbh of 40 cm, the expansion factor (as previously computed) is 7.96 trees per hectare. Again assuming a tally of six trees on 20 sample points and a volume per tree of 1.082 m³ (approximate value from Table 5-2), the average volume per hectare for this height/dbh class would be (6 × 7.96 × 1.082)/20 = 2.58 m³/ha.

Point-sampling appears to be a simple method of deriving standing tree volumes, because most of the computational work is accomplished *in advance of the field tally*. When volume-per-unit-area conversions are incorporated directly into the field tally form and trees are recorded by height classes only, a minimum of post-inventory calculations are necessary.

8-19 Sample-Size Determination The recommended method for determining *how many* point samples should be measured is to compute the standard deviation (or coefficient of variation) of basal area or volume per unit area from a preliminary field sample. When this has been done, sampling intensity may be derived by formulas described in Secs. 2-20 and 2-21. Rules of thumb, whereby point samples are compared with plot samples of various sizes, are apt to be unreliable estimators of sampling intensity.

It will be obvious that many aspects of point sampling have not been discussed in this introductory section. For additional details, the references listed at the end of the chapter are recommended.

PROBLEMS

8-1 Design and conduct a field study to compare the relative efficiencies of circular, square, and rectangular sample plots in your locality.

8-2 By regression analysis, derive a table of stump-diameter/dbh conversions for an important timber species. Base your analysis on paired measurements of at least 100 trees.

8-3 Construct a calibrated angle gauge for an appropriate baf. Then establish 10 or more sample points in a forested tract, and design a simple inventory to compare relative efficiencies of the angle gauge, the Spiegel relascope, and the wedge prism.

8-4 Derive an appropriate set of cubic-foot or cubic-meter volume conversions for point-sampling in your locality.

8-5 Establish 30 to 50 randomly selected points in a forest area. Make independent point-sample and circular-plot inventories based on the same center points. Compare results as to mean volumes, confidence limits on the sample means, average number of trees tallied per sample unit, and inventory time per sample unit.

REFERENCES

Aho, Paul E.
1966. Defect estimation for grand fir, Englemann spruce, Douglas-fir, and western larch. *U.S. Forest Serv.*, *Pacific Northwest Forest and Range Expt. Sta.* 26 pp., illus.

Avery, T. E., and Newton, Roger
1965. Plot sizes for timber cruising in Georgia. *J. Forestry* **63**:930-932.

Barrett, James P.
1969. Estimating averages from point-sample data. *J. Forestry* **67**:185.

———**and Nevers, Harold P.**
1967. Slope correction when point-sampling. *J. Forestry* **65**:206-207.

Bickford, C. Allen
1961. Stratification for timber cruising. *J. Forestry* **59**:761-763.

Bitterlich, W.
1948. Die Winkelzahlprobe. *Allgem. Forest-u, Holzw. Ztg.* **59**(1/2):4-5.

Bradley, R. T.
1971. Thinning control in British woodlands (metric). *British Forestry Commission Booklet* 32, Her Majesty's Stationery Office, London, England. 32 pp.

Dilworth, J. R., and Bell, J. F.
1968. *Variable Plot Cruising.* O.S.U. Bookstores, Inc. Corvallis, OR. 117 pp. illus.

Grosenbaugh, L. R.
1952. Plotless timber estimates—new, fast, easy, *J. Forestry* **50**:32-37. illus.

———**and Stover, W. S.**
1957. Point-sampling compared with plot-sampling in southeast Texas. *Forest Sci.* **3**:2-14.

Hovind, H. J., and Rieck, C. E.
1970. Basal area and point-sampling: Interpretation and application. *Wisconsin Conservation Dept. Tech. Bull.* 23. 52 pp., illus. (Revised.)

Hunt, Ellis V., and Baker, Robert D.
1967. Practical point-sampling. Bulletin 14, SFA State College, Nacogdoches, TX. 43 pp., illus.

Johnson, F. A., and Hixon, H. J.
1952. The most efficient size and shape of plot to use for cruising in old-growth Douglas-fir timber. *J. Forestry* **50**:17-20. illus.

Kendall, R. H., and Sayn-Wittgenstein, L.
1960. A rapid method of laying out circular plots. *Forestry Chron.* **36**:230-233. illus.

——— and ———
1959. An evaluation of the relascope. *Can. Dept. Northern Affairs and Nat. Resources Tech. Note* 77. 26 pp., illus.

Kulow, D. L.
1969. Elementary point-sampling. *Circular* 116, *West Virginia Univ. Agri. Expt. Sta.* 24 pp., illus.

Mesavage, C., and Grosenbaugh, L. R.
1956. Efficiency of several cruising designs on small tracts in north Arkansas. *J. Forestry* **54:**569-576, illus.
Myers, Clifford A.
1963. Point-sampling factors for southwestern ponderosa pine. *U.S. Forest Serv., Rocky Mt. Forest and Range Expt. Sta., Res. Paper* **RM-3.** 15 pp.

1963. Estimating volumes and diameters at breast height from stump diameters, southwestern ponderosa pine. *U.S. Forest Serv., Rocky Mt. Forest and Range Expt. Sta., Res. Note* 9. 2 pp.
Robinson, David W.
1969. The Oklahoma State angle gauge. *J. Forestry* **67:**234-236, illus.
Thomson, George W., and Deitschman, Glenn H.
1959. Bibliography of world literature on the Bitterlich method of plotless cruising. Iowa State University, Agriculture Experiment Station. 10 pp.
Wilson, Donald A., and Robbins, Wallace C.
1969. Formulas and tables for point-sampling in forest inventory, Part I, English system. Bul. 671, Maine Agri. Expt. Sta., Orono, ME. 186 pp.
——— and ———
1969. Formulas and tables for point-sampling in forest inventory, Part 2, metric system. Bul. 680, Maine Agri. Expt. Sta., Orono, ME. 303 pp.

Chapter 9

Inventory Planning

9-1 Introduction If management planning is to be effective, the state of forest conditions such as land areas, tree volumes, growth, and mortality must be known. Such information is obtained through various kinds of periodic forest inventories. Several classes of timber surveys were outlined in the preceding chapter; in actuality, there can be as many different inventory systems as there are management decisions to be made. In all instances, the objective is to plan an inventory that will be *cost effective* in attaining the specific objectives of management. It is therefore apparent that no single inventory system can be expected to suffice in all circumstances.

Insofar as this chapter is concerned, three different categories of forest inventories are considered. These are (1) intensive inventories for providing information on a stand or compartment basis, (2) management-based, or extensive, inventories designed to provide information about an entire forest property that is administered under a single ownership, and (3) regional or national inventories that are concerned with forest resource information across a wide range of vegetation types, management units, land ownership classes, and political subdivisions.

Since these three kinds of inventories are designed to serve entirely different functions, they should be regarded as complementary systems rather than as mutually exclusive options of the forest manager. Depending on individual management situations, the prevailing economic climate, and the requirements of decision-makers, each type of inventory can assume a variety of forms, e.g., whether temporary or permanent sample plots are employed. Therefore, the planning techniques described here should be regarded merely as *examples* of approaches that might be implemented by the practicing forester. For purposes of illustration, the first two inventory categories are considered in the context of large industrial forest holdings, whereas regional or national inventories are presumed to be the responsibility of governmental agencies.

STAND OR COMPARTMENT INVENTORIES

9-2 Cost-Effective Sampling It is worthy of reiteration that a timber inventory is not an end in itself; instead, it is an integral part of the complex operation and management of a forest business. And where private forest industries are concerned, one must remember that their very existence is dependent on the sale of wood products at a profit. Significant costs are incurred each time an inventory is undertaken; therefore each sampling scheme should be designed to obtain the desired information—no more and no less—for the lowest possible expenditure. In other words, each inventory should be *cost effective*.

If the forest manager who plans an inventory is also the decision-maker who will utilize the data collected, he will probably know just what information is needed, along with the sampling precision required. Conversely, if the inventory planner and the decision-maker are different persons who are widely separated in a corporate hierarchy, the choice of a particular inventory system may be based on the planner's experience or intuition. As a result, a portion of the data collected may be inadequate, or superfluous.

The preceding considerations bring us full circle to a question raised at the beginning of this book (Sec. 1-2): Why are the data needed at all? Once the needs of management have been clearly specified, the answer should become apparent—and a cost-effective inventory can be designed accordingly.

Since compartment inventories must be rather detailed and of a high level of precision (e.g., standard errors of ± 5 to ± 10 percent at a probability level of 0.95), it is obvious that a greater sampling intensity is required than that needed for the forest property as a whole. Different inventory designs are therefore dictated for the differing objectives of management.

9-3 Inventories of Cutting-Compartments These inventories are typically required at irregular time intervals for individual stands or compartments that are approaching the harvesting age. During any given year, no more than 5 percent of the total area of a forest property would likely be subject to such an inventory. And since these inventories may be scheduled only once during the stand rotation period, they are based on temporary field plots or point samples.

Where cutting-compartment inventories are designed to assess areas scheduled for logging during the following year, the decision-maker will want to know the volume and quality of wood available from each compartment or geographic locale, along with notations on average tree size, topography, accessibility, existing roads or trails, seasonal factors such as weather, and special requirements, e.g., ecological considerations.

Stand and stock tables may be compiled to show the present distribution of trees in each cutting compartment, but assessment of current stand growth is not required for those compartments about to be harvested. Of course, where stands are subjected to partial cutting, it may be desirable to obtain detailed information on trees to be left, i.e., the residual stand.

It may be possible to obtain much of the needed compartment information from recent aerial photographs, e.g., topography, access, area, stand boundaries, etc. However, for natural stands where no previous inventories have been made, it is likely that some field sampling will be required. Point samples are often used, particularly where compartments are to be clearcut and where stand volume is the primary consideration. The required number of point samples or field plots that must be measured to attain a desired level of precision is determined as previously outlined (Secs. 2-20 and 2-21).

When partial cuttings are scheduled, it may be most efficient to record the size and quality class of every nth tree as it is marked for cutting. By combining timber marking and inventory work, all essential data might be collected during a single visit to each stand.

9-4 Estimates of Plantation Yields When compartment inventories comprise the basis of cutting budgets or of long-term financial plans for intensively managed plantations, both growth and yield information are required for each management unit. In many instances, this detailed stand data cannot be obtained efficiently by conventional inventory procedures (i.e., field plots or point samples), because the required sample size would be prohibitively expensive. In these situations, growth and volume estimates may be derived from yield and projection equations that are based on plantation age, site index, and original spacing or number of trees per unit area.

Several large forest industries have developed such plantation inventory systems to the point where no field work is required, except to visit each management unit once for estimating site index. Then, stand ages are obtained from planting records, and density is estimated by counting trees on low-level aerial photographs taken prior to crown closure. All stand-volume information is generated from regression-type predictors of stand volume, and conventional tree-measurement inventory simply does not occur.[1]

MANAGEMENT-BASED INVENTORIES

9-5 Management Needs The upper levels of management in a large industrial organization desire a more-or-less continuous flow of information about the general condition of the forest property as a whole. Specific interest is centered around the quantity and quality of wood currently available, the changes expected due to growth, cutting, or mortality, the potential for increasing wood yields on the better sites, and the approximate geographic location of those tree species and stands that will be utilized during the next 5 to 10 years. For example, the seemingly simple question, What is the allowable annual cut? may require extensive efforts in data collection and analysis before a rational answer can be supplied.

Since management-based inventories are usually designed for properties of 25,000 to 50,000 ha and larger, they are apt to be of a low sampling intensity as compared with compartment inventories. Before they can be planned efficiently, however, the exact *purposes* of this expensive management tool must be established. There is no single format or design that will serve the needs of all organizations; instead, each system must be planned to supply answers to specific questions that are periodically raised by management. And, since the character of these questions may change from time to time, management-based inventories must be flexible enough to accommodate periodic variations in company policies, accounting systems, or timber-utilization standards.

9-6 Objectives and Sampling Considerations For purposes of discussion, it will be assumed here that the primary objectives of a management-based inventory are to obtain (for an entire forest property) periodic estimates of timber volumes, growth rates, and drain, i.e., volume removals resulting from harvested yields, normal mortality, and

---

[1]Ware, Kenneth D. 1973. Personal Communication.

catastrophic events. Such estimates may be derived by periodic employment of completely independent inventories based on temporary field-sample units or by use of successive inventories based on remeasurements of permanent field-sample units. In the latter instance, identical field plots and sample trees are remeasured at specified time intervals; such measurements may or may not be supplemented by temporary sample units.

For obtaining the maximum amount of information at one point in time, an independent sampling system is likely to be most efficient. However, when a continuous flow of inventory data from the forest is required, a system of permanent sample plots is often relied upon. The latter approach will be discussed here.

The periodic remeasurement of permanent sample plots is regarded as being statistically superior to successive independent surveys for evaluating changes over time. When independent surveys are repeated, the sampling errors of both inventories must be considered in assessing stand differences or changes over time. But when identical sample trees are remeasured, sampling errors relating to such differences are apt to be lower, i.e., the precision of "change estimates" is improved. In addition, trees initially sampled but absent at a later remeasurement can be classified as to the cause of removal, e.g., harvested yield, natural mortality, and so on.

Regardless of whether temporary or permanent sample units are employed for an inventory, two basic criteria must be met: the field plots must be *representative* of the forest area for which inferences are made, and they must be *subjected to the same treatments* as the nonsampled portion of the forest. If these conditions are not fully achieved, inferences drawn from such sample units will be of questionable utility.

One attempt to ensure that sample units are representative of equal forest areas is illustrated by some rigid CFI procedures whereby field plots are systematically arranged on a square grid basis; thus each plot represents a fixed and equal proportion of the total forest area. However, such sampling designs tend to be inflexible in meeting the changing requirements of management, and therefore are not recommended for most forest inventories. Even though systematic samples are sometimes quite efficient, especially from the viewpoint of reducing field travel time, it is better to use other methods of sampling that will permit calculation of the reliability of sample estimates.

9-7 The Concept of Post-Stratification Proponents of CFI systems have often assumed that stratified random sampling is unsuited to permanent plot inventories because of continually changing conditions in forest stands. In fact, however, certain forms of stratified sampling (possibly based on forest types and age or site classes) are likely to be quite useful in allocating permanent sample plots. The fact that strata boundaries may change with time can be accommodated by a procedure recommended by Cunia (1968), viz., the use of *post*-stratification rather than *pre*-stratification.

Post-stratification is made *after* the selection of the sample plots but independently of the geographic location of the plots. Sample-plot information should not be used directly in the stratification process because this may lead to biased estimates of tree growth and volumes. As an example, it may be assumed that an industrial organization wishes to stratify its forest area according to forest type and age classes. The following post-stratification procedure has been suggested by Cunia (1968):

> Maps must be prepared showing the exact distribution of these strata. Estimates of total area, average and total volumes, stock and stand tables, etc. should be calculated for each individual stratum. Given a CFI with permanent sample plots distributed over the whole forest area by an unstratified random sampling, the company prepares the management working plan using the method of post-stratification. An analysis is made of aerial photographs and old logging records available in the company files, and with the aid of check points on the ground, a detailed map showing the distribution of the forest by age-type classes is prepared.
>
> The information derived from the comparison between the data of the permanent sample plot and the plot image on aerial photographs is not used, since it is recognized that by doing otherwise a bias may be introduced in the future estimates. Each permanent plot is then located on the map and the stratum on which it happens to fall, recorded. Thus, the regrouping of all plots by the new strata is made possible. Then the area of each stratum is determined by the usual planimetering method. Using the data from all the plots belonging to a given stratum, unbiased estimates of averages per acre or totals per stratum, together with their confidence limits, are calculated for the given stratum. Consequently, the management working plan inventory data is prepared with the use of permanent plots originally distributed by unstratified random sampling and later post-stratified according to new criteria.
>
> The advantages of post-stratification over pre-stratification are several. The strata may be defined and localized on the map any time before or after the field work is completed. Because the stratification is independent of the field work, it is done only if and when it is necessary. Each stratification will serve a specific purpose and give answers to specific management questions. Finally, post-stratification, by its flexibility, can closely follow the changing needs of management and therefore may well turn out to become optimum for the overall continuous forest management.

9-8 Sample Units: Size, Shape, and Number Permanent field plots may be of fixed or variable area. The basis of variable area plots may be either plantation tree spacings (Table 8-1) or point samples utilizing a specified baf. For estimating growth, Cunia (1968) has recommended sample plots of fixed area because variable sample units involve more complex computational problems. Circular sample plots of 0.08 ha (0.20 acre) have been widely used for CFI systems in the past. Nevertheless, square or rectangular plots are recommended because (1) the sampling frame can be more reliably defined than with circular plots, and (2) the establishment of four corner stakes, however inconspicuous, improves the chances for plot relocation at a later date. Depending on the size and variability of timber stands encountered, a recommended plot size for second-growth forests might fall in the range of 0.02 to 0.20 ha. Plot areas of at least 300 m² (0.03 ha) have been suggested by Nyssonen (1967). The proper plot size for any given stand can be established only by experimentation (Sec. 2-23).

As outlined in several previous sections of this book, the number of permanent sample plots to be established and measured is dependent on the variability of the quantity being assessed and the desired sampling precision. For relatively small areas of 250 to 500 km², sampling errors of ±10 to 20 percent might be desired for current volume, with ±20 to 30 percent being accepted for growth (probability level of 0.95). This precision, projected to an entire forest of perhaps 5,000 to 12,000 km², might yield an overall precision of perhaps ±2 percent for current volume and ±5 percent for growth. The setting of higher levels of precision may be unrealistic because of uncontrollable or unknown errors in field measurements, forest area estimates, and tree-volume tables or prediction equations (Cunia, 1968)

9-9 Field-Plot Establishment Recent aerial photographs and topographic maps are invaluable aids for the initial location, establishment, and relocation of permanent sample plots. If the plots are first pinpointed on aerial photographs, they may be located by the technique described in Sec. 3-25. All pertinent data relative to bearings of approach lines, distances, and reference points or monuments should be recorded on a "plot location sheet" *and* on the back of the appropriate aerial photograph. It is essential that such information be complete and coherent because subsequent plot relocations are often made by entirely different field crews.

Plot centers or corner stakes are preferably inconspicuous and are referenced from a permanent landmark at least 30 to 100 m distant and by recording bearings and distances to two or more scribed or tagged "witness trees" that are nearer (but not within) the plot. There is some disagreement as to whether permanent plots should be marked (1) conspicuously, so that they can be easily relocated, or (2) inconspicuously, to ensure that they are accorded the same treatment as nonsampled portions of the forest (Fig. 9-1). The trend is toward essentially "hidden plots," for it

Figure 9-1 A permanent sample plot with trees conspicuously marked at dbh. (*U.S. Forest Service photograph.*)

is mandatory that they be subjected to *exactly* the same conditions or treatments as the surrounding forest, whether this be stand improvement, harvesting, fires, floods, or insect and disease infestations. Only under these conditions can it be assumed that the sample plots are representative.

Small sections of welding rods, projecting perhaps 15 to 20 cm above ground level, are useful for plot corner stakes. Where it becomes feasible to use more massive iron stakes, it may be possible to find them again with a "dip needle" or other magnetic detection devices. If individual trees on the plot are marked at all, the preferable method is to nail numbered metal tags into the stumps near ground level so that they will not be noticeable to timber markers and other forest workers. As an alternative to tagging the sample trees, individual stem locations may be numbered and mapped by coordinate positions on a plot-diagram sheet.

9-10 Field-Plot Measurements The inventory forester in charge of the permanent plot system should assume the responsibility for training field crews and for deciding what measurements should be taken on each sample plot. Standardized field procedures are emphasized because *consistency in measurement techniques* is as important as precision for evaluating changes over time.

To avoid problems arising from periodic variations in tree merchantability standards, field measurements should be planned so that tree volumes are expressed in terms of cubic measure (inside bark) for the entire stem, including stump and top. It may also be necessary to estimate the volume of branch wood on some operations. Regression equations can then be developed for predicting merchantable volumes for various portions of trees.

The field information collected for each sample unit is recorded under one of two categories: plot description data, and individual tree data. The exact measurements required will differ for each inventory system; thus the following listings merely include *examples* of the data that may be required:

Plot data	Individual tree data
Plot number and location	Tree number
Date of measurement	Species
Forest cover type	Dbh
Stand size and condition	Total height
Stand age	Merchantable stem lengths
Stocking or density class	Form or upper-stem diameters
Site index	Crown class
Slope or topography	Tree-quality class
Soil classification	Vigor
Understory vegetation	Diameter growth
Treatments needed	Mortality (and cause)

All field data are numerically coded and recorded on tally forms or directly onto machine-sort cards for automatic data processing. Plot inventories are preferably made immediately after a growing season and prior to heavy snowfall. For tracts smaller than 50,000 ha, it may be possible to establish all plots in a single season and remeasure them within similar time limitations. On larger areas, fieldwork may be conducted each fall on a rotation system that reinventories about one-fifth of the forest each year.

9-11 Periodic Reinventories Permanent sample plots are commonly remeasured at intervals of 3 to 10 years, depending on timber growth rates, expected changes in stand conditions, and the intensity of management. The interval must be long enough to permit a measurable degree of change, but short enough so that a fair proportion of the trees originally measured will be present for remeasurement. At each reinventory, trees that have attained the minimum diameter during the measurement interval are tallied as ingrowth. Also, felling records are kept to correct yields for these plots cut during the measurement interval. This information, along with mortality estimates, is essential for the prediction of future stand yields.

The data needed to calculate volume growth include stand tables prepared from two consecutive inventories, felling records, mortality estimates, and a single-entry volume table (or volume prediction equation) that is applicable to the previous and present stands. First, the stand tables for the two inventories are converted to corresponding stock tables; then, the difference in volume, after accounting for harvested yields and mortality, represents the growth of the plot.

One of the problems facing field crews who must remeasure permanent sample units is that of *finding the plots*. When plots are inconspicuously marked, relocation time can make up a sizable proportion of the total time allotted for reinventories. A study conducted by Nyssonen (1967) in Norway revealed that, after a 7-year interval, 4 to 8 percent of the permanent sample plots could not be found again. Where plots *could* be relocated, the time required for transportation, relocation, and measurement was distributed as follows:

Activity	Percent of total time
Transport by a vehicle	20.6
Walking to, between, and from the plots	22.6
Searching for the plots	12.9
Sample plot measurement	35.7
Pauses	8.2
Total	100.0

Even though time factors will obviously differ for every inventory system, the foregoing tabulation serves to illustrate some of the nonproductive aspects that should be recognized in the application of permanent plot-inventory systems.

REGIONAL OR NATIONAL INVENTORIES

9-12 Survey Needs and Objectives Inventories considered here are extensive surveys aimed at describing a regional or national timber resource base—where it is, who owns it, its general condition and productive capacity, and what portions are economically accessible or currently marketable. The extremes of circumstances under which such surveys are conducted range from "first-time" resource inventories of remote or undeveloped regions to continuous inventory systems in countries whose forests are under intensive management. This section is devoted largely to the first category, i.e., initial inventories of remote or undeveloped regions where reliance is placed on the use of aerial photographs in combination with temporary ground sample plots. The second category, typified by the U.S. Forest Survey, is described briefly at the end of the chapter.

Expanding programs of technical and economic assistance to various nations of the world provide opportunities for many foresters to work in other countries as field technicians, survey party chiefs, instructors, or technical advisors. Even the most rudimentary forest survey may enable an emerging nation to make preliminary plans for the utilization and management of its forests and other renewable resources. This section describes some of the major considerations involved in planning a timber inventory that can aid in the formulation of a constructive forest policy for regional or governmental administration.

It is now recognized that a reasonable balance must be maintained between an expanding population and the productivity of various resources available for its support. Since a nation's forest resources may comprise one of its primary tangible assets, this resource should be periodically assessed and wisely managed to ensure its supportive role in the overall economy. An initial forest inventory should therefore include descriptions of forest areas and their ownership, along with estimates of timber volumes (or weights), growth rates, and annual drain. Even though the state (i.e., government) may own or administer only a small proportion of the total productive forest area, all ownerships must be surveyed before a sound national timber policy can be drawn up and implemented.

9-13 Initial Planning Considerations The scope and sampling intensity of many primary inventories may be governed more by the funds and manpower allocated to the project than by the desired sampling precision. If the survey must also be completed within a rigid time limitation, some compromises in the survey design will become inevitable.

The first and most important step in inventory planning is to decide *exactly* what information will be required, the method of summarizing this information, and the allowable sampling errors for various categories of data. To assure that this is done, the format of all tables, graphs, and charts to be included in the final report should be outlined *in advance*. Titles, column headings, units of measurement, and estimated sampling errors should be shown for each table. A cost-effective inventory can be designed only if these decisions are made *prior* to the collection of field data.

For first-time inventories of uncharted regions, reliable base maps are essential for the determination of forest areas, for planning photographic coverage, and for regulating the pattern of fieldwork by ground survey parties. If no base maps exist, a sizable portion of the first year's inventory budget may be consumed by the cost of having them compiled. In this event, it will probably be most expedient (and certainly less expensive) to settle for planimetric rather than topographic maps.

In many countries, all regional mapping and aerial survey programs are under the direction and control of military or defense agencies. When this is the case, it will be prudent to expend a considerable effort in learning the functions of such agencies and how to gain access to key personnel. The full cooperation of these officials can be an immense contribution to the conduct and success of a large inventory project.

Once the problem of base maps has been solved, the principal cost items to be considered are those required for aerial photography, photo interpretation and field equipment, salaries of supervisory and field personnel, travel allowances, vehicles and maintenance, data processing and compilation, and the publication of a final survey report. Relative expenditures for these items will differ on each project, but the inventory planner should be cognizant of how the project funds should be and are expended. Once the total budget has been fixed, overspending during one inventory phase may require a corresponding reduction in funds for other activities.

9-14   Area Estimation and the Sampling Design   A prime objective on any timber inventory is to obtain an accurate estimate of both productive and nonproductive forest *areas*. It is usually desirable to further subdivide the productive timber-growing sites into definitive areas according to forest types or vegetation groups. As outlined earlier, reliable base maps and recent aerial photography are needed to achieve these objectives with any degree of efficiency. Furthermore, the maps and photographs can provide the basis for an efficient one-time inventory through a system of stratified random sampling.

When *no* maps or photographs can be made available for the survey, the deficiency may be partially overcome by substituting large amounts of manpower—a commodity that will often be abundant and available in developing nations. Returning to the problem of forest area estimates, these might be obtained by utilizing a plentiful labor supply to greatly intensify the ground sample. If fixed-area plots are distributed on a square grid arrangement over the entire region, forest areas (by various categories) can then be estimated from the proportion of the total number of plots falling into each classification. Total forest area can also be calculated in like fashion. For example, if 0.2-ha plots are uniformly spaced at 1 km × 1 km intervals over an entire forest, each plot will "represent" 1 km², or 100 ha. Thus if 321 plots fall into a particular forest classification, the type area is estimated as 321 × 100, or 32,100, ha. For this same design, the expansion factor for volumes and other quantities tallied on each plot would be computed as

$$\frac{\text{Area represented}}{\text{Sample plot area}} = \frac{100 \text{ ha}}{0.2 \text{ ha}} = 500$$

The *number* of sample units, i.e., the spacing between plots, could be determined by the total manpower available and the plot measurement rate. For example, if 20 field crews are made available for one year (300 days), and each crew can locate and measure 3.5 plots per day, it will be feasible to base the inventory on 20 × 300 × 3.5, or 21,000, sample plots. Whether this number proves to be sufficient or inadequate will, of course, depend on the complexity and variability of the quantities assessed and the desired levels of sampling precision. This is far from an ideal means of determining sampling intensity, but it may be the most *realistic* procedure when conditions are similar to those described here.

Whenever this method of area estimation is employed, distances between sample field plots should be carefully taped rather than paced. The general techniques outlined here are recommended *only* where forest area estimates cannot be obtained more efficiently by other approaches, because there are distinct problems encountered in attempting to compute the sampling precision for systematic designs.

Since inventory planners are often faced with the necessity of obtaining the highest possible sampling precision at a fixed cost, stratified random sampling (Secs. 2-27 to 2-29) offers a useful design for one-time regional inventories. By this procedure, forest areas are obtained from base maps and various strata are established through interpretation of recent aerial photographs. This form of sampling has the virtue of permitting different sampling intensities for strata of differing volumes (or values) and areas. It is thus recommended, especially in remote and inaccessible regions, when independent inventories are planned in conjunction with the procurement of recent airphoto coverage.

9-15 Obtaining Aerial Photography   Although existing aerial photographs may be suitable (or all that is available) under certain circumstances, contracting for new coverage is the most satisfactory plan. Since weather conditions in some parts of the world may limit air surveys to a few days per year, advance planning is essential. Specifications such as film-filter combination, season of year, and scale must be decided upon, and clearances from various governmental agencies may be required before flights can be scheduled. It will generally be useful to study all existing photography available before final decisions are made relative to exact specifications.

Photographic scales ranging from 1:10,000 to 1:20,000 have been successfully used on many forest inventories, but the exact scale specified will be influenced by allowable costs, the scale of existing base maps, and the relative skills of persons who will perform the photo-interpretation work. As a general rule, it is wise to specify the smallest scale that will accomplish photo-interpretation objectives because this will require handling of fewer stereoscopic setups.

The season of photography is important where deciduous trees are being assessed but of less concern in evergreen forests. Of course, when a high sun angle is desired, the summer months are preferred for photographic flights.

Whether black-and-white or color films are specified will be governed primarily by cost factors and the anticipated complexity of photographic interpretation. In even-aged coniferous forests of simple species structure, color images are not as essential as they might be in deciduous-evergreen mixtures or in tropical forests. Where black-and-white films are deemed acceptable, either panchromatic or infrared emulsions may be chosen; the former is often used in pure coniferous forests, while the latter works well in temperate zones where both conifers and broad-leaved trees occur in mixtures (Fig. 9-2).

The cost per square kilometer for airphoto coverage tends to decrease as photographic scales become smaller and as land areas become larger. It should be noted that when the specified scale is increased by a factor of two (e.g., from 1:20,000 to 1:10,000), *4 times* as many negatives will be required to cover a given area. A good flight crew can photograph 2,000 to 2,500 km² of land at a scale of 1:20,000 in 5 to 8 hours of flying time. Thus photography of remote project areas can be influenced as much by periodic costs of relocating the aircraft and crew to new flying bases as by the actual photographic time required.

When an aerial survey firm must be chosen on the basis of contract bids, the inventory planner should request photographic samples from each company; these provide useful guidelines to the quality of work that may be expected. And the planner should discuss all contract specifications with the selected aerial survey firm *prior* to photographic flights. A few extra days of advance planning will sometimes alleviate the need for reflights and help to prevent later disputes arising from problems with stereoscopic coverage, exposure quality, or scale deviations.

9-16 Forest Classification Systems The simplest classification system would be one that merely distinguishes between forest and nonforest areas, followed by a division of forest lands into productive and

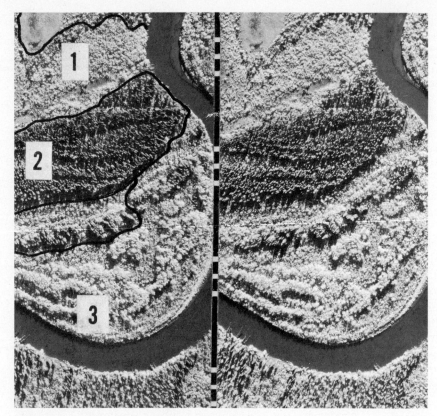

Figure 9-2 Infrared stereogram illustrating three forest associations in central Alaska. Types are (1) quaking aspen, (2) white spruce, and (3) paper birch. Scale is 1:5,000; land elevation is approximately 90 m. (*U.S. Forest Service photograph.*)

nonproductive sites. However, where good-quality aerial photographs are available, it will be useful to further classify forest lands into strata according to vegetative types—perhaps also by stand size classes. Such a subdivision will then permit the efficient adoption of stratified random sampling according to species groups, accessible versus inaccessible areas, ownership classes, and so on.

In some countries, standard systems (and symbols) for forest classification have been adopted; these should be used wherever possible, because the categories thus recognized may be directly comparable with mapping classifications used in adjacent regions. In undeveloped countries, it may be necessary to modify an existing classification scheme or develop a new one. Generalized types that are recognized internationally are coniferous, broadleaved, and mixed forests; it will usually be possible to subdivide these classes into subtypes. Ideally, these subtypes will be easily recognized—both on aerial photographs and on the ground.

The degree to which forest types and species groups can be recognized on airphotos depends on the quality, scale, and season of photography, the type of film used, and the skill and experience of interpreters. A background in forest ecology is helpful, and field experience in the specific area to be mapped is even more valuable. A general knowledge of the forest region provides the first step in the identification process: Which types can logically be encountered? Which ones are unlikely to occur in a given locality? By taking the aerial photographs into the field and marking them with spot identifications, interpreters can train themselves to recognize similar vegetation in nonvisited areas through the process of deductive reasoning.

Recognition of an individual species, often feasible only on large-scale photography, is normally the culmination of intensive study. It is obvious that the forest interpreter must be familiar with branching patterns and crown shapes of all important species in his particular region. Mature conifers in sparsely stocked stands can often be recognized by the configuration of their crowns or from shadows that fall in open areas of the stand. In similar fashion, the shapes of tree crowns in the upper canopy levels of tropical forests may provide valuable identification clues.

Aside from shadows, crown shapes, and branching patterns, the chief diagnostic features to be considered in recognizing tree species are photographic texture (fine-grained or coarse-grained images), tonal contrast, relative sizes of tree images at a given photo scale, and topographic location or site. Most of these characteristics constitute rather weak clues when observed singly, yet together they may provide the final link in the chain of identification by elimination.

For some parts of the world, vegetation "keys" have been prepared to aid in the photographic recognition of vegetative types or species. Keys are useful for training neophyte interpreters and as reference material for more experienced personnel. Depending on the method of presenting diagnostic features, photo-interpretation keys may be grouped into two general classes: *selective* keys and *elimination* keys. Selective keys are usually made up of typical illustrations and descriptions of trees in a specific region. They are organized for comparative use; the interpreter merely selects the key example that most nearly coincides with the forest stand he must identify. By contrast, elimination keys require the user to follow a step-by-step procedure, working from the general to the specific. One of the more common forms of elimination keys is the dichotomous type. With this type, the interpreter must continually select one of two contrasting alternatives until he progressively eliminates all but one item—the one being sought.

As a rule, vegetation keys are most easily constructed for northern temperate forests where conifers predominate, because there are relatively few species to be considered, and crown patterns are rather distinctive for each important group. By contrast, reliable keys are much more difficult to construct for the varied and dense vegetation of the tropics and the Southern Hemisphere.

Regardless of the classification system employed, the minimum area to be typed or recognized must be established. On extensive surveys, this minimum area may be set at 50 ha or more; for more intensive surveys, individual forest conditions down to 5 or 10 ha might be segregated.

Forest-type maps are no longer considered essential for all inventory projects, but at times their cost may be justified. A general ownership map showing principal roads, streams, and forest types may be desired for management planning and illustrative purposes. Also, in making a photo-controlled ground cruise where precise forest-area estimates are required, it may be necessary to measure stand areas on controlled maps of known scale rather than directly on contact prints; this is particularly important when topography causes wide variation in photo scales.

The wise interpreter will delineate only those forest types that he can consistently recognize. For maximum accuracy, type lines should be drawn under the stereoscope. Wherever feasible, it is recommended that forest-cover types be coded according to internationally recognized symbols. In the past, timber-type maps have assumed a wide variety of forms from one region to another, but it is advantageous to employ uniform symbols for designating tree species and stand-size classes.

After all forest types have been delineated, the desired detail can be transferred to a base map by using a vertical sketchmaster. With this instrument, a semitransparent eyepiece mirror provides a monocular view of the reflected photo image superimposed on the base map. When control points on photo and map have been matched, the transfer of detail becomes a simple tracing procedure (Fig. 9-3).

9-17 The Training of Inventory Personnel   This can constitute one of the more demanding tasks confronting the inventory planner. While technical advisors and staff supervisors may need only occasional briefings, it will often be necessary to set up formal training classes for photo interpreters, surveying and mapping personnel, and inventory field crews. On inventory projects lasting 6 months and longer, there will be a fair percentage of turnovers in the work force; thus the project must also be geared for subsequent training of new or replacement workers.

Training classes should precede the commencement of field-data collection, of course. It will be desirable to train as many crews together as possible, since this assures a minimum degree of standardization and

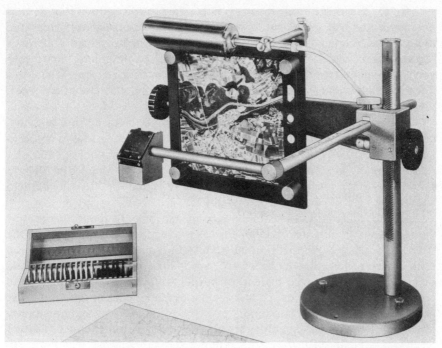

Figure 9-3 Aero-sketchmaster used for transferring photographic detail to base maps. (*Courtesy Zeiss-Aerotopograph.*)

consistency of instruction. And finally, simple but explicit field-instruction manuals should be prepared for each major activity and distributed to all party chiefs.

For the initial training sessions, it may be possible to bring in foreign experts as instructors to conduct basic classes in photo interpretation, field-plot measurements, boundary surveying, or vehicle maintenance. However, these "short-term advisors" will not be available later on when replacement personnel begin to arrive on the scene. Therefore, these new workers must be trained by the resident supervisory staff—a reality that cannot be escaped. The use of standardized field manuals and a few good slide-tape lectures can aid in meeting this recurrent training problem.

The more promising "graduates" of the training sessions should be selected as party chiefs, check cruisers, or as liaison (public relations) staff for communication with local residents and landowners. Maintaining a harmonious relationship with apathetic or suspicious landholders is an essential part of any inventory project that cannot be overlooked. And being able to enlist the support of a local populace is an asset of inestimable value, especially when the inventory is sponsored by a governmental agency regarded with some distrust.

9-18 Field Measurements Once the stratification of forest areas has been made by photo interpreters, crews are sent out to locate and measure the ground sample plots. An ideal crew usually consists of two or three persons. Safety precautions usually dictate a minimum of two persons, but more than three per crew often proves inefficient. The most knowledgeable and experienced person will usually be the party chief, unless local custom (e.g., relative age) dictates otherwise.

Each day's work should be planned to keep field parties fully occupied and moving at a reasonable rate from one sample unit location to another. For relatively inexperienced crews, fixed-area plots of square or rectangular shape are suggested. All corner stakes should be clearly marked so that a portion of the plots can be revisited for checking by field supervisors.

In the interest of consistency, tree measurements should be kept as simple and objective as possible. For example, a stick 1.3 m long can be used to locate the dbh position on each tree; diameters can be measured with tapes rather than calipers to avoid directional biases, and total heights can be measured instead of harder-to-define merchantable stem lengths. Tree measurements comprise the essential core of the inventory; careful and precise measurements must be insisted upon and constantly checked or the entire inventory results will be negated.

As stated in Sec. 9-12, the minimum data required will normally include current tree volumes, growth rates, and estimates of drain (harvested yields plus mortality). Obtaining reliable information on growth and drain can be difficult and time-consuming. Where trees do not exhibit annual rings, it may be necessary to establish a separate network of permanent "growth plots" to be remeasured at some future date. Estimates of normal mortality present a similar problem, but harvested yields can sometimes be estimated through independent surveys of primary wood-using industries in the region.

Plot and tree measurements may be recorded on handwritten tally sheets or (when crews are highly trained) directly onto machine-sort cards for use with automatic data processing machines. All tally sheets should be completely filled out in the field and turned over to supervisors or check cruisers each evening. Field crews should be aware that their work will be checked, and gross measurement errors should be corrected by having the crew revisit the plot in the presence of a supervisor.

9-19 Inventory Summaries and Reports If the field-record forms were prepared during the planning phase in conjunction with the format of final summary tables, data compilation and analysis will be greatly simplified. After the summary tables have been completed, it is customary to prepare a detailed inventory report for publication. This final report should include the inventory objectives, a description of the forest region, notes on the sampling design and data collection techniques, quantitative results, and a discussion of the implications of the results. In some instances, specific recommendations may be made regarding management and utilization of the timber resource.

The format of final reports will vary from one region to another; however, according to the Food and Agriculture Organization of the United Nations, most reports will include the following subjects:

1   General description. Geology, topography, climate, soils, and broad subdivision of the country in accordance with differences in ecological characteristics.

2   Forest history. A brief account of changes occurring in the forest during past years and the principal reasons for them.

3   Forest ownership and administration.

4   Value of the forests in the national economy, nature and extent of the demand for forest products, and the value of protection forests.

5   Description of the various classes recognized within the forest.

6   Inventory methods. Brief description of methods, sources of information, and standards of accuracy aimed at or achieved.

7   Statements of forest areas, subdivided in accordance with the standard classification.

8   Volumes of standing timber, subdivided as above.

9   Discussion of growth and drain, and the balance between them.

10   Conclusions to be drawn from the inventory survey.

For further suggestions relating to resource inventories in other countries, readers are advised that many universities maintain extensive programs of cooperative technical assistance with various nations. Information on special training programs relating to airphoto interpretation in these nations may be obtained from

International Institute for Aerial Survey and Earth Sciences
144 Boulevard 1945
P.O. Box 6
Enschede, The Netherlands

Information relating to specific inventory projects in different countries may be obtained from

Food and Agriculture Organization of the United Nations
Forest Resources Survey Section
Division of Forestry and Forest Industries
Rome, Italy

Readers who are interested in inventory assignments in other countries should strive to attain conversational proficiency in at least one foreign language. The lack of this ability is the greatest single barrier to such employment for most applicants from the United States.

9-20 The U.S. Forest Survey The Forest Survey is a periodic reinventory of the nation's forest resources on a state-by-state basis. Originally authorized by the McSweeney-McNary Forest Research Act of 1928, this nationwide inventory encompasses all ownerships of commercial forest land in each of the 50 states. Since the inception of the Forest Survey around 1930, all the 759 million acres (307 million hectares) of forest land in the United States have been inventoried at least once. Reinventories, normally planned at intervals of 8 to 15 years, have been completed on much of this land.

The Survey is essentially a continuous inventory system based on permanent sample units but supplemented by temporary sample units. Fieldwork, data analysis, and published results are the responsibility of Forest Survey projects located at Regional Experiment Stations of the Forest Service, U.S.D.A. At the conclusion of fieldwork in each state, data are collated and summarized by electronic data processing equipment; results are publicized by Forest Survey reports describing the current supply and demand for timber in that state.

Procedures for collecting and recording field data are aimed at providing answers to these general questions:

1 What is the area and productive capacity of the land available to grow timber?

2 What is the current annual growth on this area?

3 What is the present condition of this land, and how are these conditions associated with current net growth, particularly in terms of action required to increase or adjust net growth by species, age class, or tree quality?

4 How will the current net growth respond to changes in these conditions, either in the absence of disturbances or as a result of natural or man-made disturbances?

As stated in the official handbook of field instructions, the primary objectives of the Forest Survey are to provide the resource data needed to develop economically and silviculturally sound timber management plans and to provide the action programs to meet present and anticipated demands for timber. This requires information on the national forest situation as well as periodic reports appraising the timber resources of each state or geographic region covered by the survey. Therefore, at intervals of approximately 10 years, Forest Survey information from the individual states is summarized and incorporated into a national appraisal of the timber situation in the United States.

Forest Survey summary reports for the various States are available at irregular intervals from U.S.F.S. Experiment Stations.

PROBLEMS

9-1 Prepare a written report on a compartment inventory system used by a local forest industry.

9-2 Present an oral report on permanent plot remeasurement and field-tally procedures for an industrial CFI system.

9-3 List the primary factors that should be considered in planning new airphoto coverage for a tropical or Southern Hemisphere nation. Include a description of the climate, topography, and vegetation for the selected nation.

9-4 Using local aerial photographs, delineate the principal vegetative types that can be consistently recognized. Verify your identifications by ground checks. Then prepare a simple indentification key that might be used for training neophyte interpreters.

9-5 For oral presentation, prepare a 20-minute review of the most recent U.S. Forest Survey release dealing with the timber resources of your state.

REFERENCES

Anonymous
1950. Planning a national forest inventory. F.A.O., Washington, D.C. 88 pp.
Avery, T. E.
1960. Identifying southern forest types on aerial photographs. *U.S. Forest Serv., Southeast. Forest Expt. Sta., Paper* 112. 12 pp., illus.
———— **and Meyer, Merle P.**
1962. Contracting for forest aerial photography in the United States. *U.S. Forest Serv., Lake States Forest Expt. Sta., Paper* 96. 37 pp., illus.
Bernstein, David A.
1962. Guide to two-story forest type mapping in the Douglas-fir subregion. U.S. Forest Service, Region 6. 15 pp., illus.
Bonnor, G. M.
1972. Forest sampling and inventories: A bibliography. Forest Management Institute, Ottawa, Canada. 27 pp.
Cunia, T.
1968. Management inventory (CFI) and some of its basic statistical problems. *J. Forestry* **66**:342-350, illus.
Davis, Kenneth P.
1966. *Forest management: regulation and valuation.* McGraw-Hill Book Company, New York. 519 pp., illus.
Heller, R. C., Doverspike, G. E., and Aldrich, R. C.
1964. Identification of tree species on large-scale panchromatic and color

aerial photographs. U.S. Forest Service, Government Printing Office, Washington, D.C. 17 pp., illus.

Hair, Dwight
1973. The nature and use of comprehensive timber appraisals. *J. Forestry* **71**:565-567.

Husch, B.
1971. Planning a forest inventory. F.A.O., Rome, Italy. 120 pp.

Latham, Robert P., and McCarty, Thomas M.
1972. Recent developments in remote sensing for forestry. *J. Forestry* **70**:398-402, illus.

Lutz, H. J., and Caporaso, A. P.
1958. Indicators of forest land classes in air-photo interpretation of the Alaska Interior. *U.S. Forest Serv., Alaska Forest Res. Center, Sta. Paper* 10. 31 pp., illus.

Nyssonen, Aarne
1967. Remeasured sample plots in forest inventory. Norwegian Forest Research Inst., Vollebekk, Norway. 25 pp., illus.

Sayn-Wittgenstein, Leo
1961. Recognition of tree species on air photographs by crown characteristics. *Photogrammetric Eng.* **27**:792-809. illus.

Shimwell, David W.
1971. *The description and classification of vegetation.* Univ. of Washington Press, Seattle, WA. 322 pp., illus.

Society of American Foresters
1954. Forest cover types of North America, exclusive of Mexico. Committee on forest types, Washington, D.C. 68 pp., illus.

Zsilinszky, Victor G.
1963. Photographic interpretation of tree species in Ontario. Ontario Department of Lands and Forests. 80 pp., illus.

Part Three

Assessing Nontimber Resources

Chapter 10

Measuring Rangeland Resources

10-1 Introduction *Rangelands* may be defined as those lands that have the capability of producing forage for livestock and wildlife. The use of these lands is not limited to livestock and wildlife, however; rangelands may have concurrent utility for watershed protection, recreation, timber-growing, mining, or other activities. The range manager's objective is to obtain maximum coordinated use of these lands on a sustained yield basis.

The Society for Range Management, in a statement of concepts and positions, has estimated that more than 40 percent of the earth's total land area may be classed as rangeland. The Forest Range Task Force (1972) has analyzed the range resources of the United States and reported that 63 percent of the land area of the 48 contiguous states supports native vegetation that is grazable by livestock. This includes grasslands, shrublands, and grazable forests. About one-third of these lands is in public ownership, principally under the administration of the U.S. Forest Service and the Bureau of Land Management. The percentages of various lands that are grazed each year vary markedly according to region (ecogroup) and ownership, as illustrated by Fig. 10-1.

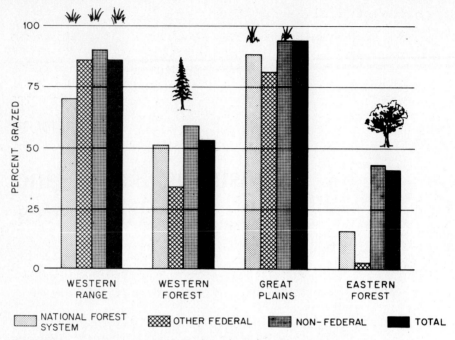

Figure 10-1 Percentage of rangelands grazed in the 48 states, by ecogroup and ownership. (*Source: U.S. Forest Service.*)

Included in this chapter are range-measurement techniques utilized by resource managers to measure characteristics of grass, grasslike, forb, and shrub vegetation. Such information is used in developing range management plans and in evaluating the results of implemented management practices.

For estimating livestock and wildlife grazing capacity, information may be needed on forage production, patterns of forage utilization, or changes in vegetative communities resulting from grazing use or specific management practices. Measurements of vegetative cover may be desired for relating management influences on water infiltration and runoff. It may also be necessary to document changes in understory vegetation that result from timber-cutting practices, since different cutting systems influence fire danger, timber regeneration, wildlife habitat, and soil erosion. And finally, vegetative measurements might be needed to determine the suitability of an area for outdoor recreational use—or to determine the effect of recreational use on changes in plant cover and composition. Thus at certain points in time, all resource managers are likely to be interested in measurements of the herbaceous and shrubby plants that are characteristic of rangelands.

PLANNING THE MEASUREMENTS

10-2   The Planning Unit   For a private ranch, the logical planning unit for which data must be collected is the property owned or leased and used in the ranch operation. On federal lands managed by the U.S. Forest Service or the Bureau of Land Management, the planning unit is often the grazing allotment, i.e., the area designated for use by a prescribed number of cattle or sheep under a single management plan (Range Term Glossary Committee, 1964). Measurements may be limited to lands within watershed boundaries, to specific plant communities, or to any other area specified as a planning unit.

Marking the boundaries of the planning unit or study area on maps and aerial photographs is the first step in deciding on the sampling procedures and measurements to be made. The size of the planning unit and the variability within the unit determine, to a great extent, the procedures and techniques that should be used. The specific data required, time available for measurements, accuracy desired, financing available, and abilities of resource personnel should also be considered prior to the collection of field data.

10-3   Use of Maps and Aerial Photographs   Topographic maps issued by the U.S. Geological Survey are recommended for locating property boundaries and for delineating planning units. The 15-min map series at a scale of 1:62,500 is useful for determining land ownership classes, section corners, etc., but the $7\frac{1}{2}$-min series at a scale of 1:24,000 is more desirable for detailed planning purposes (Sec. 3-20).

The scale of aerial photography desired for planning range measurements depends on the size of the planning unit and the intensity of the survey to be made. Scales of 1:15,000 to 1:30,000 have been successfully used for various types of rangeland surveys in the past. Indexes to aerial photography available from various federal agencies can be seen at county or regional offices of the Agricultural Stabilization and Conservation Service, Soil Conservation Service, Forest Service, or Bureau of Land Management. If existing aerial photographs are not suitable, it may be desirable to contract for new coverage (Sec. 9-15). On very large-scale (e.g., 1:600) color and color infrared photographs, it is possible to identify individual range-shrub species.

Where planning units cover hundreds of square kilometers, satellite photographs may be useful for preliminary delineation of range-type classes and physiographic units. The National Aeronautics and Space Administration has published catalogs of imagery taken from the Earth Resources Technology Satellite (ERTS). These catalogs are available at many universities and from the U.S. Government Printing Office in

Washington, D.C. ERTS photography and related imagery may be ordered from

EROS Data Center
Data Management Center
Sioux Falls, SD   57198

In ordering such imagery, the geographic area of interest must be clearly specified, because ERTS photography is indexed according to longitude and latitude, date, type of imagery, etc.

10-4 Grazing Types and Range Sites The range manager seldom encounters a planning unit that is sufficiently homogeneous for sampling without some degree of stratification. As a rule, this stratification is accomplished by ground surveillance, visual reconnaissance from low-flying aircraft, or by detailed study of aerial photographs. The recognition and delineation of various strata makes it feasible to employ more efficient means of sampling, e.g., stratified random sampling (Secs. 2-27 to 2-29).

One kind of strata recognized within planning units is the vegetation class or *grazing type*. A grazing type may be defined as "a more-or-less distinct vegetation unit which may be delimited on the basis of aspect, composition or density" (Stoddart and Smith, 1955). These authors have listed 18 major grazing types that have been widely used in designating mapping and sampling strata for range inventories on federal lands. Examples include grassland, meadow, sagebrush, mesquite, pinyon-juniper, coniferous trees, barren lands, and desert shrub. These generalized types are satisfactory for extensive inventories, but they may be inadequate for intensive surveys that require information on such items as soil conditions and plant responses to varying habitats.

The *range site* is the basic sampling unit or strata that is often identified and delineated in intensive range studies. Range site is defined as (Range Term Glossary Committee, 1964):

An area of land having a combination of edaphic, climatic, topographic and natural biotic factors that is significantly different from adjacent areas. These environmental areas are considered as units for purposes of discussion, investigation and management. Changes from one site to another represent significant differences in potential forage production and/or differences in management requirements for proper land use.

Range sites are approximately equivalent to the *habitat types* of Daubenmire (1968). Each range site may be repeated as land units within a climatic zone, and the potential or climax plant community is the same for each of these repeated units. Soils data, if available, are helpful for delineating range sites. The U.S. Soil Conservation Service designates range-site names according to soil characteristcs and topographical position within precipitation zones. Examples are clay bottoms, loam uplands, and sandy hills.

Range sites sometimes occur in such variable patterns that it is not practical to map each site separately. The mapping unit then becomes a complex of sites. The proportion of each site within the mapping unit may be determined by dot grids (Sec. 3-18). Sampling in the field may be accomplished by sites, with data interpreted and applied to the mapping unit on the basis of the percentage of the sites within the complex mapping unit.

By using acetate overlays on aerial photos, preliminary boundary location, range-site delineation, and general planning of the measurements can be quickly accomplished in the office. Preliminary site delineations can then be field checked and adjusted on the overlays where necessary.

10-5 Sampling Considerations The *time of sampling* range vegetation is important because range plant communities are composed of plants which reach their peak development at different seasons, or at different periods within a season. There are "cool-season plants" that tend to exhibit maximum growth in early spring and fall and "warm-season plants" that grow mainly in the summer, provided moisture conditions are favorable during these periods.

Near the end of the major growing season is often the best time for many vegetation surveys because species are best recognized at this time, and total herbage and browse production are near maximum. The resource manager should realize, however, that biases may exist from sampling at this time because an important species that reached peak development earlier may have largely passed from the scene. Utilization studies may be made during the grazing period to determine seasonal patterns of use, but if only a single utilization check is planned, it is best done toward the end of a grazing period and prior to a new plant growth period.

With respect to the *sampling design*, most of the techniques described earlier in this book apply equally to range inventories (Chaps. 2 and 9). The resource manager must decide on the technique that will provide the needed information and measure a sufficient number of sample units to achieve the desired level of sampling precision. Stratified random sampling will often provide a cost-effective inventory system for extensive surveys when good quality aerial photographs are available. Where systematic designs are specified, the resource manager should be aware of the pitfalls of treating such samples as if they were randomly selected (Sec. 2-25).

The American Society of Range Management (1962) lists three factors that should be considered in selecting a sampling technique:

1 *Degree of refinement desired.* The best technique is one that supplies the information required to the desired degree of reliability.

2 *Elimination of bias.* Bias may contribute to the sampling error in any technique. Minimizing error due to bias requires good sampling techniques that are highly objective.

3 *Cost.* Techniques should be considered in connection with time, manpower, and equipment available.

Allowable sampling errors for range inventories are often specified at ±10 to 20 percent at a probability level of 0.95.

10-6 Sample-Plot Shapes and Sizes Sample units for range measurements may be circular, square, or rectangular plots; point samples and lines (transects) may also be employed for special surveys. It has been stated that since vegetation often occurs in roughly circular patterns, rectangular plots should be used to include more variation within a sample plot—and hence less variation between plots. Whether this argument is valid will depend not only on plot shape, but on the relative *sizes* of sample plots and the pattern or distribution of the clumps or patches of vegetation being sampled. As in earlier chapters of this book, square or rectangular plots are recommended.

As with most forms of sampling, the plot size selected should be the smallest possible for convenience and efficiency of sampling, yet large enough so that the sampling variation between plots is not extreme.

The plot size may be chosen for the attribute being measured on the basis of previous data from the same or a similar range site, or by a preliminary study accomplished to determine the best plot size and number to achieve a specified level of sampling precision. For the latter approach, data will be needed on the *time* required to measure different-sized plots and on the influence of plot *sizes* and *number of plots* on the coefficient of variation. These relationships, along with formulas for calculating sampling intensity, are discussed in Chap. 2.

ESTIMATING VEGETATION WEIGHT

10-7 Definitions The following terms are commonly used by range managers in assessing various types of vegetation:

Herbage. The annual above-ground weight production of grasses, grass-like plants, and nonwoody, broadleaved plants (forbs). Some agencies define the term as including all current-year plant growth (U.S. Forest Service, 1965).

Browse. Current leaf and twig growth of shrubs, woody vines and trees available for animal consumption (Range Term Glossary Committee, 1964).

Forage. The herbage and browse which may be eaten by grazing animals.

The *use factor* is the percentage of herbage or browse which may be considered as forage with proper grazing management. Stoddart and Smith (1955) define use factor as

An index to the grazing use that is made of forage species, based upon a system of range management that will maintain the economically important forage species for an indefinite time. It is expressed as the percentage of the current year's weight production, within reach of stock, that is consumed.

The use factor may also be referred to as the *proper use factor.* It is determined by animal preference for individual species of plants, the relative abundance of species in a plant community, and the ability of the plants to withstand grazing. The use factor will vary from site to site, with class of animal, and with the season of the year.

10-8 Determining Grazing Capacity Livestock grazing capacity is usually expressed in terms of animal unit months (AUM). An animal unit is the equivalent of 454 kg (1,000 lb) of animal live weight, or a cow and a calf (Stoddart and Smith, 1955). The dry-weight forage required to provide for one animal unit month on rangeland is approximately 410 to 475 kg (900 to 1,050 lb).

This allowance for dry forage is high as compared to feedlot requirements because it is necessary to include the range forage that is clipped but not ingested, trampled, lost to insects, rodents or weathering, and extra forage needed to provide for the energy requirements of animals moving about on the open range to graze the forage. For example, pasture studies have shown that forage yields determined from animal production were generally 70 to 80 percent of yields determined by clipping the forage (Brown, 1954).

Animal-unit conversion factors may be used to convert the amount of forage required per AUM to forage requirements for a particular class of livestock or species of wildlife. Some conversion factors are: mule deer, 0.2; ewe and lamb, 0.2; white-tail deer, 0.14; grown horse, 1.25 (Range Term Glossary Committee, 1964).

Grazing capacity is the number of grazing animals that can be maintained on a range without depleting the range resource. The basic calculations to determine grazing capacity from herbage- and browse-weight measurements may be summarized by the following relationship:

Grazing capacity per unit area =

$$\frac{\Sigma \left(\begin{array}{l} \text{dry wt. per unit area} \\ \text{for each plant species} \end{array} \times \text{species use factor} \right)}{\text{animal-unit requirement}}$$

As an example, the following herbage and browse weights, along with corresponding use factors, may be assumed:

Range plant species	Weight/ha (kg)	Use factor (percent)
Blue grama	270	60
Burroweed	56	0
Poverty threeawn	224	20

If we further assume that the animal-unit requirement will be approximately 410 kg/AUM (900 lb/AUM), then the grazing capacity would be estimated as

$$\frac{\Sigma (270 \times 0.60 + 56 \times 0.0 + 224 \times 0.20)}{410} = \frac{207}{410} = 0.50 \text{ AUM/ha}$$

Therefore one animal unit could graze on 1 ha for 0.50 month; i.e., 2 ha would be required to yield forage for 1 AUM. Twenty-four hectares would be needed to carry one animal unit for a year.

10-9 Clipped-Plot Techniques Clipped plots may be used to determine weight of herbage and browse on range sites. The procedure is to locate plots of known area and clip herbaceous plants as near to ground level as practical, and to clip the current year's production on browse plants. Individual plant species may be clipped separately and weighed in the field, if their growth characteristics allow for easy separation. Then, samples of clipped species may be collected and dried to determine percentages of dry weights. If too much time is required in the field to separate the species, or if plants are mechanically clipped by power clippers, total herbage clipped on plots may be saved for sorting and weighing in the laboratory.

In the past, square plots that are 3.1 ft on a side (9.6 sq ft) have been popular for herbage clipping, because the plot yield in grams is converted to pounds per acre when multiplied by 10. With the advent of the metric system, however, this size will likely be replaced by a 1-m² plot, i.e., 1 m on a side. With this plot size, the herbage weight in grams, multiplied by 10, will be converted to yield in kilograms per hectare (Fig. 10-2). Various plot sizes may be used for different kinds of vegetation, of course.

Plots used to determine *total* herbage and browse weight may be clipped on range sites prior to grazing or on plots protected from grazing by wire cages. There are a number of sources of error which may be associated with clipped plots unless precautions are taken during clipping. Care must be taken to clip accurately at the plot boundary; otherwise data will be biased upward or downward. The inclusion of previous-year dry-matter production along with current growth will result in an overestimation of annual production. And carelessness in the height of clipping can introduce bias because a high proportion of the weight of some plants (e.g., bunch grasses) is near the base.

Since clipped-plot samples are expensive and time-consuming, they are largely employed in conjunction with other estimation techniques. Ocular estimates of vegetation weight, in combination with clipping and weighing, are sometimes used in range analysis. The estimator trains him-

Figure 10-2 Clipping herbage on a square sample plot. (*U.S. Forest Service photograph.*)

self to recognize plant-weight units of 5 or 10 g, or some other convenient unit (Pechanec and Pickford, 1937), and then proceeds to estimate the number of these units for each plant species on sample plots. Ocular estimates have proven most successful when few species are present on the plots.

Clipped plots and ocular estimates can be combined in a system of double-sampling (Wilm, Costello, and Klipple, 1944). By this technique, ocular estimates are made for all sample plots, from which a subsample (perhaps 1 plot in 10) is clipped and weighed. The relationship between estimated and clipped plots is established by regression analysis, and all estimated data are then adjusted by using the regression line. The application of regression techniques to relate an easily measured attribute to herbage or browse weight is a common approach for determining plant-weight production on a range site.

10-10 Other Weight Techniques Plant-weight production may also be estimated by determining the weight of average plants or plant parts, followed by simple counts of these units on sample plots. Or, in some instances, it may be feasible to develop regression equations to predict herbage and browse weights from precipitation and plant-production data recorded over previous years (Hutchings and Stewart, 1953). Various units of cover (e.g., foliage cover or basal area) may also have value for predicting weights of range vegetation (Hutchings and Mason, 1970). The greatest difficulty in developing regressions based on weight-cover relationships is that the regression line is modified by changes in plant vigor and resulting height-growth differences.

In general, the greatest single limitation in determining grazing capacity from forage weight is the time (and cost) involved in obtaining a reliable sample of weight data from the planning unit. Additional problems arise in establishing reasonable use factors and animal unit requirements. Use factors can vary greatly, and the decision on forage weight required per AUM is often a rough estimate, because of variable forage losses on different range sites. Grazing-capacity estimates from dry-weight data are also influenced by the *quality* of the forage, e.g., net energy, digestible protein, minerals, and vitamins. Despite these limitations, however, estimates of grazing capacity from forage weight are useful to the range manager, particularly when they are applied in conjunction with other types of measurements.

RANGE-UTILIZATION ESTIMATES

10-11 The Need for Utilization Estimates The utilization of forage plants is commonly expressed as the percentage of the current year's herbage or browse weight that is removed by grazing animals.

There are many different techniques for determining utilization, but the simplest method is to select a *key species* (a palatable and abundant plant) and estimate the percentage use on this species along transect lines through the range sites.

One use of the utilization percentage is for calculating a grazing capacity. If a range is stocked for 60 days with 40 animal units (80 AUM), the proper use factor for a key species is 60 percent, and the current use is estimated at 20 percent, grazing capacity may be calculated by this relationship:

$$\frac{80 \text{ AUM}}{0.20 \text{ current use}} = \frac{x \text{ AUM}}{0.60 \text{ proper use}}$$

The grazing capacity is thus calculated as 240 AUM. One-third of this amount (80 AUM) is currently being used; therefore, there are 160 AUM remaining to be utilized.

Utilization studies are also needed to determine *where* a range is being grazed. The key species selected for this type of evaluation should be widely distributed, palatable, and a species for which use can be easily estimated. The pattern of usage should be mapped, with notations on areas that are overgrazed or undergrazed. Armed with this information, the range manager can plan management improvements, e.g., water development, fencing, herding, or trails to obtain more uniform use on a range.

Another benefit derived from utilization studies is that of learning which plants are used during different seasons of the year. This information is useful in evaluating the effects of grazing on plant vigor and in planning grazing levels and systems that will maintain the vigor of preferred herbage species.

10-12 Utilization Techniques Ocular estimates of utilization are often employed. The resource manager trains himself to make such estimates by clipping plants to various levels, estimating the weights removed, and then verifying the actual utilization by clipping and weighing remaining plant parts. Such estimates may be made over general areas, on sample plots of fixed area, or on individual plants along transect lines.

Ocular appraisal of the use of primary forage plants is a technique for estimating general utilization on an area according to nine "use classes" (Deming, 1939):

1 Unused
2 Slight use
3 Light use
4 Moderate
5 Proper

6 Close
7 Severe
8 Extreme
9 Destructive

An entire range-planning unit may be surveyed, with use classes delineated on maps or aerial photographs. This method provides a rapid technique for determining *where* a range is being grazed.

Another technique employes *paired* sample plots, plants, or plant parts to estimate utilization. One of the pair is clipped *before* grazing and the other *after* grazing; the difference, expressed as a percentage of the ungrazed weight, is the utilization. For pasture studies, the forage weight differences may be obtained from caged versus open (grazed) plots, but such techniques are too expensive and require too many sample units to be cost effective for most range inventories.

Measurement of *twig length* before and after grazing is a technique used in some browse-utilization studies. In this case, use is not a percentage of total plant weight, but the method does provide an estimate of the *relative* degree of plant utilization. The greatest difficulties with this approach are those associated with twig growth between measurements and the problem of obtaining an unbiased and adequate sample.

The *number of grazed twigs* on browse plants may also be used to estimate relative plant utilization. With this method, individual plants and branches from each plant should be selected at random. Ten twigs (or some other convenient number), beginning at the tip of the branch, are then observed. The percentage of total twigs that are grazed provides an estimate of relative utilization for the plant species sampled. Averages for large numbers of plants may be required to obtain a reliable estimate for an entire site.

Regression techniques are useful for relating relatively "easy-to-measure" characteristics to plant utilization. Relationships between percent of utilization and average height of grazed plants or number of plants grazed can be developed for specific range sites; then, for future studies, use estimates are greatly simplified (Fig. 10-3).

A technique known as the *grazed-class method* may also be used for ocular estimates of forage utilization (Schmutz, Holt, and Michaels, 1963). By this approach, photographic guides of key species are used to place sample plants into one of six grazed classes: 0, 10, 30, 50, 70, or 90 percent utilized (Fig. 10-4). Sample data can be used to calculate the degree of current forage use, relative proper use of species, or distribution of grazing on an area. Workable photo guides have been developed for a

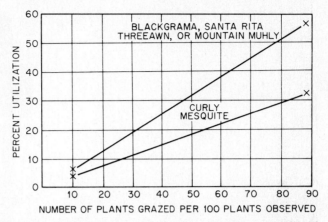

Figure 10-3 Relationship of percentage utilization to number of plants grazed. (*Courtesy Arizona Inter-Agency Range Committee.*)

number of key species in the southwestern United States (Schmutz, 1971).

As a rule, field sampling is done after seasonal growth on the key species has ended. If 50 plants of the key species comprise the sample, field tallies are doubled to determine the percentage of grazed plants by classes. Then, the percentage of current use is determined by multiplying the percentage of grazed plants in each class by the respective class midpoint and totaling the products, as shown in the following example:

Grazed class midpoint (%)	Field tally (No. plants)	Grazed plants by classes (%)	Current use by classes (%)
0	6	12	0
10	8	16	2
30	10	20	6
50	15	30	15
70	7	14	10
90	4	8	7
Total	50	100	40

In this example, the average utilization of the key species sampled is approximately 40 percent. The method is rapid, and with practice, good agreement can be attained among different observers. One of the major problems encountered on utilization surveys is that of evaluating use during a period when regrowth may occur; this is the main reason for planning field observations near the end of the growing season for key species.

0

10

30

50

70

Figure 10-4 Grazed-class photo guides for estimating utilization of Arizona fescue. Estimated utilization in percent is shown next to each photograph. The backdrop in these pictures was added for the sake of highlighting the fescue. (*Courtesy E. M. Schmutz.*)

90

RANGE CONDITION AND TREND

10-13 Concepts and Definitions It has long been recognized that overgrazing of certain plant communities can be documented by changes in the species composition of those communities (Sampson, 1917). It has also been shown that grazing capacity is influenced by the stage of plant succession on a range area, with higher grazing capacities usually associated with stages of succession closest to herbaceous climax vegetation.

Range condition is the status or stage of succession that a plant community expresses as compared with the potential or climax vegetation possible for the site. Thus the condition may be classed as excellent, good, fair, or poor, depending on present characteristics of the range site. Impacts of grazing and other influences on a range site are reflected by changes in species composition, plant cover, numbers of plants, relative vigor of plants, and soil erosion.

Trend is the direction of change—whether stable, toward, or away from the potential for the site. A trend toward poorer range conditions might be caused by such factors as excessive grazing, drought, fire, plant diseases, or mechanical disturbances of the soil. The range manager must be able to determine the causes of site deterioration. A poor range condition is usually an indication that improvements in management are needed to restore the site to its maximum productivity and use. Although range condition and trend evaluations tend to emphasize grazing influences, these concepts may also be extended to measure impacts of any origin on the range vegetation.

10-14 Plant Cover, Density, and Frequency These are the attributes of vegetation that are most frequently measured to determine condition and trend on range sites in response to grazing or other impacts.

Plant crown cover is the proportion (or percentage) of the ground surface under live aerial parts of plants. *Plant basal cover* is the percentage of the ground covered by plant bases, and *total cover* may include the combined aerial parts of plants, mulch, and rocks. Cover may be determined from ocular estimates of sample plots, by charting or mapping vegetation on plots, or it may be estimated from low-altitude aerial photographs. In the last instance, the estimate would correspond to crown closure (Sec. 5-15).

The proportion of cover may also be estimated along taped transects, or "point-frames" may be employed (Fig. 10-5). A frame holding 10 vertical or inclined pins is a standard measuring device; the pins are lowered through the vegetation, and the percentage of "hits" provides an estimate of cover.

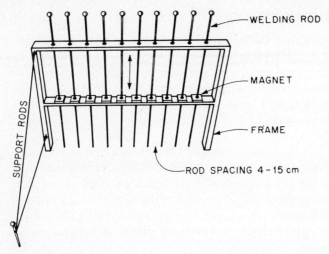

Figure 10-5 A point frame for sampling range vegetation.

Density is defined as the number of plants or specific plant parts per unit area of ground surface, e.g., number of mesquite plants per hectare. The counting of individual plants on sample plots of known area is a simple means of deriving density estimates. For sod-forming plants, however, it is difficult to decide on which plant units to count. And in some vegetation areas, number of plants per unit area are so large that counting is not practical. Density does not give an indication of the size of individuals unless counts are made and recorded by size classes.

Frequency is the number of plots on which a species occurs divided by the total number of plots sampled. Frequency data are used to detect changes in plant abundance and distribution on a range site over time, or to identify differences in species responses to varying management plans. Estimates of frequency are simple and objective; the resource manager must merely identify the species and record its presence if it is found on the sample plot.

Selection of the proper plot size is extremely important for estimating frequency, and more than one plot size may be needed for varying plant species and plant distributions. Frequency data are easily obtained, but numerous sample plots must often be evaluated before reliable estimates can be derived.

10-15 Range Condition from Species Composition The relative proportion of each plant species on a given range site is termed the *species composition*. It may be expressed in terms of weight, cover, or density (Range Term Glossary Committee, 1964). A technique has been

developed for quantifying species composition in the determination of
range condition (Dyksterhuis, 1949). This method is used by the Soil
Conservation Service for range condition analyses.

Species are grouped into three categories based on their response to
grazing. Plants that are present in the potential plant community but
decrease with heavy grazing are called *decreasers*. Plants that become
more abundant, at least initially, with heavy use are *increasers*, and
species not present in the potential vegetation but which invade the site as
cover of the native plants is reduced are called *invaders*. Range *condition
guides* are developed by gathering species composition data from sites
which are producing the potential for that particular locale. A sample
guide for a range site in southern Arizona appears in Table 10-1.

Such a guide can be used by range managers to estimate range condition from evaluations of species composition on a given site. First, the
percent species composition by weight, determined from field sampling, is
listed as shown in Table 10-2. The last column of the table includes all
"decreasers" but only the maximum allowable percentages for "increasers." None of the "invaders" contribute to the climax portion,
because they are not expected to be present in a true climax situation. The

**Table 10-1   Range Condition Guide for a Loamy Upland Range
Site**

Decreaser plants (Count all found)	Increaser plants (Count no. shown)	Maximum composition (% by weight)	Invader plants (Count none)
Bush muhly	Three awns	5	Whitehorn
Plains lovegrass	Fluffgrass	T	Mesquite
Bristlegrass	Slender tridens	T	Burroweed
Fall witchgrass	Pappus grass	T	
Hall's panic	Dropseeds	T	
Sideoats grama	Rothrock grama	T	
Wolftail	Burro grass	T	
Cottontop	Purple muhly	T	
Sprangletop	Slender, sprucetop or purple grama	10	
Black grama	Tobosa	5	
Cane beardgrass	Curly mesquite	10	
Vine mesquite	Blue or hairy grama	35	
Twinberry	Snakeweed	T	
	Waitabit	T	
	Fairy duster	10	
	Yucca	T	
	Perennial forbs	5	
	Native annuals	5	

Table 10-2 Calculation of Range Condition from the Guide in Table 10-1

Species*	Species composition (% by weight)	Climax portion allowable (%)
Sideoats grama	5	5
Wolftail	5	5
Blue grama	50	35
Sprucetop grama	15	10
Three awns	15	5
Native annuals	5	5
Burroweed	5	0
Total	100	65

*The first two species listed are decreasers, the next four are increasers, and the last one is an invader plant.

total of the climax portion column indicates that 65 percent of the potential climax vegetation is present on the site.

The Soil Conservation Service classifies range site condition as follows:

Total climax vegetation (%)	Range condition class
76–100	Excellent
51–75	Good
26–50	Fair
0–25	Poor

The foregoing example from Table 10-2 would thus be categorized as a range site in good condition. A higher percentage climax portion for the same site a few years later would indicate an upward trend, and a lower percentage climax portion would indicate a downward trend.

10-16 The Three-Step Method A three-step method of condition and trend measurements (U.S. Forest Service, 1965) has been utilized for range analyses on lands managed by the U.S. Forest Service and Bureau of Land Management. The first step is to establish a cluster of two or three permanent transects. At regular intervals along each transect, a 2-cm-(3/4-in.-) diameter loop is lowered vertically from the tape marking the transect. A tally of plant "hits," rock, litter, and bare soil within the loops is made. Then, plant cover, total ground cover including rocks and litter, and plant composition can be estimated from the data.

The second step is to use ocular appraisals and a summary of transect data to classify current condition and trend of the site. Vegetation condition is determined by "scores" based on plant composition, cover, and plant vigor. A soil condition rating is also determined.

The third step is to take a closeup photo and a photo of the general view of the transect for future reference. These are permanent study transects, and when data are collected for the same site at a future date, a new estimate of condition is attained, trend is indicated, and adjustments in management can be made accordingly.

10-17 Impacts on Rangelands Range measurements provide data on site productivity in terms of existing livestock and wildlife grazing capacity and enable the resource manager to predict or document changes in capacity or impacts. These data are essential for making rational management decisions. Emphasis is also on documenting changes in range vegetation due to impacts other than grazing. These influences might be industrial contaminants, off-road vehicles, or conflicting uses for land. Range measurement techniques are becoming more and more important as resource managers are required to document environmental impacts or justify management practices, especially on public lands (Fig. 10-6).

Figure 10-6 Coordinated management of longleaf pine forests and rangelands on a national forest in Texas. (*U.S. Forest Service photograph.*)

PROBLEMS

10-1   Using aerial photographs of a local range area, locate the boundaries of a pasture and delineate the range sites. Then determine the area of each site with dot grids or a planimeter.

10-2   Calculate the grazing capacity for each range site recognized in Problem 10-1. Obtain the essential vegetation weight estimates and proper use factors from your instructor.

10-3   Using plant-composition data for several locations within each range site, determine range condition from local SCS condition guides.

10-4   Obtain utilization data for a key species for those locations in each range site where range condition has been evaluated. Would you infer that current utilization is correlated with range condition?

10-5   Using data obtained from 50 ten-point frame settings, calculate plant composition and the percentage of vegetative basal cover.

10-6   Obtain frequency data at two different points in time for a local range site. Then determine whether range condition is upward, stable, or downward.

REFERENCES

American Society of Range Management
1962. *Basic problems and techniques in range research*. National Academy of Sciences—National Research Council, Pub. 890, Washington, D.C. 341 pp., illus.

Arizona Inter-Agency Range Committee
1972. Proper use and management of grazing land. 48 pp., illus.

Brown, Dorothy
1954. Methods of surveying and measuring vegetation. Bull. 42, Commonwealth Bureau of Pastures and Field Crops, Commonwealth Agricultural Bureau, Farnham Royal, Bucks, England. 223 pp., illus.

Curtis, J. T., and McIntosh, R. P.
1950. The interrelations of certain analytic and synthetic phytosociological characters. *Ecology* **41**:434–445.

Daubenmire, Rexford
1968. *Plant Communities: A Textbook of Plant Synecology*. Harper & Row, Publishers, Incorporated, New York. 300 pp., illus.

Deming, M. H.
1939. A field method of judging range utilization. Div. of Grazing, U.S. Dept. of the Interior, Washington, D.C. (mimeo. paper).

Dyksterhuis, E. J.
1949. Condition and management of range land based on quantitative ecology. *J. Range Manage.* **2**:104–115, illus.

Forest-Range Task Force
1972. The nation's range resources—A forest-range environmental study. *Forest Resource Report* No. 19, U.S. Forest Service, Washington, D.C. 147 pp., illus.

Hutchings, Selar S., and Stewart, George
1953. Increasing forage yields and sheep production on intermountain winter ranges. USDA Circ. 925. 63 pp., illus.
———— **and Mason, Lamar R.**
1970. Estimating yields of gambel oak from foliage cover and basal area. *J. Range Manage.* **23**:430–434.
Hyder, D. N., Bement, R. E., Remmenga, E. E., and Terwilliger, C., Jr.
1965. Frequency sampling of blue grama range. *J. Range Manage.* **18**:90–93.
McGuire, John R.
1973. Status and outlook for range in the new politics. *J. Range Manage.* **26**:312–315, illus.
Park, G. N.
1973. Point height intercept analysis. *New Zealand J. Botany* **11**:103–114, illus.
Paulsen, H. A., Jr., and Ares, F. N.
1962. Grazing values and management of black grama and tobosa grasslands and associated shrub ranges of the southwest. *USDA, Forest Service Tech. Bull.* No. 1270. 56 pp., ilus.
Pechanec, J. F., and Pickford, G. D.
1937. A weight estimate method for the determination of range or pasture production. *J. Amer. Soc. Agron.* **29**:894–904.
Pierce, William R., and Eddleman, Lee E.
1970. A field stereophotographic technique for range vegetation analysis. *J. Range Manage.* **23**:218–220.
Range Term Glossary Committee
1964. A glossary of terms used in range management. American Society of Range Management, Portland, OR. 32 pp.
Sampson, A. W.
1917. Succession as a factor in range management. *J. Forestry* **15**:593–596.
Schmutz, Ervin M.
1971. Estimation of range use with grazed-class photo guides. *Univ. of Arizona Coop. Ext. Serv. and Agr. Expt. Sta., Bull.* A-73. 16 pp., illus.
Stoddart, Lawrence A., and Smith, Arthur D.
1955. *Range management*, 2d ed. McGraw-Hill Book Company, New York. 433 pp., illus.
U.S. Forest Service
1965. Range Analysis Field Guide-Southwestern Region. (mimeo. paper). 153 pp., illus.
Wells, K. F.
1971. Measuring vegetation changes on fixed quadrats by vertical ground stereophotography. *J. Range Manage.* **24**:233–236.
Wilm, H. G., Costello, D. F., and Klipple, G. E.
1944. Estimating forage yield by the double-sampling method. *J. Amer. Soc. Agron* **36**:194–203.

Chapter 11

Measuring Wildlife Resources

11-1 Introduction Management of the wildlife resource implies an effort to attain a degree of balance between the food and cover available and the animal populations that are favored. Thus the inventory problems are twofold:

1 Estimating, through periodic sampling techniques, numbers of animals, composition, trend, and the natural range of various wildlife populations

2 Determining the food and cover requirements of different species, and evaluating the adequacy of various habitat units for supporting wildlife populations.

In many respects, the problems associated with wildlife measurements are similar to those described in evaluating rangeland resources for domesticated livestock. This is particularly true with respect to wildlife habitat assessments, i.e., the determination of carrying capacity, forage production, forage utilization, or condition and trend. With wild animals, however, the exact population size is rarely, if ever, known. Therefore census techniques, along with estimates of animal productivity and population trend, are also of special importance.

The evaluation of wildlife resources is more difficult (and often less precise) than similar assessments of rangelands because many game species obtain a large proportion of their forage from browse species (woody plants), fruits, and nuts. Also, many wild animals are more mobile than domesticated livestock, and their movements are ordinarily beyond human control. There is no simple and reliable technique for determining population size, and only rough estimates can be made of the number of animals being supported within a given area.

Except on federal lands, wildlife censuses in the United States are usually conducted by state agencies, e.g., game and fish departments. This is because game animals belong to the citizens of each state, and the possession of such animals (dead or alive) is carefully regulated in accordance with state game laws. Thus, any studies involving the capture or confinement of wild animals must be "cleared" through proper administrative authorities. Studies relating to the *effects* of resident wildlife on various habitats may be the responsibility of land management agencies or they may be jointly financed by land management and conservation agencies.

FACTORS AFFECTING WILDLIFE POPULATIONS

11-2 Composition and Productivity A reliable wildlife census is not merely a count of the total number of animals; it is an evaluation of the population *composition* as well. Information is needed on numbers of animals in each age group, sex ratios for each age group, preferred seasonal habitats, general health status, productivity rates, mortality rates, average life span, adaptability, mobility, and the extent of "home ranges." In other words, the life history of each species must be known and understood before census or trend data can be utilized effectively.

Both hunted and nonhunted populations require periodic censuses and estimates of *productivity*. Nonhunted species vary in number because of natural mortality, and the productivity of hunted species is directly affected by the character of the game harvested. If half of the mature bucks (but no does) are removed from a herd of deer, an initial 50:50 sex ratio is modified considerably. The *percent* of production may rise, however, because deer are polygamous.

11-3 Changing Population Patterns As a rule, the smaller the mammal or bird, the faster their production, normal mortality, and regeneration of the population each year. Rabbits reproduce rapidly, for example, but surplus production is continually removed by man, predators, weather, disease, and other factors. Similarly, the typical squirrel or bobwhite quail has a lifespan of a year or less, and so there is a constant turnover or replacement by new individuals in the population. Since the composition is changing each year, the annual rate of increase (or decrease) will change accordingly.

Periodic evaluations of population composition is even more important with long-lived animals. In an elk population, for example, details on age groups and sex ratios are especially important, because such animals may live more than one-third of the life-span of man. When complete population data are available, it is feasible to predict the annual reproduction rate, the uniformity of annual changes, and the pattern of change, i.e., whether the population is increasing, stable, or declining. Such knowledge is essential for the reliable forecasting of periodic eruptions or catastrophic declines in wildlife populations.

Some form of continuous census is desirable to gauge the response of populations to changes in their environment. The complete census should be designed to detect changes and trends in wildlife populations, for it is the yardstick by which the success or failure of management is measured.

11-4 Mortality Estimates It is usually quite difficult to determine the causes of natural mortality in wildlife populations. All species are subject to some form of predation, disease, parasites, extreme weather, or starvation. In many instances, the only evidence of mortality is the detection of an annual decrease in the number of survivors. Thus a continuous census may offer an indirect means of estimating mortality losses over time.

The mortality of game animals from legal hunts is best estimated at manned stations where hunters are required to check into and out of an area. Less expensive (and less reliable) data on the legal kill by hunters can be obtained through spot checks, wing collection boxes, or mail questionnaires. Crippling losses resulting from hunts can be roughly estimated by making inquiries at check points, but they are more reliably determined from field surveys.

11-5 Movement Patterns and Activity Cycles A knowledge of the mobility and normal home range of certain species, especially large mammals, is important in estimating numbers of animals in relation to their ecological density. Since the value of census information is related to estimates of carrying capacity in numbers per unit area, it is important to know the size of the land base that supports the population. And the key to the land base is found in studies of the basic nature of animal movements, home ranges, and responses to environments (Jenkins and Marchinton, 1969).

Population movements and home ranges may be estimated by a variety of techniques, including those based on the distribution of nests or burrows, browse lines on favored plants, the banding of birds, and so on. Where the larger land mammals are involved, *radio telemetry* offers an efficient means of tracking and studying the behavior of animals. Dependable miniaturized telemetry systems are available at reasonable costs, and such devices have been used extensively for studying herds of white-tailed deer.

While telemetry is not employed as a strict census technique, the data thus derived may be used to refine basic census methods for obtaining population estimates. For example, most direct census methods require that animals be in a relatively open area for consistent detection. Movement pattern and activity cycle information from radio telemetry permit the wildlife manager to estimate the percentage of a given population that is likely to be exposed during a particular season or time of day (Fig. 11-1).

Movement patterns are also valuable for calibrating track-count censuses, since the distance traveled per unit of time is related to the number of tracks made. Thus it is important to be able to predict the mobility and activity cycle for the "average animal" in the population during the time interval when tracks are being formed.

POPULATION AND TREND ESTIMATES

11-6 Census Methods The various techniques for measuring populations of vertebrates may be grouped into three classes: *direct* census, *indirect* census, and *ratio* methods. A direct census implies the counting of the animals or birds themselves; such counts may be made on drives, by visual surveillance from aircraft, from aerial photographs or thermal imagery, and by ground observations on flushing strips.

For an indirect census, observations other than animal counts are recorded, and the population estimate is derived from this indirect evidence of animal presence. Included here are bird-call counts, track counts, and pellet-group counts.

Ratio methods are based on a measured change in a population. For example, a known number of game birds may be captured, banded, and returned to the population. When these birds are seen, recaptured, or taken by hunters at some later point in time, the ratio of the total banded birds to those recaptured can be used for estimating the population size.

11-7 Drive Census This method requires a line of observers or "beaters" moving steadily through an area to flush out the desired species. Recorders are stationed at the opposite boundaries and along the

Figure 11-1 Gray squirrel with harness and radio transmitter. (*Courtesy Virginia Polytechnic Institute and State University.*)

edges of the tract to count the animals pushed out. If vegetation is sparse and the line of beaters is widely spaced, each person records all birds or animals that go back through the line on their right side. A fair amount of noise is often desirable, and regular calling back and forth among beaters (to be sure that all observations are recorded) will aid in obtaining a reliable count.

The drive census is one of the oldest methods in use, and where sufficient manpower is available, it will provide reliable population estimates. The fact that 25 to 50 persons may be needed to cover an area of 2 or 3 km² tends to limit the application of the method to level terrain that is already surrounded by clearings such as firebreaks or logging roads. Under the limited circumstances where drives are economically feasible, the data derived serve as a useful control or base for evaluating alternative census procedures.

11-8 Aerial Surveillance Visual observation of wildlife from low-flying aircraft is an effective census technique in areas where animals tend to congregate and where overstory cover is relatively sparse. The method is mainly applicable to large mammal counts in open plains country and for migratory waterfowl wintering on open coastal waters.

A common procedure involves low-level flights in a grid pattern with a pilot and observer. Helicopters, though more expensive, may be effectively used to count desert bighorn sheep in rough, low mountains or to enumerate elk that are concentrated on winter ranges with sparse tree cover. In some states, visual surveys are also used to census moose and to count breeding waterfowl on systematically spaced aerial transects.

Helicopter counts are apt to be more reliable than surveys from fixed-wing aircraft, and the slower flights may enable observers to obtain a listing of species sighted by sex and age classes. The basic census procedures are simple for good observers and pilots, especially where the exact flight paths and areas to be covered are carefully mapped out in advance.

11-9 Aerial Photographs and Thermal Imagery Wildlife species that can be counted on visual surveys are also susceptible to enumeration on aerial photographs. Large-scale photography has been successfully used to count waterfowl along the Pacific Coast flyway and to determine trends in gull populations by combining visual estimates of numbers with photography of nesting areas and associated flocks. Such trend estimates do not provide a complete picture of the population, but they may be useful in detecting large annual changes, i.e., variations of 25 percent or more. For inventories of waterfowl and large mammals, photographic scales of 1:3,000 and larger are recommended; color or infrared color films should be specified to provide the maximum of contrast between the wildlife species and associated backgrounds or native habitats (Fig. 11-2).

Thermal (infrared) scanning systems also show promise for making aerial inventories of large, warm-blooded mammals, except where such animals are under dense overstory canopies. This heat-sensing imagery is commonly obtained from low-level flights (e.g., altitudes of ± 300 m) with thermal scanners that record heat emissions in the wavelength range of 8 to 14 micrometers.

In theory, infrared scanners will detect temperature differences of 1°C for objects that are about 1 m in diameter and larger. Most practical tests, however, have indicated that a differential of several degrees may be needed to enumerate such animals as livestock, deer, elk, and antelope.

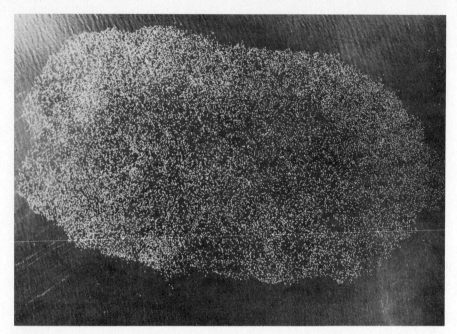

Figure 11-2 Airphoto of greater snow geese at Backbay, Virginia.
Reliable counts can be made from such pictures. (*Courtesy Virginia
Polytechnic Institute and State University.*)

From flight altitudes of 100 m or less, it is possible to differentiate between two or three species when there are significant differences in their
sizes and body temperatures (Parker and Driscoll, 1972).

Since thermal scanners are independent of visible light, they can be
employed at night or early morning when animals may be more readily detected. However, they are severely limited by angular resolution capabili-
ties that will image only larger animals, and by lack of adequate penetration through rainclouds and coniferous tree canopies. To overcome this
latter problem, microwave imagery (radar scanning) shows some promise
as a wildlife remote sensor for the future.

11-10 Strip-flushing Census This one-man method may be
used for species that will hold to cover until an observer approaches, and
then fly or run away when flushed. Ruffed grouse, woodcock, and even
white-tailed deer may be enumerated by this technique.

The procedure is similar to a strip system of timber cruising sometimes used by foresters. The observer walks along parallel lines or transects through a tract and records the *flushing distance* each time an
animal is sighted. From this data, the *average* flushing distance is

calculated, and twice this distance comprises the average strip width covered by the survey.

The average strip width multipled by the length of all strips walked provides an estimate of the *sample area* actually traversed on foot. The relation of this sample area to the total tract area is used to expand the number of animals flushed to a population estimate for the area:

$$\text{Population } (N) = \frac{\text{total area}}{\text{sample area}} \times \text{no. of animals flushed}$$

The method is fairly simple, but it assumes that the flushed species is randomly distributed throughout the tract—possibly a dangerous assumption. In practice, the technique tends to be limited to fairly level and open terrain where walking is very easy and where good visibility conditions prevail.

11-11 Call Counts Indirect census methods are commonly used for smaller, short-lived animals and for big game that is relatively inaccessible because of weather, terrain, or cover. Such surveys may be less precise than a direct census, but they can provide valuable information on population trends.

Call counts are used to assess population trends for game birds such as the mourning dove. When doves migrate northward in spring, the males establish territories and attempt to attract a female by calling (cooing). In many states, a series of 32-km routes have been established in dove habitats for checking during the calling season. Observers begin their routes just before daylight, stopping at specified intervals to count all dove calls heard during a 3-min interval. Doves seen perched or flying across the road between stops are recorded separately.

Most male birds that proclaim territories by calling can be counted by various modifications of this method. Male call counts alone do not constitute a complete census, but they may be used in conjunction with sex-ratio data to provide population estimates and trends.

11-12 Track Counts This indirect census method is best adapted to land areas that are criss-crossed with a grid pattern of nonsurfaced (i.e., easily imprinted) roads and trails. Checking these roads a few hours after heavy rains appears to give the best results. The technique has received limited endorsement, because counts are often highly variable, especially for low population densities (Fig. 11-3).

The behavioral pattern and activity cycle of the species should be well known to observers before this census procedure is attempted (Sec. 11-5). Track counts are most useful for assessing populations when a

Figure 11-3 Tracks of the gray fox. (*Courtesy Virginia Polytechnic Institute and State University.*)

species is migrating or when herds are moving from one seasonal range to another.

11-13 Pellet-Group Counts This method is based on the assumption that periodic accumulations of animal defecations are related to population density. For example, studies have shown that mule deer and elk leave about 13 clusters of fecal pellets on the ground every 24 hours. Thus the number of pellet groups on a range unit may be converted to one deer or elk day for each 13 groups found. To convert deer days to numbers of animals, it is necessary to know how long the deer has been on the area (which can be determined for migratory herds), or the survey must be cleared of pellet groups and then counted *after* a known time interval, e.g., 1 month.

Pellet groups are counted on sample plots or strips that preferably are located by random selection. Circular plots of 0.004 ha have proven efficient for many surveys. The number of pellet groups (PG) per square kilometer is computed by

$$PG/km^2 = \frac{\text{no. of groups} \times 100 \ (ha/km^2)}{\text{area in sample plots (ha)}}$$

Then, the defecation rate (13 in this example) and the time interval (in days) are used to estimate the number of animals per square kilometer:

$$\text{Animals/km}^2 = \frac{\text{PG/km}^2}{\text{no. of days} \times 13}$$

In humid and heavily forested regions, pellet-group counts may be confined to winter because the growth of plants on the forest floor and falling leaves make counts difficult during other seasons. The method has limited value in heavy rainfall areas and in regions where dung beetles are prevalent.

11-14 Ratio Methods: Lincoln Index The more commonly used ratio methods fall into two categories—those based on the banding or marking of animals and those based primarily on kill data from legal hunts, along with a knowledge of population structure.

The first method is illustrated by a calculation procedure known as the *Lincoln index*. A number of animals are captured, marked or banded, and then released back into the population (Figs. 11-4 and 11-5). When animals from the population are later recaptured or returned by hunters, the ratio of total banded animals to the banded individuals killed can be used to calculate the size of the population (N):

Figure 11-4 Trapped Abert squirrel with ear tag. (*U.S. Forest Service photograph.*)

Figure 11-5 Banding the leg of a golden eagle. (*Courtesy Virginia Polytechnic Institute and State University.*)

$$N = \frac{\text{total no. banded}}{\text{no. of banded killed}} \times \text{no. of unbanded killed}$$

The accuracy of the method depends upon an adequate sample size, and the banded or unbanded individuals must have an equal chance of being captured, seen, recaptured, or killed—as the case may be. Recapturing animals with food bait may result in a biased sample if "trap-happy" animals return for the bait more frequently than individuals who have not previously found it.

11-15 Kelker's Ratio This method of population estimation requires data on population structure and changes in sex and age ratios resulting from legal hunts. The following deer-survey data may be used as an example:

	Before hunting	*After hunting*
Ratio of does to bucks	2.78:1	3.85:1
Ratio of fawns to does	0.81:1	0.69:1

If "any deer" hunts are permitted, the number of bucks remaining *after* the hunting season may be calculated by the formula

$$\text{Bucks} = \frac{(d_1 \times kb) - kd}{d_2 - d_1}$$

where d_1 = number of does to bucks before hunting
d_2 = number of does to bucks after hunting
kb = total kill of bucks
kd = total kill of does

By using the ratios previously listed, and assuming a kill of 1,748 bucks and 1,117 does, the number of bucks (after hunting) would be

$$\frac{(2.78 \times 1,748) - 1,117}{3.85 - 2.78} = \frac{4,859 - 1,117}{1.07} = 3,497 \text{ bucks}$$

On the post-hunt survey, there were 3.85 does per buck, and so there would be a total of $3,497 \times 3.85 = 13,463$ does. The post-hunt fawn/doe ratio of 0.69, multiplied by the number of does (13,463) yields an estimate of 9,289 fawns. Thus the total post-hunt herd is estimated as $3,497 + 13,463 + 9,289 = 26,249$ deer.

This ratio technique is relatively easy to apply for certain game animals that are regularly hunted, since sex ratios and kill data are readily available. However, it would not be applicable in parks and other areas closed to hunting. Populations determined from such ratio methods must be regarded as approximations, since the procedure assumes that nonhunting mortality is minimal.

11-16 Trend Estimates Game species are sometimes counted by walking or riding along predetermined routes during specified seasons or diurnal periods. The total number of deer, elk, rabbits, or quail seen per kilometer of travel provides an indication of population trend—or a means of estimating sex and age ratios for various species. Thus trend estimates may be used to keep track of a wildlife population without actually enumerating that population.

Large mammals are best counted during breeding seasons because they are less wary at such times. Trend measurements alone are not adequate for intensive management of big game that are either at low population levels or sensitive to legal kill, e.g., bighorn sheep. They may be adequate, however, for lightly hunted deer herds with good cover on their fall ranges and for smaller game species.

Road or horseback routes can sometimes detect enough broods of young quail, pheasant, or turkey poults to derive an average brood size and serve as an index to the annual productivity. As a result, the game manager may recommend a hunting season similar to previous years if spring trend counts and breeding are normal and if summer broods average as high in number as those of several preceding years.

Trend counts do *not* constitute a complete census. In many instances, they are merely used to supplement data taken on the entire population. When management is based on trend estimates alone, it is likely to be second-class management.

HABITAT MEASUREMENTS

11-17   The Elements of Habitat   Populations of wildlife tend to differ in numbers because of variations in hunting pressures, species characteristics, adaptability, and the quality of available habitats. The essential habitat components are water, food, and cover (i.e., protection from inclement weather and predators, including man).

Some of the habitat requirements for individual species of wildlife will differ from domestic livestock requirements. For example, there is evidence that jackrabbits, squirrels, and some grouse species do not need a continual supply of open water; instead, they may survive on succulent vegetation, insect food moisture, and similar sources. Conversely, turkey or white-tailed deer will ordinarily have a habitat requirement of open water. With regard to food requirements, many kinds of natural foods are consumed, but an individual species may be quite selective about *which foods* are regarded as palatable.

Different types of plant cover used for nest sites, resting, bed grounds and other purposes will also vary with the wildlife species, its size, and mobility. It is necessary to evaluate the cover requirements for each species, since adequate cover for the cottontail will be inadequate for deer. Of equal importance to the elements of water, food, and cover is the *spatial arrangement* of these components. Without the proper arrangement of the essential habitat elements, there will be a poor population or none at all. Most wildlife needs *all* these elements within their normal daily range of movement. And if the basic elements periodically reoccur in several locales over a landscape, a highly productive population is much more likely to develop.

11-18   Available Food   Procedures previously described for estimating forage yields, use, condition, and trend of rangelands will apply equally to wildlife habitats. Measurements of the edible herbage utilized from shrubs or trees is based on twig lengths before and after browsing (Sec. 10-12). Carrying capacities for various habitats are computed by the same procedure used for determining livestock grazing capacity. In fact, in some instances, a given range may be utilized by either domestic or semiwild animals (Fig. 11-6). Animal unit requirements will differ for each species, of course.

An important source of wildlife food that is of minimal concern to domestic livestock is plant fruit, including acorns, nuts, and seeds. Measurements of fruit production are difficult because of variations in time of ripening and the length of time they are held on the producing plant.

Efforts to estimate fruit yields have been generally confined to acorns, nuts, or large fleshy fruits. Sampling may be based on fixed-area plots by setting funnel-type traps to collect dropped fruits or by counting fruit on sample branches of the woody plant. With trap samples, the number of fruits per trap is expanded to the number for the total crown area; four to six traps per tree are often used for estimating acorn yields.

When numbers of fruits on sample branches are used for estimation purposes, tree totals may then be expanded by determining yields from various classes of tree size, form, and species in stands of known composition and density. Area sampling consists of collecting data from small

Figure 11-6 American bison have been reintroduced to several parts of the United States. These are near the former site of Model, Tennessee. (*Courtesy Tennessee Valley Authority.*)

plots distributed over the entire stand. Open, unprotected plots on the ground may be useful if samples can be taken frequently during the fruiting season. Otherwise, traps must be used to protect against losses due to deterioration and animal consumption.

Wildlife forage estimation based on clipped plots is an expensive and time-consuming process (Sec. 10-9). However, a procedure known as the *rank set* method shows some promise for decreasing the number of clipped plots or for increasing sampling precision without increasing sample size. The description that follows is from Ripley and Halls (1966).

> As an example, it may be assumed that nine sets of three random samples are defined and ranked by ocular judgment on the basis of forage yields. Forage from the highest ranking sample in the first set is clipped and weighed; in the second set the second ranked sample is measured; and the third ranking sample from the third set is clipped and weighed. The sequence is then repeated for the remaining sets, and the nine samples clipped out of the twenty-seven samples inspected would include three samples in each of the three ranks. The average of the sample estimates of the means in each stratum (rank) is the unbiased estimate of the population mean.

During a browse and herbage sampling experiment in a pine-hardwood forest in East Texas, it was determined that sampling variation was reduced by nearly one-half through the use of the rank set method. It was concluded that precision equal to that from simple random sampling could be achieved with about half the number of clipped plots.

11-19 Determining Forage Preferences To evaluate food habits, preferences, and nutritional requirements for various wildlife species, it is usually desirable to work with experimental animals, e.g., captured and confined wild animals or semitame individuals that were raised in captivity. Study conditions are greatly simplified when a sufficient number of experimental animals can be held and maintained in paddocks or large enclosures that approximate typical range conditions.

When large numbers of animals are needed, some means of live-trapping is needed. Methods include baited box-type traps, the driving of deer or elk into corrals with spotlights, or herding large animals into enclosures by use of light aircraft and helicopters. Another technique is to shoot larger mammals with a special dart gun. The dart injects a paralyzing or disabling drug which immobilizes the animal for several hours, thus permitting its capture and confinement.

When only a few animals are required for studies of forage preference and consumption, it may be feasible to capture young specimens and tame them for experimental purposes. Special care must be exercised in feeding such animals so that they do not develop a taste for table scraps in lieu of a normal range diet.

Several studies have employed tame or semitame antelope and deer to observe their food preferences in the habitat of their wild counterparts (Parker, 1968). In limited instances, tame animals have been employed in experiments to determine the effect of different vegetation types and seasons, grazing treatments, or range manipulations on kinds and quantities of forage taken. The resulting experience demonstrates that some wildlife species can be trained and handled for effective use in forage utilization studies (Fig. 11-7).

Advantages of the tamed-animal system are

1   Opportunity for positive identification of all foods taken

Figure 11-7   Observing a tamed deer to determine forage preferences. (*Courtesy Arizona Game and Fish Department.*)

2 Recognition of species, parts, or phenological stages of plants that are unacceptable as forage

3 Ability to relate selections and rejections to availability in a desired time and place

4 Opportunity for sampling in conformance with predesigned plans as well as the incorporation of forage consumption measurements in an experimental design without additional cost for fencing or facilities in the experiment itself

The tamed-animal approach is subject to several obvious limitations. There is no reliable means of *quantifying* intake, and methods for demonstrating an acceptable degree of similarity between tame and wild animals are open to question. There are large variations between individual animals, thus creating a problem in expanding data to population levels. And finally, the time and costs involved in rearing such animals are considerable. In summary, if the objective is to determine the *kinds* of forage consumed, the technique works quite well. However, where a knowledge of *amounts* consumed is also needed, the method will require further refinements before it can be regarded as completely reliable.

11-20 The Edge Effect One measurable quantity that is related to the *arrangement* of the basic habitat elements is the amount of *edge* present on a given range. Edge may be defined as the total linear measure of the borderline between two distinct vegetation types; i.e., it must be distinct in the eyes of the wildlife species under consideration. Animals find these borders between classes of vegetation attractive because they often provide food supplies near nesting grounds, cover for travel, or a clear escape route near a bed ground.

Edge is a quantity that is often used to compare a productive range with a habitat of unknown ability to support wildlife. It is also a quantity that is subject to periodic change because of events such as forest fires and timber harvesting. A square opening of 9 ha surrounded by forest has only about one-fourth of the border or edge provided by nine scattered 1-ha openings. This fact can be an important consideration in planning clearcut logging in conjunction with wildlife habitat requirements.

There are many techniques for measuring edge on a selected range (e.g., on type maps or aerial photographs), but the land manager must exercise keen judgment in deciding *which edges* will be of interest and importance to a given species of wildlife. For example, a deer might not consider a difference between two grass types to be significant, whereas a grass-bush border would probably constitute an important edge.

The concept of edge is particularly important for species that are characterized by a limited home range and a small radius of daily mobility.

It is a criterion by which management efforts on a game range can be quantified and evaluated. As a rule, the population potential of a given wildlife range is proportional to the sum of the edge in that range.

11-21   Damage and Losses from Wildlife   The unwanted utilization of forage, herbage, seeds, planted seedlings, and cultivated crops by wildlife must occasionally be assessed in order to formulate control methods. In addition, predatory animals may impose a threat to the existence of certain rare wildlife species.

Large mammals can consume ample amounts of food, resulting in severe damage to managed forests or farm crops. And small animals can eat or destroy quantities of seeds and stored grains. Once a problem situation is recognized, hunted species can be easily reduced in number to restore the balance between population size and range carrying capacity. The rational control of nuisance animals (e.g., rodents) and predators (e.g., coyotes) presents a more formidable problem to the resource manager, however.

The first step in damage evaluation is to identify the species or group of animals causing the damage. Teeth marks on browse, tracks, droppings, and food caches may provide useful clues; identification is usually a relatively simple process. Next, the seriousness of the loss should be established, preferably in quantitative terms such as number of tree seedlings browsed or seed losses per hectare.

Finally, a course of action must be decided upon. Choices often include the use of repellents (in lieu of poisons), capture and relocation of offending animals (by state agencies), or manipulation of the habitat to make it less attractive to the damaging species. The last alternative is perhaps most desirable in theory, but the length of time required to accomplish such changes may rule in favor of more immediate measures. Extreme methods such as poisoning or the introduction of a bounty system should be avoided altogether, if at all possible.

11-22   Management Priorities and Inventory Needs   Vertebrate wildlife populations are always influenced, for better or for worse, by *any* modification of wild lands. In many parts of the world, the management of the major game species is integrated with the production of timber, water, domestic livestock, fish, and outdoor recreation. As each product from the land becomes more important, it tends to be more intensively managed. Thus changes made to increase water yields may either increase or reduce forage for livestock and wildlife. Or a forest area that is modified to provide greater opportunities for human recreation may reduce the potential for growing sawlogs. As a result, management priorities for various wild-land outputs are under constant review and adjustment (see Chap. 14).

Attitudes are also changing *within* the field of wildlife resource management, with greater emphasis being placed on rare and unusual species, including those considered as "varmints" in years past. Thus the wildlife manager must consider the niche of the alligator, the pileated woodpecker, and the coyote in the overall ecosystem, for tomorrow's citizens may well equate songbirds rather than game birds with well-managed public lands.

Changing public attitudes and a greater emphasis on nonhunted wildlife populations will eventually necessitate new and more refined inventory techniques. The inevitable increase in the relative value of wildlife resources should make it economically feasible to more thoroughly investigate the use of both remote sensors (e.g., microwave imagery) and human observers (e.g., volunteer census takers) in the immediate future.

PROBLEMS

11-1 Design and participate in a drive census or a strip-flushing census for an important game species in your locality. Compare results with similar surveys conducted by public agencies. Describe the main problems encountered during your census, and suggest possible ways to improve the efficiency of the method.

11-2 Design and conduct some form of indirect census for a wildlife species, e.g., bird-call counts, track counts, or pellet-group counts. Prepare a written report on your findings.

11-3 Use the Lincoln index or Kelker's ratio, along with essential data from your state game and fish department, to calculate the population size for a hunted game animal.

11-4 Construct and deploy a set of "varmint-proof" traps to collect plant fruits over a predetermined period of time. Then develop mathematical conversions to expand the volume or weight of collected fruit to a unit-area basis. In a brief written report, illustrate your trap design in a schematic drawing, and discuss your findings.

11-5 For your geographic region, list any animals that habitually cause significant economic damage or loss. How is the problem being handled by local game authorities? Can the losses be readily measured or expressed quantitatively?

11-6 What rare, unusual, or endangered species of wildlife occur in your locality? What steps are (or should be) taken to ensure their survival? Which species (if any) are being killed under a bounty system? *How many* of these species have you personally seen (unconfined) in the last 5 years? Can you develop a sampling technique to estimate how many of these animals (e.g., the coyote) remain in your state today?

REFERENCES

Bump, G., Darnaw, R. W., Edminster, F. C., and Crissey, W. F.
    1947. *The ruffed grouse: Life history, propagation, and management.*
    N.Y. State Cons. Dept., Albany, NY. 915 pp., illus.
Burt, Henry B., and Grossenheider, R. P.
    1952. *A field guide to the mammals.* Houghton Mifflin Company, Boston,
    MA. 200 pp., illus.
Giles, Robert H., Jr. (ed.)
    1969. *Wildlife management techniques.* The Wildlife Society, Washington,
    D.C. 623 pp., illus.
Hanson, William R.
    1963. Calculation of productivity, survival and abundance of selected ver-
    tebrates from sex and age ratios. *Wildl. Monographs* **9**:1-60.
Hewitt, Oliver H.
    1967. *The wild turkey and its management.* The Wildlife Society, Washing-
    ton, D.C. 589 pp., illus.
Jenkins, James H., and Marchinton, R. Larry
    1969. Problems in censusing the white-tailed deer. Symposium Proceedings,
    Nacogdoches, TX. Pp. 115-118.
Kelker, G. H.
    1940. Estimating deer population by a differential hunting loss in the sexes.
    Proc. Utah Academy of Science, Arts, and Letters **17**:65-69.
McKell, Cyrus M., Blaisdell, J. P., and Goodin, J. R.
    1972. Wildlands shrubs—Their biology and utilization. *U.S. Forest Serv.,
    Intermount. Forest and Range Expt. Sta., Tech. Report* INT-1. 494 pp.,
    illus.
Murie, Olaus J.
    1954. *A field guide to animal tracks.* Houghton Mifflin Company, Boston,
    MA. 374 pp., illus.
———
    1951. *The elk of North America.* The Stackpole Co., Harrisburg, PA, and
    the Wildlife Management Institute, Washington, D.C. 376 pp., illus.
Parker, H. Dennison, and Driscoll, Richard S.
    1972. An experiment in deer detection by thermal scanning. *J. Range
    Manage.* **25**:480-481.
Parker, Kenneth W. (ed.)
    1968. Range and wildlife habitat evaluation: A research symposium. *U.S.
    Forest Serv., Misc. Pub.* 1147, Government Printing Office, Washington,
    D.C. 220 pp., illus.
Patterson, Robert L.
    1952. *The sage grouse in Wyoming.* Sage Books, Inc. Denver, CO. 341 pp.,
    illus.
Ripley, Thomas H., and Halls, L. K.
    1966. Measuring the forest wildlife resource. L.S.U. Forestry Symposium
    Proceedings, Baton Rouge, LA. Pp. 163-184.

Rosene, Walter
　　1969. *The bobwhite quail.* Rutgers University Press, New Brunswick, NJ.
　　418 pp., illus.
Taylor, Walter P. (ed.)
　　1956. *The deer of North America.* The Stackpole Co., Harrisburg, PA. 668
　　pp., illus.
Trippensee, Reuben Edwin
　　1948. *Wildlife management: Upland game and general principles.*
　　McGraw-Hill Book Company, New York. 479 pp., illus.

Chapter 12

Measuring Fisheries Resources

12-1 Introduction Fisheries scientists are concerned with the biology, economics, and social value of fisheries resources. As with other wildlife resources, the objective of management is to achieve and maintain a balance between the production of desired species and annual utilization. This brief introduction to fisheries measurements stresses methods of measuring individual fish, population estimates, and aquatic habitat evaluations.

The term *fisheries* implies a degree of utilization by man, and the harvesting of fish constitutes an added form of mortality on fish populations. For man to obtain long-term utilization of a fisheries resource or to protect an endangered species, he must have an intimate knowledge of their biology. Only after the complete life history is documented can the fisheries scientist make biologically sound management decisions that will ensure optimal utilization and preservation of the resource.

Fish are collected for study with a variety of gear and sampling techniques. A 1.2×3 m (4×10 ft) small-mesh minnow seine, pulled by two

persons, is used to collect fish in shallow areas along the shorelines of
lakes and streams. Electroshocking devices are also used in shallow
water, i.e., less than 1.5 m deep. Offshore fish in lakes are caught with gill
nets that capture fish around the body as they swim into the net. Bottom
fish in lakes and marine waters are captured with an otter trawl pulled by a
boat, or with some type of trap net in which the fish may enter easily but
cannot escape. Fish poisons are used to collect fish in special circumstances. Each method is "selective" for certain species and/or sizes of
fish. A great deal of care must be taken to ensure that the collecting gear
and sampling methods are appropriate for the goals of the investigator.

INDIVIDUAL FISH MEASUREMENTS

12-2 Methods of Aging Fish Measurements of individual fish
constitute the basis for deriving the age composition of the population, the
age of sexual maturity, and the growth rate of the population. Individual
measurements are also used to back-calculate the length for each year of
life and to determine the "condition" of the fish. Growth rate and condition are valuable biological indicators of the environmental suitability for
the species. They may also suggest management manipulations, i.e., the
need to provide a suitable forage fish or the need to control rough or
coarse fish. Knowledge of the age or size at sexual maturity is important
in formulating fishing regulations that will ensure an adequate annual
breeding stock.

There are four general methods used to age fish: the scale method,
the otolith and bone method, the length-frequency method, and the
known-age method. The *scale method* is the most common means of
aging fish. Scales, like other structures of bone, show seasonal changes in
growth rate (Fig. 12-1). The aging of fish by the scale method is possible
in waters where there is a definite change in growth rate associated with
water temperature, i.e., decreased growth in winter. Annual growth marks
(annuli) on scales reflect a period when growth was slow or stopped. A
special scale projector is used to illuminate the outline and detail of a scale
for interpretation and measurement.

Seasonal change in growth is also reflected in *otoliths* (ear bones) and
other bones, i.e., vertebrae and spines. Usually, they must be stained or
polished to bring out the distinctive banding. Periods of rapid growth
show up as light bands, while slower growth is represented by darker
bands.

If a large number of fish are collected from a population, the variations in length within each age class will be (ideally) scattered about the
mean in a normal distribution. When the entire population data are plotted (i.e., number of fish versus length), there will be groupings of fishes of

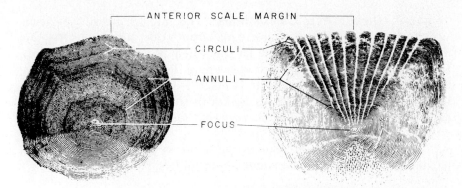

Figure 12-1 The cycloid scale of a whitefish (left) and the ctenoid scale of a sunfish (right), showing year marks (annuli) and general scale features. Both fish were 2 years old. (*Courtesy U.S. National Marine Fisheries Service.*)

particular ages around particular lengths, making possible a graphical separation by age groups (Fig. 12-2). The requirements of this method are (1) a large sample size (usually several hundred fish), (2) a short collection period (usually one day), and (3) a representation of all sizes and age groups. It may not be possible to separate *all* age classes by *length-frequency analysis* in fish populations that have extended breeding seasons (spring through summer breeders) or where the fish are long-lived and are characterized by growth rates that decrease with age.

Observations of fish of *known age* may be used to verify other methods of age determination. Young-of-the-year fish placed in a pond and periodically recaptured for length evaluation will provide growth rates for fish of known age. *Marked fish* (i.e., tagged, fin-clipped, etc.) of known age may also be released into a natural population and recaptured later to provide growth-rate information.

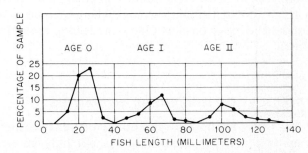

Figure 12-2 Hypothetical length/frequency graph showing how fish age can be estimated from a large sample of fish of varying sizes.

12-3 Growth-Rate Calculations The rate of growth for each year of a fish's life is often calculated from scale measurements; this approach is feasible because the length growth of a fish scale is proportional to the length growth of the entire fish. A sample of body-length/scale-length measurements is taken from fish of all sizes. Scale length is measured from the *focus*, anteriorly to the margin of scale. There are several formulas that may be used, but they all assume some body-growth/scale-growth relationship.

The direct-proportion relationship assumes that the ratio of body length to scale length is a constant (b) for all lengths of fish:

Body length = $b \times$ scale length

The value of the constant b will vary according to the species of fish, of course. Another method of calculating body length from scale measurements is based on a simple linear regression of the form $\hat{Y} = a + bX$ (Sec. 2-32):

$\hat{Y}$ (body length) = $a + (b \times$ scale length)

12-4 Condition of Fish The general well-being of a fish species is often reflected by a "condition" factor. A length/weight relationship of a fish is used to calculate a coefficient of condition. This value expresses the condition of the fish in numerical terms (relative leanness or plumpness). The coefficient of condition K is commonly computed by the relationship

$$K = \frac{\text{fish weight (g)}}{[\text{fish length (cm)}]^3} \, (100)$$

The coefficient of condition will vary with different aged fish, fish of different sex, and even within a single individual after a seasonal change (i.e., before and after spawning). Therefore, any comparisons of K values should be based on fish of the same length, age, sex, and season of collection.

POPULATION AND TREND ESTIMATES

12-5 Homogeneity and Movement Patterns A complete census of a fish population requires not only an estimate of numbers of individuals but also information on interactions of various species, the degree of homogeneity or intermingling, movement and behavior patterns, reproductive activities, and mortality rates.

A group of fish capable of independent exploitation and management is termed a *stock*. On occasion, it may be necessary to determine whether the harvest of a stock at one end of a large lake has a direct effect on the same species of fish at the other end. Several methods can be used to determine the degree of homogeneity or intermingling among fish populations of a single species.

Morphometric measurements involve evaluations of such characteristics as number of dorsal-fin rays or gill rakers on individuals from various areas to ascertain whether there are significant differences in morphology. The detection of such differences may indicate a degree of reproductive isolation between the individuals sampled.

It may also be possible to establish important species differences through blood-group tests, biochemical variations, or the marking of captured fish and their return to the population. When marked fish are recaptured at a later date, information is provided on the degree of intermingling in various areas and on movement and behavior patterns of observed species.

Investigations of movement patterns attempt to find out where fish will be at a particular time or when they might appear at a specific locale. Answers to these questions are important to commercial and sport fishermen and also to the scientist investigating the effects of water pollution on fish populations.

Knowledge of a fish's "liability to capture" is also essential to ensure fishing efficiency. In most situations, man is attempting to harvest a rather elusive resource in his fishing efforts, and it is obvious that certain types of gear tend to catch more (or larger) fish than other kinds. This fact is partially due to behavior patterns of the species being sought, i.e., the reaction to the particular fishing apparatus and the technique employed. Research studies therefore seek to establish activity cycles for various fish and responses to different fishing approaches.

12-6   Reproduction and Mortality   At the time of spawning, a new generation of fish is produced. When spawning is successful, man may be able to harvest a part of the surplus population that would otherwise be lost to natural mortality. Thus spawning activities are studied to determine which ecological factors are critical to the fish species for ensuring a successful spawn.

Spawning investigations provide insights into possible deleterious effects on fish reproduction when breeding habitats are altered by human pollution or natural elements. Certain land management practices, even "approved" timber-harvesting or strip-mining operations, may alter a stream environment to the extent that fisheries resources are severely damaged or destroyed.

Studies of natural mortality are conducted to determine which environmental factors may cause a fish species to be particularly susceptible to physical and chemical habitat changes, diseases, or predation. These studies may also include the effects of sublethal pollution on such activities as migration and breeding.

Survival and mortality rates may be estimated by comparing the numbers of a marked stock that are alive at successive ages or by separating the fish caught in successive catches into age classes. A creel census is valuable for collecting information on fishing mortality. If large numbers of fish are marked before a creel census begins, an estimate of total mortality can be obtained from assessments of fishing mortality.

12-7 Direct Population Estimates Population size in terms of weight is useful as a measure of the utilization of aquatic space. Accordingly, the terms *standing crop* and *carrying capacity* may be used by fisheries biologists with reference to fish populations of inland waters.

A standing crop is the total weight of one species or all species in a stream, lake, or reservoir at a given time. The standing crop provides a rough estimate of productivity, and it is usually expressed in terms of weight per unit area. Carrying capacity is defined as the theoretical maximum weight of a species of fish that a specific habitat may support during a stated interval of time.

The basic methods for estimating fish populations are essentially the same as those outlined in the previous chapter, viz., direct census, indirect census, and ratio methods.

A direct census of fish may be accomplished by (1) draining a body of water and counting the entire population, (2) counting migrating adults as they move upstream to spawn, (3) using sonar (echo-sounding) devices, (4) trapping all fish in random locations and extrapolating the sample to a population estimate, and (5) using a proportion based on the catch per unit of fishing effort. Where the fishing intensity is high, the total catch provides an indication of population size. If fishing pressures are light, the catch per unit of fishing effort is found to be roughly proportional to stock abundance.

12-8 Indirect Population Estimates When fish themselves are not amenable to sampling, some other attribute that can be easily measured is used to predict population size or trend. For example, a breeding population size might be estimated through regression analysis by relating the number of eggs laid by females to the number of spawning sites occupied by adults.

For some marine species, population estimates are derived from the number of pelagic (neutral buoyancy) eggs that are collected at sea per unit of time. The mean number of eggs per female (fecundity), the sex ratio, and some estimate of the total number of eggs laid during a spawning season must be known. Such information may be difficult to obtain, but for many marine species, this method provides a good estimate of population trend.

12-9   Mark/Recapture Ratios   These ratios are especially useful for estimating population size for freshwater sports fishing stocks when good catch information is available. The underlying principle is to establish a marked fish population that will be subject to the same probability of recapture as the unmarked population. Where only a short catch period is involved, population size is estimated by use of a "single recapture relationship" as described in Sec. 11-14.

When fish are caught, marked, released, and recaptured over a period of several days, a "multiple capture estimator" is used:

$$\hat{N} = \frac{\Sigma(M_t\,C_t)}{\Sigma(R_t)}$$

where M_t = total marked fish at large on day t

C_t = cumulative total catch as of day t

R_t = cumulative total of marked fish recaptured as of day t

A hypothetical application of this multiple census estimator is presented in the tabulation that follows. In this example, a population of bluegill sunfish is estimated as approximately 1,800 individuals after 10 days of sampling:

Day No.	$\Sigma(M_t C_t)$	$\Sigma(R_t)$	$\hat{N}$
1	1,500	1	1500
2	3,560	3	1187
3	5.783	4	1446
4	8,542	7	1220
6	20,320	12	1693
8	28,471	16	1779
9	36,304	20	1815
10	39,500	22	1795

The employment of mark/recapture ratios for estimating fish-population size assumes that there is (1) no death caused by marking, (2) no loss of marks, (3) no recruitment to the unmarked population, (4) no difference in "catchability" of the two populations resulting from tagging, and (5) a random distribution of the marked fish in the unmarked population. The principal difficulties associated with such estimates are those encountered in establishing a marked population that is large enough to get a good number of recaptures and is subject to the same probability of capture as the unmarked population.

12-10 Trend Estimates   The primary objectives of fisheries management are to predict and maintain the quantity and quality of the fisheries output at a high level. The appraisal of methods used to improve and maintain the stock depends on a knowledge of previous and current harvests, i.e., records of fishing efforts and successes. Poor catches are often the first clue to the need for more intensive management.

Commercial fisheries records are maintained by government agencies, while sports-fishing data are collected by fisheries biologists. These analyses are referred to as production studies in commercial fisheries and creel-census studies in recreational fisheries; they are designed to provide information on changes in fishing regulations, stocking or transplanting, environmental improvements, and changes in fishing methods.

The general *creel census* is aimed at obtaining broad information on *trends* in kinds of fishing, time of fishing, time spent, species and sizes of fish caught, and catch per unit of effort (number of legal fish per fisherman hour). An example of a creel-census questionnaire is illustrated by Table 12-1.

To maximize the physical yield or production of fisheries, attempts are made to control the total catch and the rate of exploitation through annual removal of a certain percentage of the population. For each fish species and habitat, there is (theoretically) a given level of fishing at which the stock will stabilize and reach a position of equilibrium. At this level of harvest, the production of biomass is maximum, thus providing a stable output of fish resources over a long period of time. The relationship of fishing effort to the equilibrium yield of the population is termed the maximum sustained yield (MSY) of the stock (Fig. 12-3). Some investigators advise against fisheries management for MSY alone; instead, maximum economic return—in conjunction with physical yield—is recommended.

AQUATIC HABITAT EVALUATIONS

12-11 Sampling Vegetation and Bottom Organisms   Fish populations make up only one element of a typical aquatic community. This community is composed of varied plants and animals that form complex interrelations with each other and with their environment. An understanding of the food-chain relationships between fish and other organisms in the aquatic habitat is invaluable to the manager of fisheries resources.

Table 12-1   Creel Census Questionnaire*

Check: If stream_____If lake_____County_____

Name of lake or stream_____Date_____

Time of interview_____

Species caught	*Number*	*Avg. fork length*
1 Sunfish		
2 Channel catfish		
3 Crappie		
4 Rainbow trout		
5 Etc.		

Time fished   AM_____   Total hours fished_____

                 PM_____

Number of anglers in party_____Male_____Female_____

_____

Residence: City and state_____

Type of fishing

Boat_____   Still fishing_____

Shore_____   Trolling_____

Other_____   Casting_____

                                               Other _____

Bait used_____

_____

*One card to be used by each fishing party, whether or not fish were caught.

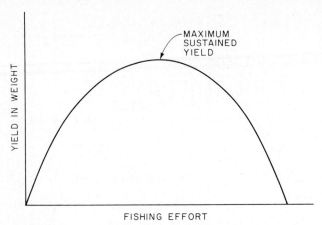

Figure 12-3 The theoretical relationship between fishing effort and yield.

This section describes sampling techniques and methods of quantifying the life (excluding fish) in aquatic habitats. Such information is used by the fisheries manager to rate habitats as poor, marginal, or good for the well-being of certain sport fishes, to assess changes in the aquatic habitat as a result of man-related or natural pollution, and to enhance a fisheries through biological or environmental manipulation.

Rooted *aquatic vegetation* is often sampled by hook or rake from shore or from a boat. Vegetative abundance is computed in terms of dry weight per unit area. Plants form the basis of the food chain that terminates with the top consumer—usually a carnivorous fish. Living aquatic plants provide oxygen and food for consumers, a supporting substrate for a host of insects, and shelter from predation for young fish.

The sampling and quantification of *bottom food organisms in still waters* is accomplished with some type of dredge or bottom "grab" device. These devices take a standard-sized "bite" out of the lake bottom. Then the dredge is pulled to the surface, and all bottom organisms are sieved from the sediment and trash. Later, the weight or volume of organisms per square meter is determined, along with the species composition. The number of samples necessary to give a correct estimate of abundance depends on the lake size, type of bottom, and variations in the organisms collected.

Bottom fauna in streams are sampled with a device such as that shown in Fig. 12-4. Stones within the frame are washed off in front of the net, and the bottom is vigorously disturbed; this washes all bottom organisms downstream into the net. The material is sorted, and the weight or volume of organisms is determined, along with the species composition.

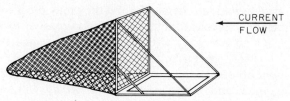

Figure 12-4 A stream-bottom sampler. Mesh size is approximately 2 × 2 mm.

Several samples are usually taken across the width of the stream, and all habitats should be included.

12-12 Sampling Plankton Plankton are submacroscopic plants and animals that float in water free of the bottom; they form the base of the food chain, and their relative abundance indicates the *productivity* of a body of water. Plankton are sampled with a variety of small, fine-meshed nets (Fig. 12-5) that are pulled behind a boat or are raised vertically from the bottom to the surface.

Computations of plankton density and species composition are expressed in relation to the volume of water sampled. The volume or weight of plankton per cubic meter of water may be determined by the relationship

$$\text{cm}^3/\text{m}^3 \text{ or } \text{g}/\text{m}^3 = \frac{\text{plankton volume (cm}^3\text{) or weight (g)}}{\text{net mouth area (m}^2\text{)} \times \text{length of haul (m)}}$$

12-13 Water Temperature Details of evaluating water quality are discussed in the next chapter; this section is concerned largely with the *relevance* of several aspects of water quality to fish production. Even small changes in water chemistry (temperature, dissolved oxygen, or pH) can adversely affect fish populations. Fish have optimum ranges of toler-

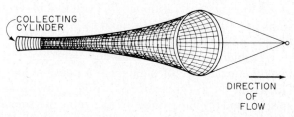

Figure 12-5 Diagrammatic plankton net. Mesh size would approximate that of linen.

ance to various chemicals, and they may die if overexposed to noxious elements. Physical factors such as excessive turbidity and sedimentation can also adversely affect fish populations and their habitats.

Water-temperature changes can also influence the survival, distribution, breeding, and growth rates of organisms, the solubility of dissolved oxygen, and water stratification. Many human activities can result in elevated water temperatures—often to the detriment of the fisheries resource. For example, the clearcutting of shade trees along stream banks may result in stream temperatures above the tolerance level of trout and salmon. And heated effluents discharged into lakes and streams are likely to be highly destructive to some fish populations.

Recommended *maximum temperatures* for various fish (from Water Quality Criteria, 1968) are as follows:

33°C—growth of catfish, white bass, and threadfin shad
32°C—growth of large-mouth bass, bluegill, and crappie
28°C—growth of northern pike, yellow perch, walleye, and small-mouth bass
26°C—spawning and egg development of catfish and threadfin shad
20°C—growth and migration routes of salmon and trout; egg development of yellow perch and small-mouth bass
12°C—spawning and egg development of salmon and trout
 8°C—spawning and egg development of walleye and northern pike

12-14 Dissolved Oxygen, pH, and Turbidity For good growth and condition of warm-water fish populations, the dissolved oxygen (DO) concentration should be above 5 ppm or 5 mg/l; it may decrease to 4 mg/l for short periods during a 24-hour period. For cold-water fish (trout and salmon), the DO concentrations should not be below 6 ppm. At spawning, the DO concentration should not be below 7 ppm. The DO concentration may range between 5 and 6 ppm for short periods of time but should never fall below 4 ppm.

Very hard waters are often toxic to fish, whereas soft waters may have a poor productive capacity. For the general well-being of fish, a pH of 6.5 to 8.5 is best, although fish will live in waters where the pH ranges from 5 to 10. No material should be added to the aquatic habitat to lower the pH below 6.0 or raise it above 9.0.

Turbidity causes (1) reduced light penetration and lessened photosynthetic activity of plants, (2) a possible loss of much of the bottom fauna and flora, (3) reduced feeding, growth, and activity in some fish species, and (4) impairment of spawning in some fish species. Natural turbidity probably causes no mortality among fish, but it may be responsible for low productivity and a poor standing crop of fish.

Measurements of turbidity are expressed in terms of Jackson Turbidity Units (JTU).[1] The permissible turbidity level should not exceed 50 JTU in warm-water streams or 25 JTU in warm-water lakes. Up to 10 JTU may be acceptable in cold-water or oligotrophic lakes, but the limit is much lower (0.10 JTU) in cold-water streams.

12-15 Sedimentation The addition of sediment to streams harms fish life and lowers the productive capacity of the aquatic habitat. Suspended sediments create turbid water, which can have deleterious effects on fish and habitats. When sediment settles on the gravel of a stream bed, the effects on fish are quite subtle. If the gravel is used by trout and salmon for spawning, sedimentation can (1) reduce intragravel water flow and the amount of oxygen available to developing eggs and fry, (2) physically trap fry in the gravel and prevent them from emerging, or (3) influence fry survival after they emerge from the gravel, if the sediment accumulates in gravel crevices and eliminates them as sources of refuge from predators. The quantity of bottom-dwelling aquatic insects available for fish food may also be reduced by the accumulation of sediment.

If the silt deposited in a reservoir contains elements rich in organic matter, the productive capacity will likely be increased; if the material is clay or sand (and poor in nutrients), the productive capacity may be reduced. Even minor amounts of sediments inhibit the growth of normal stream or lake fauna. Waters that normally contain 25 to 80 mg/l of suspended solids are indicative of good-to-average waters for freshwater fisheries. Waters with 80 to 400 mg/l of suspended solids do not usually support productive fish populations.

PROBLEMS

12-1 Your instructor will supply numerical data on body-length/scale-length measurements for a local fish species. Use these paired measurements to develop a simple linear regression for predicting the growth rate of the species.

12-2 Determine the coefficient of condition for a fish species. Base your calculations on measurements of at least 20 to 30 specimens.

12-3 Use a mark/recapture ratio, along with essential data from your state game and fish department, to calculate the population size for a local fish species.

12-4 Your instructor will supply numerical data for two comparable species that have been marked and planted in a lake. After a given time interval, it has been determined that different *percentages* of the two species have been caught by anglers. Use the chi-square test to determine whether these differences can be explained by chance alone.

[1] One JTU = 1 mg SiO_2/l.

12-5 Design and conduct a creel census to determine the mean fork lengths of two comparable species caught by fishermen. Then use the Student's *t* test to ascertain whether the difference in mean fork lengths is significant.

REFERENCES

Bennett, George W.
  1971. *Management of lakes and ponds.* Van Nostrand-Reinhold Company, New York, 375 pp., illus.
Calhoun, Alex
  1966. *Inland fisheries management.* California Dept. of Fish and Game, Sacramento, CA. 546 pp., illus.
Federal Water Pollution Control Administration.
  1968. *Water quality criteria.* U.S. Dept. of the Interior, Washington, D.C. 234 pp., illus
Freese, Frank
  1960. Testing accuracy. *Forest Sci.* **6**(2):139-145.
Krygier, J. T., and Hall, J. D.
  1971. *Forest land uses and stream environment.* Oregon State University Press, Corvallis, OR. 252 pp., illus.
Lagler, Karl F.
  1956. *Freshwater fishery biology.* Wm. C. Brown Company Publishers, Dubuque, IA. 421 pp., illus.
Lux, F. E.
  1966. *Age determination in fishes* (revised). U.S. Dept. of Commerce, National Marine Fisheries Serv., Fishery Leaflet 637. 7 pp., illus.
Ricker, W. E.
  1968. *Methods for assessment of fish production in fresh waters.* IBP Handbook No. 3, Blackwell Scientific Publ., Oxford, England. 313 pp., illus.
Royce, William F.
  1972. *Introduction to the fishery sciences.* Academic Press Inc., New York 351 pp., illus
Schwoerbel, J.
  1970. *Methods of hydrobiology.* Pergamon Press, London. 200 pp., illus.

Chapter 13

Measuring Water Resources

13-1 Introduction Water is important to resource managers in its liquid, solid, and vapor forms. It is one of our most dynamic natural resources, and at times it may completely dominate or limit the use and management of other resources on the land. During periods of heavy rainfall, runoff, or snow cover, for example, water may limit access to the land, timber harvesting, grazing, and other operational functions.

In both liquid and solid forms, water influences the production rates of timber, forage, and wildlife. In the form of snow, water provides winter recreational opportunites, and liquid water on and from wild lands affects fishing, swimming, boating, and other water-based recreational activities. In many localities, streamflow runoff derived from liquid and solid precipitation constitutes an important water-supply source for municipal, industrial, and agricultural applications downstream. Runoff may also provide significant sources of power to aid in satisfying energy needs. Excessive runoff may cause upstream and downstream damage as a result of erosion, flooding, or sedimentation. Thus, the quantity, timing, and quality of water produced from wild lands are of critical importance; either too much or too little water can be as limiting as water of impaired quality.

In vapor form, water is a factor in determining evaporation and transpiration rates from wild lands. And its contribution to atmospheric humidity may exert a significant influence on the forest-fire hazard because of the effect on fuel moisture contents.

Interactions between water and the utilization of other resources on the land can also be important. As an illustration, the harvesting of trees may increase streamflow yields, at least temporarily. At the same time, poor access-road engineering on watersheds may increase rates of erosion and sedimentation. It is therefore apparent that water not only affects other resources, but the use and management of those resources affects water quantity and quality. To assess the significance of water both on and off the land, the resource manager should be able to inventory water in its various forms, just as is done for timber, rangelands, and wildlife resources.

13-2 Factors Affecting Runoff The flow of a stream is essentially controlled by two factors, one depending on the physical characteristics of the watershed and the other upon weather and climatic characteristics (e.g., precipitation) that directly affect the watershed. Land managers concerned with water resources must have an appreciation of the mensurational aspects of both sets of factors to achieve desired water resource objectives and to properly evaluate available management opportunites.

A watershed is an area of internal drainage, the size and shape of which is determined by surface topography. A watershed is completely encircled by a divide or ridge line. Precipitation falling on one side of the divide drains toward the outlet or mouth of the watershed on that side of the divide; precipitation falling on the other side of the divide drains toward outlets of other watersheds. The resource manager uses the watershed as his basic land unit for planning and management purposes; in this sense, it is roughly comparable to the forester's working circle or the range manager's grazing allotment.

In essence, the watershed is a limited unit of the earth's surface within which climatic conditions can be assessed; it also represents a system where a balance can be struck in terms of the inflow and outflow of moisture. Various sizes of watersheds may be recognized and delineated, depending on the objectives of users. Small, experimental watersheds may encompass only a few hectares in area, while large watersheds may be composed of entire river basins.

PHYSICAL CHARACTERISTICS OF A WATERSHED

13-3   Area   Perhaps the easiest characteristic of a watershed to measure is its areal extent. Such evaluations are commonly made by using a planimeter or dot grids to measure the delineated area on planimetric maps, topographic maps, or aerial photographs. Area is an important consideration because the total volume of water carried by a stream is directly related to watershed area. Larger watersheds generally produce greater amounts of water, although this generalization may not hold for some of the more arid portions of the world.

Another important consideration is the effect of watershed area on peak flows. As with total water yields, higher peak flows are usually associated with larger areas. However, when such outputs are expressed in terms of *flow per unit of watershed area*, it is the smaller watersheds that characteristically have the greater rates of flow.

13-4   Shape   The outline form or shape of a watershed can sometimes have a marked effect on streamflow patterns. For example, a long, narrow basin would be expected to have attenuated flood-discharge periods, whereas basins with round or oval shapes are expected to produce sharply peaked flood discharges. Although watershed shape is a difficult parameter to quantify, various indices have been developed for comparing the configurations of different basins. One such index, based on the degree of roundness or circularity of a watershed may be computed by

$$\text{Shape index} = \frac{0.28 \times \text{watershed perimeter (km)}}{\sqrt{\text{watershed area (km}^2)}}$$

When a watershed is circular in shape, the index value will be approximately 1. The closer a shape-index value is to unity, the greater the likelihood that precipitation will be quickly concentrated in the main stream channel, possibly resulting in high peak flows. Watersheds that are noncircular in shape will have index values greater than unity.

13-5   Slope   The slopes of various land surfaces within a watershed, usually expressed in percentage terms, can greatly influence the velocity and associated erosive power of overland flow. In addition, slope is related to infiltration, evapotranspiration, soil moisture, and the groundwater contribution to streamflow.

For small areas, watershed slope can be estimated by computing the average slope from several on-the-ground measurements obtained with an

Abney level or clinometer. For larger areas, or for evaluating a number of different watersheds, slope estimates can be computed from topographic maps issued by the U.S. Geological Survey. One procedure consists in randomly selecting locations within each watershed and measuring slopes directly on the contour maps; the slope for the entire watershed can then be approximated by computing an arithmetic average of these values. Watershed slope can also be estimated by the following relationship, based on determining the area between contour lines within a watershed:

$$\text{Slope (\%)} = \frac{c \times l}{a} \, (100)$$

where c = contour interval (m)
$\quad l$ = total length of contours (m)
$\quad a$ = area of watershed (m²)

For those occasional situations where slopes are relatively uniform over an entire watershed, an estimate of average slope may be derived by the relationship

$$\text{Slope (\%)} = \frac{e}{d} \, (100)$$

where e = elevational difference between the highest and lowest points on the watershed (m)
$\quad d$ = horizontal distance between high and low elevations (m)

13-6 Elevation The mean elevation and the variations in elevation of a watershed are important factors with respect to temperature and precipitation patterns, especially in mountainous topography. Temperature patterns, in turn, are associated with evaporative losses and with the timing of periods of snowpack accumulation and melt. Precipitation patterns, such as annual amounts or the proportion of annual precipitation that falls as snow, may also be related to elevation and are important in assessing the total water flow from a watershed.

The relationship of elevation to area within a watershed can be illustrated by a hypsometric curve (Fig. 13-1). Such a curve can be used to estimate the proportion of a watershed that lies above or below any selected elevation.

13-7 Orientation Transpiration and evaporation losses on a watershed, factors that affect the amount of water available for streamflow, are influenced by the general orientation or aspect of the basin. Also, the accumulation and melting of snow is related to the orientation of a water-

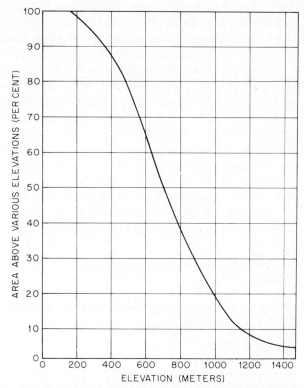

Figure 13-1 Hypsometric curve for a drainage basin.

shed. For example, if the orientation is southerly, successive snowfalls may soon melt and infiltrate into the ground or produce runoff. For those watersheds with a northerly orientation, individual snowfalls may accumulate throughout the winter and melt late in the spring, producing high volumes of streamflow.

The orientation of a watershed is normally expressed in degrees azimuth or in terms of the major compass headings (i.e., N, NE, E, etc.); the designation indicates the direction that the watershed "faces." The direction of flow for the main stream channel can also be used to indicate the general orientation of a watershed.

13-8 Drainage Network The pattern or arrangement of natural streams on a watershed is an important physical characteristic of any drainage basin for two primary reasons. First of all, it affects the efficiency of the drainage system and thus its hydrographic characteristics. Secondly, the drainage provides the land manager with a knowledge of soil and surface conditions existing on the watershed; more specifically, the erosive forces of stream channels are related to and restricted by the type of materials from which the channels are carved. Most drainage patterns can be classed as dendritic, i.e., an irregular branching of tributaries, often with no predominant direction or orientation.

A quantitative approach to classifying streams in a basin can consist in systematically *ordering* the network of branches and tributary streams. Each nonbranching tributary, regardless of whether it enters the main stream channel or its branches, is designated a first-order stream. Streams receiving only nonbranching tributaries are termed second order; third-order streams are formed by the junction of two second-order streams, and so on (Fig. 13-2). The order number of the main stream at the bottom of the watershed indicates the extent of branching and is an indication of the size and extent of the drainage network.

Another method of quantifying the drainage network of a watershed consists in determining drainage density by the following relationship:

$$\text{Drainage density (km/km}^2) = \frac{l}{a}$$

where l = total length of perennial and intermittent streams on a watershed (km)

a = watershed area (km²)

Drainage density is an expression of the closeness of spacing of stream channels on a watershed. In general, low drainage densities are favored in regions of highly permeable subsoils, dense vegetative cover, and low relief.

WEATHER AND CLIMATIC CHARACTERISTICS OF A WATERSHED

13-9 Precipitation The measurement of precipitation (i.e., the amount of water falling upon the earth) is basic to nearly all water resource evaluations. Several forms of precipitation exist, although the two most commonly identified are rain and snow. Precipitation amounts are gauged by measuring the vertical depth that accumulates above a horizontal surface. The three broad catagories of precipitation gauges in general use are known as standard, storage, and recording gauges.

Standard gauges are approximately 66 cm tall and 20 cm in diameter. Precipitation is "caught" by the collector and funneled into a receiving tube where it can be measured with a graduated stick. Concentrating the precipitation in the receiver serves two useful purposes: (1) it allows greater precision in measurement, and (2) it protects the stored precipitation from wind and sun, minimizing evaporative water losses. The stand-

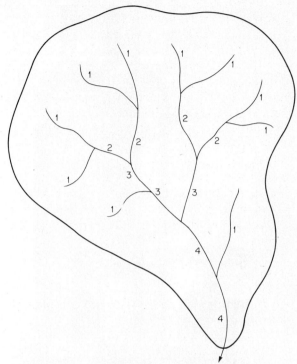

Figure 13-2 One system of designating stream orders.

ard gauge holds approximately 5 cm of precipitation in the receiving tube and 50 cm in the overflow cylinder.

Storage gauges are used to measure total seasonal precipitation, usually in remote areas; thus they have a relatively large capacity for stored precipitation. Small amounts of oil and antifreeze are often added, the first to prevent evaporation and the second to prevent freezing. Precipitation amounts are usually measured several times a year.

Two common types of recording gauges are the weighing gauge and the tipping-bucket gauge. The tipping bucket is suitable for measuring rainfall intensities; however, only the weighing gauge is satisfactory for measuring both rain and snow (Fig. 13-3). With this instrument, the weight of the receiving can, plus the precipitation that has fallen, is monitored continuously by a recording mechanism.

Precipitation measurements can be influenced by such factors as the wind velocity, the form of precipitation, and the height of the gauge above ground. A suitable location for a precipitation gauge would be one where

Figure 13-3   Universal weighing and recording rain gauge. (*Courtesy Belfort Instrument Company.*)

little or no wind occurs. Sites with individual trees, buildings, or small groups of objects nearby may cause unusual wind currents near the gauge and should therefore be avoided. In areas of rugged terrain or mountainous topography, locations near the tops of ridges where strong winds may predominate should also be avoided. Suitable exposures are often found in openings of forest or shrub vegetation. Whenever possible, a gauge should not be located closer than 1 to 2 times the height of surrounding objects. The top of the gauge is usually located about 1.2 m above the ground surface; in regions of heavy snowfall, however, the gauge is positioned at a greater height.

Precipitation in the form of snow creates a number of problems in measurement. Probably most important is the effect of wind on the amount of snow caught by a gauge. To reduce this effect, windshields are often installed around the gauge orifice (Fig. 13-4). Shielded gauges will usually have a greater precipitation "catch" than unshielded gauges. Except in the case of weighing gauges, the snow must be converted to a liquid before measurements can be made. Often, the collector funnel is removed so that the gauge is less subject to "capping" by snow.

13-10 Snow Measurements   Snowfall is the depth of fresh snow that has fallen over a limited time period (generally 24 hours), and it is measured with a "snowboard." A snowboard merely consists of a flat

Figure 13-4 Field installation of a precipitation gauge with windshield. (*U.S. Forest Service photograph.*)

piece of material with a vertical rod or dowel attached. It is placed on the ground or on the old snow surface prior to each snowfall event. After a snow storm, the depth of new snow on the board is recorded. If snowfall has not been measured, it can be estimated as follows:

Snowfall (cm) = precipitation (cm) × 10

The assumption that 10 cm of snow results from 1 cm of precipitation is not necessarily valid for any one storm, but it provides a useful estimate when a number of storms are averaged together.

Snow depth refers to the total depth of old and new snow on the ground. In areas of heavy snowfall, permanent snow stakes are installed so that the depths can be read directly. These measurements are particularly sensitive to the effects of wind on snow-accumulation patterns. Snowboards and snow stakes should be located in areas that are both representative of snowfall accumulation and sheltered from the effects of wind. Where wind is a problem, a large number of measurements must be made to obtain reliable estimates of snowfall and snow depth.

The term *snowpack* refers to snow that has accumulated on a watershed from one or more individual storms. Snowpacks are an annual occurrence in many parts of the world. The buildup or accumulation phase of a snowpack takes place during the winter months, when snowfall events are common and losses from the snowpack relatively limited. With the onset of warmer weather in the spring, the snowpack disappears due to melting and evaporation, collectively referred to as *ablation*.

The amount of water in a snowpack is termed the *water equivalent*. The water equivalent is defined as the vertical depth of liquid water over a horizontal surface that results from melting of the snow. To the watershed manager, snowpack water-equivalent measurements provide useful information on the amount of liquid water stored in a winter snowpack. In many areas, this "stored water" represents a major source of streamflow and water supply for downstream areas. Relationships between snowpack water equivalent and total streamflow can be developed to predict early spring and summer runoff volumes (Fig. 13-5).

The snowpack water equivalent is usually determined with a metal snow-sampling tube and a spring balance. The tube has a sharp, serrated cutting edge at the lower end and is designed to penetrate various types and densities of snow. The spring balance is calibrated for direct readings of the water equivalent of the core.

In western United States, the Soil Conservation Service uses snow-sampling tubes to measure snowpack water equivalents on hundreds of snow courses each winter. These courses are measured at two-week in-

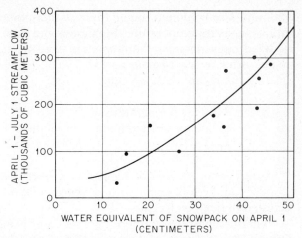

Figure 13-5 Relationship of snowpack water equivalent and streamflow for a single snow course.

tervals, beginning in mid-January and continuing into April of each year. Each snow course is a permanently marked location, often consisting of ten or more sampling points established at 8- to 30-m intervals along predetermined lines or transects. Snow courses are selected to provide an index to the amount of streamflow that results from water stored in winter snowpacks.

An alternative to periodic sampling of snowpack water equivalent is provided by a "snow pillow" placed on the ground surface to continuously monitor the water equivalent of the overlying snowpack. A snow pressure pillow is a flat, liquid-filled container varying from 1.5 to 3 m in diameter. Antifreeze solution is used to fill the pillow. The accumulation of snow (or snow melt) atop the pillow increases or decreases the pressure on the liquid inside. This pressure, which corresponds to a particular value of water equivalent, can be either recorded in place or transmitted to a receiver many kilometers away.

13-11 Other Weather Measurements Collectively, the measurement of air temperature, relative humidity, wind, evaporation, incoming solar radiation, and precipitation are used to characterize weather conditions. Evaluated over time, these day-to-day weather measurements provide an index to the climate of a particular area. A thorough knowledge of the climatic conditions associated with a given watershed is a valuable tool to the practicing watershed manager.

A variety of instruments is available for measuring *air temperature.* Liquid-in-glass thermometers containing mercury or alcohol are most common. The volume of liquid in these thermometers changes uniformly with changes in temperature. Maximum and minimum thermometers are modified liquid-in-glass thermometers used to measure temperature extremes, often over a 24-hour period. These values can then be used for estimating the mean[1] daily air temperature:

Mean daily air temperature =
$$\frac{\text{maximum temperature} + \text{minimum temperature}}{2}$$

Continuous records of temperature over daily, weekly, or monthly periods can be obtained with a thermograph. Air temperatures are recorded in degrees Celsius.

Thermometers and thermographs are usually mounted inside a shelter with louvered sides so that air can circulate freely. This is necessary to prevent direct sunshine or precipitation from affecting air temperature measurements. The shelter is commonly located about 1 to 1.5 m above ground in an open area at a distance of at least 2 times the height of any obstructing object.

Relative humidity is a measure of the amount of water vapor in the atmosphere. More precisely, relative humidity is a ratio, expressed in percent, of the amount of water vapor actually present to the amount that can be held at saturation for a given temperature. Relative humidity can be measured with a sling psychrometer. This device consists of two thermometers, one of which has a close-fitting, moistened wick attached. Whirling the psychrometer causes a cooling of the wick and a depression in temperature for the wet-bulb thermometer. The difference, or depression, in temperature is related to the relative dryness of the air. Using the sling psychrometer and psychrometric tables, estimates of relative humidity can be obtained. A hygrograph is an instrument that continuously records relative humidity. Hygrothermographs are used to simultaneously record both relative humidity and air temperature (Fig. 13-6).

Wind, defined as air in motion, represents a highly variable yet often important factor in many hydrologic processes. To describe this motion, two characteristics of wind are usually observed: direction and speed (or velocity). Wind direction refers to the direction *from* which the wind is blowing; it is usually recorded in degrees azimuth from true north or as compass points. A wind vane can be used to determine wind direction.

Wind speed is the rate at which air passes a given point on the earth's surface; it is usually expressed in distance per unit of time, such as meters

---

[1]Although commonly referred to as *mean* temperature, the value more nearly approximates the median rather than the arithmetic mean.

Figure 13-6   Hygrothermograph with cover raised. (*Courtesy Belfort Instrument Company.*)

per second. Because of large variations in windspeed during short time intervals, the average velocity over a period of 10 minutes is often used to estimate windspeed. By accumulating or totaling the number of "kilometers of wind" that have passed a location over relatively long periods of time, the wind run, expressed in kilometers per day or kilometers per month, is obtained. Cup anemometers are often used to measure windspeed. Anemometers are usually placed at a height of approximately 6 m above open, level terrain.

Evaporation is the net loss of water molecules from a liquid surface. Energy availability and vapor-pressure gradients determine the rates and total amounts of evaporation from a free water surface. Estimates of evaporative losses can be obtained with evaporation pans. Throughout the United States, a device known as a *Class A* pan is used as the standard of measurement (Fig. 13-7). This pan has an inside diameter of approximately 120 cm and is 25 cm high. The water level is maintained about 5 cm below the rim, and changes in water level over time are measured with a "hook gauge" in a small stilling well placed inside the pan. Daily evaporation is computed as the difference in water level on successive days, corrected for any precipitation during the period. Pan evaporation is generally greater than evaporation from the surface of a reservoir or other natural body of water. To allow for this difference, a correction coefficient is used to reduce annual pan evaporation to an es-

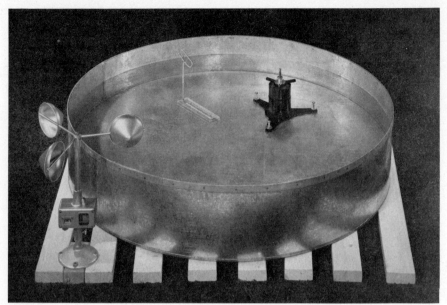

Figure 13-7 Evaporation station. (*Courtesy Belfort Instrument Company.*)

timate of lake or reservoir evaporation. This coefficient varies from approximately 0.6 to 0.8, depending upon the depth and surface area of the lake or reservoir.

Incoming solar radiation represents the primary energy source for many processes on natural watersheds, i.e., photosynthesis, evaporation from soils and lakes, transpiration, snow melt, warming of soil and air, etc. The amount of incoming solar radiation, although variable in space and time and influenced by numerous factors, can be measured with an instrument known as a *pyranometer* (Fig. 13-8). The amount of radiation is expressed in langleys, where a langley is defined as a unit of radiant energy equivalent to 1 cal/cm^2. Langleys can be accumulated for various time periods such as minutes, days, months, etc.

MEASUREMENT OF WATER QUANTITY

13-12 Stream-gauging Of the various types of hydrologic information, one of the most important to a watershed manager is streamflow data. Such data can provide the manager with information on daily, seasonal, and annual runoff volumes, as well as peak and low flows. Streamflow from natural watersheds is basically a result of precipitation. This relationship is greatly modified, however, by factors such as weather, soils, vegetation, and topography. For some portions of the United States, where watershed characteristics do not differ greatly from

Figure 13-8 Pyranometer for measuring incoming solar radiation. (*Courtesy Weather Measure Corporation.*)

one area to another, the streamflow measured on one watershed may be used to index flows from nearby or adjacent watersheds. Regression methods can be used for establishing these relationships. In other areas, however, the diverse nature of natural watersheds and the large number of factors affecting streamflow will often prohibit such extrapolations. Because of this situation, direct measurements of streamflow may represent the only method of accurately determining runoff from a particular watershed.

To obtain an estimate of the quantity of streamflow from a watershed, a measurement of discharge is necessary. Discharge Q, or rate of flow, is the volume of water that passes a particular location per unit of time. Two types of information are required for discharge estimates: the cross-sectional area a of the channel and the mean velocity v for this cross-sectional area. Discharge can then be computed by

$$Q = a \times v$$

Since the discharge of a stream is the product of its cross-sectional area and mean velocity, accurate measurements of both quantities are necessary. Units of discharge are cubic meters per second or liters per second.

Perhaps the simplest way of estimating discharge (and one of the least accurate) is to observe how far a floating object, tossed into the stream, travels in a given length of time. Dividing this distance by the time interval provides a rough estimate of the velocity of the water. Because the velocity at the surface is greater than the mean velocity of the stream, a reduction factor is necessary to obtain an estimate of mean velocity. This factor is commonly assumed to be about 85 percent. Using this corrected velocity and a measurement of the cross-sectional area of the stream, the discharge can be computed from the preceding formula.

Another method of measuring streamflow is based on the following relationship:

$$Q = \frac{a \times r^{2/3} \times s^{1/2}}{b}$$

where Q = discharge (m³/s)
  a = cross-sectional area (m²)
  r = hydraulic radius (m²/m)
  s = slope of channel (m/m)
  b = roughness coefficient

The hydraulic radius is computed by dividing the cross-sectional area a of the stream by the wetted perimeter. The roughness coefficient b must be estimated from conditions of the channel and may vary from approximately 0.030 to 0.060 for natural channels; an average value for natural streams is about 0.035. The main source of error in applying this formula to natural channels results from estimating the roughness coefficient. An error of 0.001 represents about a 3 percent error in discharge. This method, often referred to as the *slope area method*, can perhaps best be used for estimating the discharge of peak flows in natural channels where sufficient high-water marks can be determined.

A more common and accurate method of estimating stream discharge than either of the foregoing procedures is to use a stream-current meter. A current meter is an instrument used to measure the velocity of flowing water by means of a rotating element. When placed in a flowing stream, the number of revolutions per unit of time is related to the velocity of the water. To make these velocity determinations, the current meter is either mounted on a hand-held rod or suspended from a cable.

The velocity of a stream varies from point to point in a given cross section, and a number of velocity measurements with a current meter are necessary to obtain a reliable estimate of discharge. Because of stream-bed roughness, channel configuration, and turbulence, velocity profiles of natural streams are subject to considerable variation. To properly weight the various velocities found in a given stream, the stream is divided into several vertical sections, and the mean velocity and area are determined separately for each section. The discharge Q for the entire stream can then be obtained by summing the product of area a and velocity v for each section:

$$Q = a_1v_1 + a_2v_2 + \cdots + a_nv_n$$

where n is the number of sections. The greater the number of sections, the closer the approximation to the true discharge. Ten may be adequate under ideal conditions, but an evaulation of 15 to 20 sections is desirable. The actual number taken depends primarily on the size of the stream channel and the amount of turbulence.

The velocity and depth of each vertical section can be measured from cable cars, boats, and bridges, or simply by wading. For depths greater than 0.5 m, two measurements are made for each section: at 0.2 and 0.8 of the depth of the water. These two velocities are averaged to obtain the mean velocity for that section. For depths less than 0.5 m, the current meter is set at 0.6 of the depth as measured from the water surface. For deep streams, velocity measurements are made at relatively close intervals, and the actual velocity profile is estimated; however, this method is both costly and time-consuming.

Once the discharge rate has been determined, the volume of flow can be calculated for any specified time period by

Volume of runoff = discharge × time

13-13 Developing a Rating Curve A measurement of discharge is applicable only to those stream conditions and flow levels existing at the time of measurement. Yet, flow levels in natural streams usually change with time, and a relationship of discharge to some other variable is desirable. In practice, the "stage" or depth of water above a given datum at a specified stream cross section is used. When a sufficient number of stages and their associated discharges have been measured, a steam-rating curve can be constructed. This relationship, along with a record of the stage of a stream, can be used to estimate discharge for those periods when the stage is not constant (Fig. 13-9).

Rating curves are affected mainly by channel characteristics and thus must be developed individually for all gauging stations utilizing natural channels. Stage measurements may be obtained from systematic readings of the water-level surface on a gauge or graduated rod or from automatic water-stage recorders.

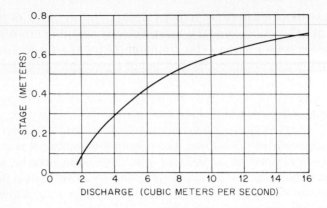

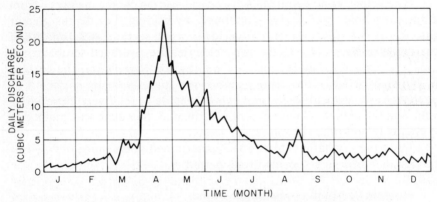

Figure 13-9 Rating curve for a natural stream channel (above) and a streamflow hydrograph developed from a rating curve and record of stage (below).

13-14 Weirs and Flumes On smaller streams, the channel configuration may be modified to alter the flow characteristics along a particular stretch of channel. This is done to obtain more accurate measurements of streamflow. Two general categories of structures, viz., weirs and flumes, may be utilized, depending upon the characteristics of the stream channel.

Weirs are among the oldest and most reliable types of structures that can be used to measure the flow of water in small streams. A weir is usually a simple overflow structure built across an open channel to create an upstream pool. The discharge over the crest of the weir is determined by the vertical distance between the crest of the weir and the water surface in the upstream pool; this height is usually referred to as the *head*. Depending upon the shape of the opening, weirs may be identified as V notch, rectangular, or trapezoidal.

Weirs can be used most effectively whenever there is a fall of 0.33 m or more over the crest. An advantage of standard weirs is that equations exist to estimate stream flow directly without the necessity of special calibration. Weirs should not be used on streams that have considerable bedload or suspended sediment load.

Flumes are somewhat similar to weirs, and numerous types are employed, depending upon channel and stream characteristics. In contrast to weirs, flumes do not create an upstream ponding effect but instead provide a smooth length of channel that allows the stream to pass through freely. In addition, the velocity of flow is usually sufficiently high so that any suspended sediment or bedload will not be deposited. The more common types of flumes have been precalibrated, although some field measurements may be necessary to check the calibration.

Streamflow measuring devices such as weirs and flumes are usually selected to meet the specific needs for each location. Flow occurs on some watersheds only as the result of an occasional large storm. Other watersheds may have streams that flow continuously. In most cases, it is necessary to measure streamflow at low, medium, and high rates as accurately as possible. Whenever possible, equipment with a precalibrated stage-discharge relationship should be used to gauge the entire flow.

MEASUREMENT OF WATER QUALITY

13-15 Water-Quality Sampling Water-quality samples are obtained so that the various kinds and amounts of substances present in water can be evaluated. A sampling program is often necessary because of the difficulties in attempting to continuously monitor the water quality of a lake or stream. Knowing when, why, and where to collect samples is basic to obtaining good water-quality measurements. This requires not only a knowledge of the system being sampled but also the expected time and space distribution patterns of the variables being sampled and their behavior in solution. Nonrepresentative sampling is perhaps the major source of error in obtaining water-quality information.

One of the goals of a water-quality investigation may be to provide information from which the general composition of water can be precisely determined. Other investigations may concentrate only on specific water-quality problems. The distribution of materials in an aquatic environment is influenced by the source of the material, mobility, phase (solid, dissolved, or gaseous), and type of system (stream, lake, reservoir). Sampling sites should be both assessible and representative of major sections of a stream or lake system.

For some streams, a "grab sample" obtained with a clean glass or plastic container may provide a satisfactory sample for preliminary analysis. This method of sample collection usually assumes that stream turbulence causes adequate mixing and that the sample is representative of the entire stream cross section. A single grab sample, however, should be regarded as representative of the discharge only at the time of sampling.

Samples collected weekly, or even monthly, can provide a reasonable indication of water quality for many streams. Systematically sampling a number of locations about the same time is of value for reconnaissance purposes. If at all possible, flow measurements should also be available at sampling sites. If streamflow and water quality are closely related, a record of stream discharge provides a convenient means for attempting an extrapolation of the chemical record.

Once obtained, the water samples may have to be treated immediately to protect against degradation of the contents. For example, provisions for freezing or otherwise preserving the sample must be available, if water samples are to be used later for organic analysis. A possible alternative is to measure certain variables in the field.

If a water sample is to be retained for later analysis in the laboratory, the sample container should be marked or tagged so that its identity is not lost. Information such as time, date, water temperature, where the sample was obtained (i.e., middle of lake, edge of stream, etc.), and streamflow may be necessary to correctly interpret the results of a water quality analysis.

13-16 Sediment Measurements Sediment generally refers to rock and mineral particles that have been transported by water, whereas sedimentation is the process of deposition of these transported particles from water. For convenience, sediment discharge is often divided into two broad categories: suspended load and bedload. Suspended sediment and bedload measurements are usually made separately because of differences in sizes of particles and their distribution in a stream.

13-17 Supended Sediment Suspended sediment usually consists of the smaller particles (clays, silts, and fine sands) that are kept aloft from the channel bottom by the turbulence of flowing water. The maximum size of particles held in suspension depends on both streamflow velocity and turbulence of flow. Suspended sediments usually have the same velocity as the water.

Perhaps the most difficult problem in determining suspended-sediment discharge for a stream is obtaining a representative sample. Sediment concentration is usually least near the surface and increases with depth. Concentration may also vary with the distance across the stream. Because of these problems, the method of sampling may have a large effect on estimates of sediment discharge. Sediment-sampling sites should be located near stream-gauging stations whenever possible because of potential relationships between sediment movement and streamflow discharge.

Various techniques have been developed for sampling streams to obtain an estimate of suspended sediment load. Some of these methods are also used to obtain samples for other types of water-quality analyses. The collection of one or more grab samples is the most common procedure for small streams. However, because of the problems previously outlined, this method may not always be reliable for sediment sampling.

Single-stage samplers consist of a container with an inflow and outflow tube at the top (Fig. 13-10). This type of sampler is used on small, fast-rising streams, where it is often impractical to obtain other types of samples. The single-stage sampler begins its intake when the water level exceeds the height of the lower tube and continues until the container is full. Consequently, this type of device samples only the rising state of the hydrograph, which may limit the utility of data collected. A single-stage sampler is inexpensive and can collect a point sample automatically. A variety of stages can be evaluated by installing a "bank" of these samplers at selected heights.

The sampling bias involved in obtaining suspended-sediment samples by the methods outlined can be minimized by using a depth-integrating sampler. A depth-integrating sampler has a container that allows sediment-laden water to enter as the sampler is lowered and raised at a constant rate in the stream. This procedure obtains a relatively uniform sample for a given vertical section of the stream. Depending upon the size of the stream, a number of these samples may be taken at selected intervals across the channel.

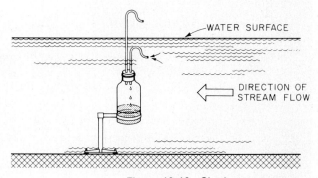

Figure 13-10 Single-stage sampler.

A continuous record of suspended sediment can be obtained with a splitter (Fig. 13-11). Splitters are usually used on small streams in conjunction with a weir or flume. As the water flows over the crest of the weir, a small fraction is "split off," or separated, by a mechanical divider. This water is retained in large containers for later analysis of the suspended-sediment concentrations. By using a multiple splitter, relatively large streams may be sampled by this method.

After a sediment sample is obtained, the liquid portion is removed by centrifuging, filtering, or evaporating, and the amount of sediment is weighed. The dry weight can then be expressed as a concentration in milligrams per liter or in ppm.

As an alternative to the physical separation of suspended sediments

Figure 13-11 Sediment dam equipped with a "splitter." (*U.S. Forest Service photograph.*)

from the liquid portion of the sample, turbidity measurements may be used to index the suspended sediment load of a stream. Turbidity refers to the optical property of a sample that causes light to be scattered and absorbed rather than transmitted. Historically, the Jackson Candle Turbidometer has been a standard instrument for turbidity measurement, with results reported in Jackson Turbidity Units (JTU).[1] Due to limitations of the Jackson Turbidometer, photometric methods are becoming more common. These methods are readily adaptable to both field and laboratory conditions. In addition, formulations of formazin turbidity suspensions have come into use for calibrating turbidometers (Taras et al., 1971). Correlations between turbidity and the concentration of suspended particles can be developed for many streams. However, because turbidity measurements are based on the optical properties of the particles in suspension, attempts to extrapolate such relationships to other streams may not always be successful.

13-18 Bedload Bedload refers to the larger and heavier sediments (i.e., sands, gravels, cobbles, etc.) that are sliding, rolling, or bouncing along the bottom or bed of a stream. The average velocity of the bedload materials is less than that of the water (Fig. 13-12).

No single device for measuring bedload in streams has proved to be reliable, economical, and easy to use. Thus, although a variety of bedload samplers exist, none are universally used. Estimates of bedload can sometimes be obtained by measuring the amount of material deposited in sediment traps or sediment basins. Water flowing through the basin or depression slows sufficiently to drop out the heavier bedload (and in some cases the suspended sediment) material. Following major runoff events, field surveys are conducted to quantify the volume of material trapped. Reservoirs and stock ponds provide additional locations for estimating bedload transport of streams.

13-19 Chemical Quality The chemical constituents of natural water are derived from many different sources, including gases and aerosols[2] from the atmosphere, weathering and erosion products of rocks and soil, decomposition of plants and other organic matter, and contamination from human activities, such as sewage, sprays, and detergents. Some of the more common ions and their concentrations in various types of water are indicated in Table 13-1. Actual concentrations for a given sample may vary greatly from these tabulated values. Many natural

---

[1] One JTU = 1 mg SiO_2/l.

[2] A system of colloidal particles dispersed in a gas, smoke, or fog.

Figure 13-12   Bedload deposited in a stream channel downstream from a V-notch weir. (*U.S. Forest Service photograph.*)

resource management activities can directly affect both the kind and amount of chemical constituents present.

For some of the more common chemical substances, instrumentation has been developed to permit direct measurement of a particular constituent in the aquatic environment. For example, standarized oxygen and pH

Table 13-1   Concentrations (Milligrams per Liter) of Selected Chemical Constituents in Various Waters*

Constituent	Rain and snow	River water	Well water	Sea water
Chloride (Cl)	0.2	7.8	82	19,000
Sodium (Na)	0.4	6.3 ⎫	611	10,500
Potassium (K)	—	2.3 ⎭		380
Sulphate (SO₄)	2.1	11	1,010	2,700
Magnesium (Mg)	—	4.1	24	1,350
Calcium (Ca)	1.4	15	37	400
Bicarbonate (HCO₃)	—	58	429	142
Silica (SiO₂)	—	13	7.9	6.4
Iron (Fe)	—	0.7	0.2	0.01
Dissolved solids	—	90	1,980	—
Hardness as CaCO₃	—	55	191	—

*From Hew, 1970.

probes are available to measure the dissolved oxygen and hydrogen ion concentrations in natural streams or lakes. Similarly, electrode probes can be employed for determining many individual chemical ions. Basic data used in the determination of water quality are obtained by the chemical analysis of water samples in the laboratory or by on-site sensing of chemical properties. In either case, evaluations can usually be accomplished by photometric or titrametric methods. More sophisticated techniques for determining the chemical quality of water are also available but are beyond the scope of this text.

Photometric or colorimetric methods relate the intensity of color (following the addition of a measured amount of reagent to a standard volume of sample) to the concentration of the substance present. Basic photometric instruments consist of a light source, a photocell, and a meter. Interposed in the light beam are a color filter and the sample (Fig. 13-13). The amount of light absorbed is proportional to the amount of substance present. Photometric methods of analysis are usually adaptable to field use.

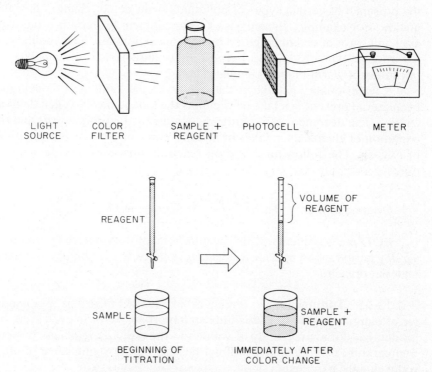

LIGHT
SOURCE

COLOR
FILTER

SAMPLE +
REAGENT

PHOTOCELL

METER

REAGENT

VOLUME OF
REAGENT

SAMPLE

SAMPLE +
REAGENT

BEGINNING OF
TITRATION

IMMEDIATELY AFTER
COLOR CHANGE

Figure 13-13 Photometric (above) and titrametric (below) methods for determing the chemical quality of water.

Titrametric or volumetric methods are based on the slow addition of reagents of known concentration to a standard volume of sample. This procedure is designed to give an abrupt color change after a certain amount of reagent is added. The concentration of the chemical constituent being determined is proportional to the amount of reagent added. Titrametric methods are perhaps better suited to laboratory conditions, and they usually provide more accurate results than photometric methods. Both methods require specific reagents for the particular chemical constituent being evaluated.

Graphical presentations of chemical analyses or groups of analyses provide a convenient method of relating chemical relationships among various waters. Relationships of water quality to hydrologic parameters such as stream discharge can often be accomplished by either graphical or regression methods.

13-20 Biological Quality The complete enumeration of the numbers and kinds of all microorganisms in a water sample is a difficult task. To simplify the problem, indicator organisms may be used to index the presence of certain types of pollutants or to detect changes in water quality. For example, an analysis of fecal coliform bacteria is often used as an indicator of recent pollution by humans or animals. Fecal coliform is a particular type of coliform bacteria that characteristically inhabits the intestines of warm-blooded animals.

A water-quality parameter that relates to the amount of biodegradable material present in a lake or stream is the biochemical oxygen demand (BOD). The decomposition of organic matter by microorganisms and the oxidation of chemicals in lakes or streams consumes extensive quantities of oxygen. The following oxidation reaction illustrates this decomposition:

$$\text{Organic matter} + O_2 \xrightarrow{\text{microorganisms}} CO_2 + H_2O$$

BOD measurements, which require a laboratory determination over a 5-day period, often provide a satisfactory index to the amount of organic material present.

13-21 Temperature Stream or lake temperature acts as a regulator of biological activity and is thus an important factor in evaluating the productivity of a given body of water and the type of organisms present. Temperature may also have a direct bearing on the significance of other water-quality parameters.

Surface-water temperature for lakes or streams can be measured with standard liquid-in-glass thermometers. Thermocouple elements are commonly used to obtain temperatures at depths in lakes and reservoirs. For fast-flowing streams, care must be taken to protect the temperature-sensing element from damage. In clear, slow-flowing streams, the sensor should also be shaded to prevent warming from incoming solar radiation.

13-22   Sources of Additional Information   Federal agencies are primarily responsible for the collection and publication of hydrologic and meterological data. The National Oceanic and Atmospheric Administration publishes monthly and annual summaries of climatological data. These data have been collected by a network of National Weather Service (formerly U.S. Weather Bureau) stations. Climatological summaries for a particular state can be ordered at nominal cost from

> Superintendent of Documents
> U.S. Government Printing Office
> Washington, D.C.   20402

Information concerning the availability of climatic data for specific locations can be obtained from any National Weather Service office. Daily streamflow data, with monthly summaries for each of 16 regions, are published by the U.S. Geological Survey in annual Water Supply Papers. Water Supply Papers can be obtained from the address previously indicated. The Geological Survey also publishes an annual series of water resources data for each state. These data are contained in two volumes: Part 1, entitled *Surface Water Records*, contains information on daily, monthly, and annual streamflow for gauging stations; Part 2, entitled *Water Quality Records*, contains physical and chemical water-quality data. Both volumes can be obtained from the District Office of the Geological Survey for a particular state.

Although most hydrologic and meterologic information is collected and published by the agencies specified, other federal, state, and private organizations collect and publish additional data. Much of this information can be obtained through public or university libraries.

PROBLEMS

13-1   Delineate the boundaries of two gauged watersheds on topographic maps. Determine the area, slope, elevation, and orientation of each watershed. In addition, obtain hydrographs from each watershed for storms that are similar in magnitude and duration. Compare these hydrographs, based on your knowledge of the physical characteristics of each watershed.

13-2 Obtain topographic maps of two watersheds in different portions of the United States. Delineate the watershed boundaries and classify streams on each watershed by stream order. Plot the number of streams versus stream order for each watershed on the same graph. Compute the drainage density for each watershed.

13-3 Compute the intensity of precipitation for each 10-minute interval for a storm on a recording precipitation gauge chart. Express intensities in millimeters per hour.

13-4 Obtain a thermograph (or hygrothermograph) chart for a 3-day period. Use 2-hour intervals to obtain air temperatures for computing the mean for each day. Also, compute the mean daily temperature for each day based on maximum and minimum temperatures. Compare the advantages and disadvantages of these two methods.

13-5 Obtain a hygrograph (or hygrothermograph) chart for a 3-day period. Using the procedures of the previous problem, compute the mean daily relative humidty for each of the 3 days. Compare methods.

13-6 Obtain a chart from a recording anemometer showing wind speed over a 3-hour period. Randomly sample this chart to obtain 25 point estimates of wind speed, and plot a frequency distribution. Do the plotted points approximate a normal frequency distribution? Calculate the standard deviation. Determine the average wind speed for each 10-minute period, and compute the standard deviation of these values. How does this compare with the standard deviation computed from the point samples?

13-7 Using snow-course data (snow depth and water equivalent) for five to ten sampling locations, compute the mean density of the snowpack at each location. Plot the relationship of water equivalent versus snow depth, and determine a straight line of "best" fit for the data points.

13-8 Using basic stream-depth, -width, and -velocity measurements that have been obtained with a current meter, compute the discharge in cubic meters per second. Assuming the streamflow remained at this level of discharge over a 24-hour period, determine the volume of water represented. Express this in millimeters of water over the watershed.

13-9 Using sediment-concentration and streamflow data for a particular watershed, compute the total volume of sediment yield on a weekly, monthly, or annual basis. Compute the sediment yield per square kilometer of watershed area.

13-10 Select a watershed 100 to 500 km² in size. Determine the type, source, and quality of various hydrologic and meterological data that are available for this watershed.

REFERENCES

Anonymous
    1962. Field manual for research in agricultural hydrology. *USDA, Agri. Res. Serv., Agri. Handbook* 224. 215 pp., illus.

Blair, Thomas A., and Fite, Robert C.
1957. *Weather elements*. Prentice-Hall, Inc., Englewood Cliffs, NJ. 414 pp., illus.

Day, John A.
1966. *The science of weather*. Addison-Wesley Publishing Company, Inc., Reading, MA. 214 pp., illus.

Fischer, William C., and Hardy, Charles E.
1972. Fire-weather observers' handbook. *U.S. Forest Serv., Intermount. Forest and Range Expt. Sta.* 152 pp., illus.

Guy, H. P., and Norman, V. W.
1970. Field methods for measurement of fluvial sediment. *From*: Techniques of water resource inventory, book 3, ch. 2. U.S. Geol. Survey, Washington, D.C. 59 pp., illus.

Hew, John D.
1970. Study and interpretation of the chemical characteristics of natural water. U.S. Geol. Survey, Washington, D.C. *Water Supply Paper* 1473. 363 pp., illus.

Leopold, Luna B., Wolman, M. Gordon, and Miller, John P.
1964. *Fluvial processes in geomorphology*. W. H. Freeman and Company, San Francisco, 522 pp., illus.

Linsley, Ray H., Kohler, Max A., and Paulhus, Joseph L. H.
1975. *Hydrology for engineers*, 2d ed. McGraw-Hill Book Company, New York. 416 pp., illus.

Sawyer, Clair N., and McCarty, Perry L.
1967. *Chemistry for sanitary engineers*. McGraw-Hill Book Company, New York. 518 pp., illus.

Stringer, E. T.
1972. *Techniques of climatology*. W. H. Freeman and Company, San Francisco. 539 pp., illus.

Taras, Michael J., Greenberg, Arnold E., Hook, R. D., and Rand, M. C. (eds.)
1971. Standard methods for the examination of water and waste water. Amer. Public Health Assn., Washington, D.C. 874 pp.

U.S. Department of Agriculture
1972. Snow survey and water supply forecasting. *Soil Conservation Serv., National Eng. Handbook*, Sec. 22. 198 pp., illus.

Vennard, John K.
1965. *Elementary fluid mechanics*. John Wiley & Sons, Inc., New York. 570 pp., illus.

Wisler, C. O., and Brater, E. F.
1965. *Hydrology*. John Wiley & Sons, Inc., New York. 408 pp., illus.

Chapter 14

Measuring Recreational Resources

14-1 The Problem There appears to be an ever-growing demand for forest recreational facilities in the United States. This heightened interest is generally attributed to such factors as the pressures of urban living, increases in leisure time, and the mobility of a large segment of the population. Whatever the reasons, the recreational resource can be as important to the land manager as the more conventional products of wood, wildlife, and water yields.

Many public lands, e.g., national and state parks, are managed *primarily* for recreational benefits, with much lower priorities assigned to the more tangible products of the forest and range ecosystem. As a result, the resource manager should have some objective means of describing, comparing, assessing, or measuring recreational resources and the benefits or user satisfactions derived therefrom.

Among the more basic questions that arise in planning recreational inventories are (1) deciding precisely *what* to measure and (2) devising a cost-effective estimation technique for obtaining the desired information. The first question is the more difficult to answer, for it presumes that a decision-maker requires a certain kind of information in a particular format and time frame. If the inventory information is *not* being accumulated for purposes of decision-making, the resource manager should question whether the data are needed at all. For example, a count of the number of vehicles that pass through the Great Smoky Mountain National Park is significant only if such numerical data are useful in formulating a policy or management decision.

While wood yields from a forest can be expressed in terms of cubic meters per hectare and grazing capacities can be stated in animal unit months, it is much more difficult to define the direct product of recreational-esthetic resources. Is it sufficient, for instance, to enumerate visitor-days, tents per campground, or fishing boats launched per week? More importantly, do such tabulations make up logical units for summarizing the production and utilization of recreational resources?

Many resource managers and recreational specialists feel that the direct products of recreational-esthetic resources are the *satisfactions derived* from the recreational experience; in other words, the quality of the experience may be as important (or more so) as the total number of persons utilizing a recreational site. Unfortunately, we have not yet devised operational inventory systems that will provide reliable definitions and measurements of such products. And until user satisfactions can be defined in objective units, it may be difficult for the resource manager to plan recreational facilities that provide maximum user benefits (Fig. 14-1).

In the meantime, there *are* attributes of the recreational resource that *can* be measured to some degree. Workable techniques have been devised for describing the visual aspects of various landscapes, for estimating visitor use on exisiting recreational sites, and for assessing potential recreational areas. It is with these procedures that the ensuing discussions are primarily concerned. At the end of the chapter, a special section has been included on the presentation of multiple-resource measurements.

LANDSCAPE DESCRIPTION

14-2 Visual Impacts of Landscape It has been determined that a large proportion of human perception is based on sight; as a result, landscape managers are concerned with the visual impacts of various management practices on observers. Even when land management practices are acceptable from a scientific viewpoint (e.g., clearcutting and reseeding of even-aged forest plantations), they may not produce visually acceptable landscapes. As an essential first step in striving for landscapes of beauty as well as utility, several systems of landscape description and classification have been devised.

Figure 14-1 Can the satisfactions and benefits of family camping be defined in objective units? (*Courtesy Tennessee Valley Authority.*)

One of the primary purposes of a landscape-description system is to promote communication and understanding among those persons responsible for improving the esthetic appeal of vistas that result from various land management practices. Such systems are not completely objective, and the distinction between desirable versus undesirable landscapes is often unclear—or is left to the individual observer. Nevertheless, rational methods of description *do* provide useful guidelines for administering forest lands in such a way that visual impacts have a positive effect on human psychological welfare. The system outlined here is from the U.S. Department of Agriculture (1973).

14-3 Landscape Character In the national forest approach to landscape management, there are three underlying concepts based on an observer's visual reaction to his environment—that each landscape has an identifiable character, that visual variety in landscapes is a preferred attribute, and that deviations from a characteristic landscape can often be designed to achieve a degree of acceptable variety. The "character" of a landscape is the composite impression that is created by its combination of visual features, e.g., land, water, vegetation, and structures.

Even though landscape character cannot be rigidly determined, several descriptive terms are employed to describe the character of landscapes or segments within landscapes (Litton, 1968). These terms are as follows:

Type of landscape	Example or description
Panoramic	A clear view from foreground to horizon, e.g., rolling prairies, shorelines, etc.
Feature	Includes a dominant object or objects, e.g., monadnocks or extinct volcanoes
Enclosed	Spaces surrounded or enclosed, e.g., a meteoritic crater or a small lake encircled by trees or cliffs
Focal	A landscape that leads the observer's eye to a point of convergence, e.g., a river gorge or a straight road through a mature forest
Canopied	A landscape that is covered overhead, e.g., a tree-enclosed pathway
Detail	Characterized by minute features or small, distinctive foreground objects, e.g., patches of small wildflowers or individual leaf patterns
Ephemeral	A landscape that produces an unusual visual impact because of such influences as clouds, fog, reflections, wild animals, birds, or insect life

14-4 Dominance Elements and Principles Within any given landscape, the four elements that compete for dominance are form, line, color, and texture (Fig. 14-2). *Form* is the shape or mass of an object or a combination of objects that appears unified. *Line* refers to a feature arranged in a row or sequence—or the intersection of two planes. *Color* enables the observer to differentiate among features that may otherwise be similar in form, line, or basic characteristics. And *texture* refers to the apparent coarseness or fineness of features, depending on the distance from which they are viewed. In terms of relative visual impact, these four elements are defined in order of importance, with form being the strongest factor and texture the weakest.

The visual dominance of form, line, color, and texture in a landscape is affected, in turn, by six additional factors or principles. These are contrast, sequence, axis, convergence, codominance, and enframement. An understanding of these principles may assist the resource manager in analyzing the visual impact of landscape modifications resulting from various management practices.

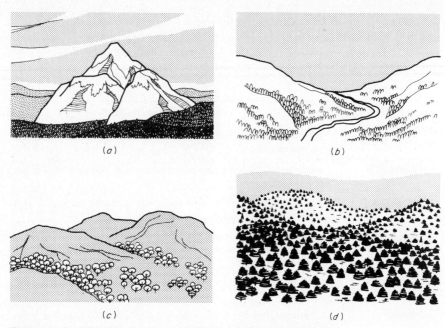

Figure 14-2 The four elements of dominance in a landscape are
(a) form, (b) line, (c) color, and (d) texture. (*Adapted from sketches
by U.S. Department of Agriculture.*)

Contrast requires no definition; it should suffice to emphasize that
the greater the contrast between features, the greater the visual impact.
The elements of form, line, or color may occur in a *sequence* within a
landscape and thus direct the eye along a specific vista or toward a distant
feature. A well-planned sequence of visual experiences can often enrich
an observer's appreciation of a landscape. An example might be a tree-
lined footpath alongside a mountain stream that terminates at a waterfall
or a fish hatchery.

An *axis* is a well-defined line of direction, motion, growth, or extension. Examples might include a cleared right of way, a canal, mall, or
straight stretch of road bisecting the landscape. The vista created by an
axis focuses observer attention primarily on the terminus and its
background.

As the term implies, *convergence* occurs when the major landscape
features or elements focus attention on a point or a small area.
Codominance is the result when two or more major features are essentially identical, e.g., twin buttes. And *enframement* can be represented by
a valley highway that is "framed" by walls of trees or cliffs on either side.
The reader should be cognizant of the fact that the elements and princi-

ples of dominance can occur in a myriad of combinations, thus creating the desirable impact of *landscape variety* from one vista to the next.

Finally, there are a number of variable or changing conditions that can influence just *how* landscape elements are seen (Fig. 14-3). These variables must be carefully considered by the resource manager who wishes to create the greatest visual impact for various landscapes. When all the landscape factors enumerated in this brief introduction are given due consideration, the resource manager should be able to plan such activities as timber harvesting, surface mining, or road construction so that scenic vistas are at least maintained, if not improved.

VISITOR USE OF RECREATIONAL FACILITIES

14-5 Recreational Characteristics Forest recreation is a commodity that is consumed on-site; therefore, location is an important attribute of recreational resources. Also, recreation is a final consumer product, as are wildlife and fish. A third characteristic is the nonstorability of recreational opportunities. Recreation is a good or service

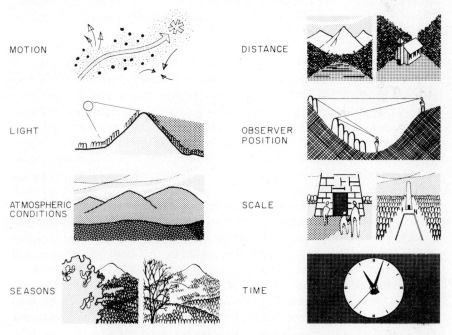

Figure 14-3 Variable factors that can influence the visual impact of landscapes. (*Adapted from sketches by U.S. Department of Agriculture.*)

that is time-intensive, and its usage is measured in time-related units such as visitor-days. A campsite not used today does not increase camping capacity tomorrow.

A fourth feature of forest recreation is that it makes up less of a physical product than other benefits derived from the land. The visitor who avails himself of land resources to produce his recreational experience would ordinarily take few physical objects away with him; thus the recreational experience is somewhat analogous to that of watching or participating in an athletic event. And finally, the total recreational experience represents a composite or package of benefits and recollections that are not susceptible to partitioning or subdivision.

The output of recreational management is commonly measured in terms of visitor use, i.e., visitor-days.[1] This information is valuable for scheduling visitor information programs, maintenance operations, and planning additional recreational sites or facilities. Use data are also of assistance in the prediction of the rates at which facilities depreciate. When the intensity of use on a site is compared with its capacity, patterns of use or activity changes over time can be ascertained.

Recreational use is the result of the interaction of the *supply* of opportunities provided, and the *demand* of the public for such opportunities. Thus, in economic terms, use may be regarded as the *quantity* of recreation that is consumed.

14-6 Visitor Registration Systems An obvious means of measuring use at a recreational site is to obtain a *complete registration* of visitors entering or leaving an area. To employ this method effectively requires absolute control over access to the site, and a registration station must be manned around the clock. This approach is seldom used on a year-round basis, and it is usually limited to facilities where fees or permits are needed for entry (Fig. 14-4). Many parks maintain entry checkpoints or registration stations during peak-use seasons, but they are rarely operated on a 24-hour basis because of the expense involved. Where such systems are feasible, they do provide an opportunity to gain detailed visitor information, e.g., number of persons per vehicle or family unit, length of visit, types of activities pursued by different age groups, and so on.

For estimating visitor use on dispersed or undeveloped recreational sites such as wilderness areas, various systems of *self-registration* have been employed. One major problem is that many people do not voluntarily register their presence; thus this method has not worked well in areas where there are numerous routes for ingress and egress. It is sometimes

---

[1] A visitor-day is usually defined as 12 visitor-hours; i.e., 2 visitor-days equal 1 calendar day.

Figure 14-4 Registration of visitors at the entrance to a recreational facility where a fee-permit system is employed. (*Courtesy Tennessee Valley Authority.*)

feasible to designate a "calibration period" whereby the proportion of visitors who do register can be estimated to determine whether nonregistrants differ from registrants in terms of their activity and use characteristics.

For both estimating and regulating visitor use on dispersed sites, there appears to be considerable merit in a permit or license-fee system. By this approach, registration data can be obtained in the same manner as currently supplied by applicants for hunting and fishing licenses.

14-7 Sampling Visitor Populations Because of the problem of counting or registering *all* visitors at recreational sites, some form of sampling may be employed to estimate visitor use. This approach, of course, creates a new problem—which persons and what proportion of the total number of visitors should be counted, registered, or interviewed? As with any public opinion poll, a *representative sample* is the objective, but this is not easily achieved with mobile populations of varying age groups, differing activity patterns, and divergent recreational preferences.

If the only information desired is the total visitor use during a particular season, a number of sample days might be selected, followed by tallies of visitors present on those dates. To account for weekly cycles of visitor use, a sampling design must be developed to select "measuring dates" having a representative proportion of weekdays, holidays, and weekends; otherwise any extrapolations from such estimates may be severely biased.

A variation of this technique is to stop all persons leaving the site on certain dates to determine how long they have been at the recreational facility; this approach permits an estimate of use in terms of visitor-days. One difficulty of applying such estimates is that they are valid only for the current season; the sampling must be repeated during subsequent years to update or revise use evaluations.

The sampling design must be even more carefully selected where individual visitors are interviewed to determine such characteristics as family size, occupation, or recreational preferences. The inherent dangers of arbitrarily selecting individuals may be exemplified by a visitor survey conducted nearly half a century ago on the Superior National Forest in Minnesota. Two or three rangers were instructed to interview forest visitors to determine which occupational groups were represented. It happened that these survey duties had to be scheduled on weekends, when (unknown to the rangers) there were several ships at anchor in the port of Duluth. As a result, the survey indicated that 80 percent of all the visitors on the national forest were U.S. Navy sailors!

14-8 Indirect Estimates of Use One method of minimizing the annual problem of sampling use is to find an indicator that is more cost effective for predicting use than direct counts of people themselves. This approach is analogous to the indirect census techniques previously outlined for wildlife and fish populations. Indicator measurements that have been employed include a diversity of inventory data such as traffic counts, water consumption, number of boat launchings per unit of time, weight of garbage collected, and quantity of sewage effluent (Fig. 14-5).

The essential characteristic of an indicator variable is that it should be highly correlated with the kind or pattern of recreational use to be predicted. The basic procedural steps that have been followed on many surveys are:

1   Select the season of year for which predictions of visitor use are desired.

2   Choose an indicator (e.g., traffic counters) that presumably rises and falls in the same pattern as the recreational use to be predicted. Obtain indicator data continuously—throughout the season.

3   Randomly select several sample days (perhaps 10 to 30 days during the selected season) with equal representation of weekdays, holidays, and weekends. On the sample days, measure the recreational use of interest, e.g., by interviews, camper registration, turnstile counts, etc.

4   By regression analysis, attempt to establish a relationship between the indicator data and recreational use, based on paired measure-

Figure 14-5   Would the number of boat launchings per day be a reliable indicator of visitor use for this site? (*Courtesy Tennessee Valley Authority.*)

ments for the sample days. Calculate the precision of the prediction equation.

 5 For future seasons (assuming that use patterns are similar), continue to obtain indicator data only. Use the regression equation to predict recreational use.

 14-9 Axle Counts The indicator most frequently used at developed, unsupervised recreational sites is an axle count obtained from an automatic traffic counter. Not only is this technique much used, but it is also much abused. The popularity of such devices may be attributed to two characteristics: they are relatively cheap, requiring little maintenance, and they produce numbers. Unless they are intelligently located, however, the data that results can be quite misleading (Fig. 14-6).

 In a study of recreational sites in the Appalachian Mountains, James and Ripley (1963) found strong correlations between visitor use and axle counts. In one instance, a linear equation of the form $\hat{Y} = a + bX$ was fitted to the relationship with this result:

$$\hat{Y} \text{ (total visits)} = 110 + 0.3X \text{ (axle count)}$$

 For some variables, of course, the relationship between an indicator variable and visitor use may be curvilinear. The sampling precision for

Figure 14-6 How would you measure visitor use for this circular trailer park? If traffic counters are used, where should they be installed? (*Courtesy Tennessee Valley Authority.*)

this type of use-prediction equation may be less than that obtained in predicting other products of resource management. For example, many use surveys (based on 10 to 12 sampling days per site) produce sampling errors of ± 25 percent of the estimated variable at a probability level of 0.68.

14-10 Water Consumption as an Indicator Where water is supplied to developed recreational sites through a metered system, consumption may be closely related to hours of recreational use. In a study of a recreational site in Arizona, for example, it was found that water consumption was more highly correlated with the number of visitor-days than were axle counts. A comparison of the two indicator estimates is given in Table 14-1.

Where water meters are pretested to ensure that they accurately record low-water flow, they may have several advantages over such indicators as pneumatic traffic counters. Even though they may be more expensive to install, a single meter may suffice for certain sites where two or

Table 14-1 Estimates of Recreational Use on an Arizona Campground*

Activity	Based on water meter		Based on axle count	
	Estimate	Sampling error†	Estimate	Sampling error†
	Visitor-days	Percent	Visitor-days	Percent
Camping	27,420	5.7	27,276	7.5
Spectator	485	21.3	408	24.2
Viewing scenery	303	18.7	266	19.9
Misc. activities	272	—	171	—
Total use	28,480	5.3	28,121	7.3

*From James and Tyre (1967).
†Probability level of 0.68.

more traffic counters might be needed. Also, water meters require little maintenance, they are less susceptible to vandalism, and they are unaffected by snow and ice. And finally, meters provide added information on site water requirements, including the need for pumps or sewage disposal facilities.

ASSESSING POTENTIAL RECREATIONAL SITES

14-11 Inventory Criteria The preceding sections were concerned with measurements of visitor use, i.e., the *output* of recreational planning and management. Here we are concerned with the inventory of natural resources with respect to their potential as *inputs* in the production of recreational use on developed or undeveloped areas.

Many of the measurement techniques discussed in other parts of this book are applicable to inventories of potential recreational sites. For example, the recreational planner will often require information on vegetative types, timber volumes, water resources, and wildlife populations. He may differ from other resource managers in the way he assesses these values as recreational input factors, but his physical inventory requirements may be quite similar.

Existing techniques are readily available for the physical inventory of recreational sites; the real problem is that of establishing inventory criteria, i.e., standards based on what potential visitors consider a recreational resource. Until this can be done, inventory criteria will continue to be based on the judgment of planners and administrators.

As a rule, inventory criteria employed in the past have been based on a combination of physical characteristics and administrative considerations. For example, the criteria for locating potential campgrounds would include some *physical* requirements regarding the amount of slope, kind of vegetation, and the availability of water supplies. There would also be *administrative* criteria concerning the minimum site area and the maximum distance from population centers.

14-12 Inventory Procedure The inventory itself is often conducted in a manner similar to that of preparing a land-use or a vegetation-type map. Standards are established to (1) discover potential sites, (2) designate selected areas for development, and (3) rank the proposed sites by desirability classes or assign them to various management categories. The sites that meet the original standards may then be shown on a map—a presentation that makes up the finished product of the inventory. Except for statistical summaries of site areas, carrying capacities, and demographic information, few calculations are involved.

14-13 Aerial Surveys The prime objective of an aerial survey is to locate potential recreational sites and transfer these areas to a base map of suitable scale. With up-to-date photographs in the hands of skilled interpreters, a preliminary recreational survey can be accomplished with a minimum of field work.

Most types of photographic films are suitable, although color emulsions are generally preferred. Exposures should be planned during the dormant season when deciduous trees are leafless and/or during the season when the greatest numbers of people would be likely to utilize potential features. Photographic scales of 1:5,000 to 1:12,000 have been successfully employed; if large regions must be covered by a preliminary survey, the smallest scale that can be reliably interpreted should be chosen to avoid the handling and steroscopic study of excessive numbers of exposures.

The photo-interpretation phase will require the identification and delineation of such features as

Natural vegetation	Existing structures
Land-use patterns	Historical features
Scenic terrain features	Access roads
Water resources	Paths or trails
Beaches and inlets	Soils and drainage
Potential docks or ramps	Topography

The more promising potential sites are then checked on the ground to verify interpreter assessments of current land use, present ownership, site availability, and potentially undesirable features (e.g., polluted water, excessive noise, industrial fumes, or lack of suitable access).

After elimination of those areas that are unavailable or undesirable, a final report is prepared to summarize and rank the recreational potential of each site recommended. The report should be accompanied by both ground and aerial photographs that have been annotated to emphasize salient features, needed improvements, and possible trouble spots (Fig. 14-7).

PRESENTATION OF MULTIPLE-RESOURCE MEASUREMENTS

14-14   Multiple Products and Uses   In attempting to implement the concept of multiple-use management on wild lands, it is important to recognize the utilization potentials or yields of *all* available natural resources. As pointed out in preceding sections of this book, these diverse

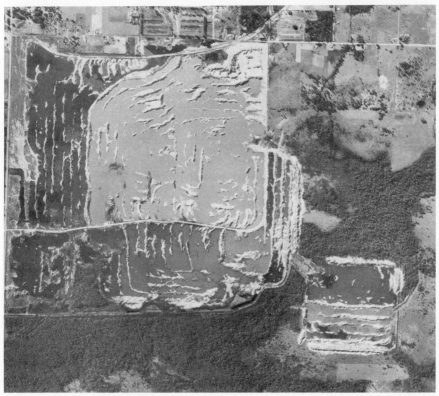

Figure 14-7   Vertical airphoto of an open-pit phosphate mine in Florida. When surface mines have been worked out, they are sometimes revegetated and converted to water-based recreational sites.

yields may be expressed in terms of wood volumes, grazing capacities, numbers of fish and wildlife, water yields, recreational visitor-days, or other units. Obtaining an optimum "mix" of these varied outputs and uses is the elusive objective sought by many resource managers.

Although the multiple-use concept is viewed as the guiding light for the management of wild lands, specific areas are often managed for only one or two primary products, such as timber and grazing, recreation and wildlife, water and timber, etc. Nevertheless, the trend is away from single-use management and toward the production of multiple resources from the land. As this trend continues, more conflicts will inevitably arise, for the cutting of a timber stand or the damming of a stream will have *some effect* on the production of other natural resources. Thus, if the goal of land management is to provide the maximum *total benefit* from all resources, consumers must be prepared to accept something less than the maximum yield from any single benefit or product.

14-15 Resource Interrelationships Relationships between several resource products on a management unit may be regarded as competitive, complementary, or supplementary. A *competitive* relation exists when one resource must be sacrificed to increase another, as for timber versus water or timber versus forage. With a *complementary* relation, two or more resource products may increase together, as might occur for forage and water once the timber has been removed. A *supplementary* relation implies that a change in one resource product has no influence on another; this might be illustrated by changes in relative numbers of livestock and wildlife—at least within limited ranges.

On a given land management unit, it is important to know whether the relationship among various resource outputs is competitive, complementary, or supplementary. If a supplementary relationship exists between wildlife populations and recreational use, for example, the land administrator will not be able to influence the production of one resource by manipulation of the other. These considerations are important to those persons who inventory various natural resources, because the measurement of yields from wild lands constitutes the basis for determining "before-and-after" responses to alternative management practices.

14-16 Inventory Tabulations Measurements of wild-land resource products on a given management unit can be summarized in tabular form as a *product mix*. Such a tabulation may also reflect the *changes in resource yields* that result from the implementation of various management practices, assuming that an inventory system is sufficiently sensitive to detect such changes.

The hypothetical tabulation that follows illustrates how a product mix might form the basis for deciding whether to continue a present management system or whether to opt for an alternative plan. Except for the fisheries resource, numerical values are based on a presumed land area of approximately 10 km².

Resource yields and measurement units	Management alternatives		
	Status quo	Plan A	Plan B
Timber-growth (m³)	5,000	7,500	2,500
Grazing capacity (AUM)	250	400	1,000
Wildlife (no. of deer)	6	10	4
Fish (hundreds of trout)	18	12	3
Streamflow (m³/sec)	4	8	16
Recreation (visitors/year)	5,000	1,000	500

To make the tabulation more meaningful, it may be further assumed that the "status quo" represents an overstocked ("wilderness-type") forest with few openings, that plan A results in a second-growth forest of moderate stocking with large openings, and that plan B calls for conversion of the management unit to about two-thirds rangeland and only one-third forest. Under plan B, it can be seen that streamflow might be greatly increased, but clearing of the land would result in increased solar heating of the stream (due to removal of shade trees) and a consequent reduction in the trout population. As another example, the number of deer might be greatest under plan B because of the creation of an optimum habitat in terms of cover, browse, and edge.

14-17 Measurement Units and Benefits Even though the persons who plan and conduct inventories of the various resources may not be responsible for deciding among the management alternatives, they *should* develop a capability for producing product-mix tabulations of this kind by striving to develop more sensitive measurement techniques for detecting change. And while *all* products listed will rarely occur together on a single management unit, it is noteworthy that there are 15 different combinations of two products each that can result from the six classes of yields shown here.

A product mix can be of considerable assistance to decision-makers responsible for selecting management alternatives, but it hardly constitutes an ideal matrix. What is needed is a *single measurement unit* by which the benefits of varied resource outputs can be gauged.

Monetary return can be used as a common denominator for yields such as timber or livestock production, but it is more difficult to translate other benefits (e.g., hiking in a wilderness area) into purely monetary values. Nevertheless, decisions directly affecting resource yields *are* going to be made, and the need for a common "meter stick" is long overdue.

PROBLEMS

14-1 Take your own set of photographs or color slides to illustrate five of the seven characteristic landscapes described in Sec. 14-3.

14-2 Investigate the possibility of counting hikers or cross-country skiers by means of a remote sensor, e.g., hidden camera, infrared scanner, photoelectric beam, etc. In a brief report, describe the cost and expected reliability of the system, along with a proposed location for installation.

14-3 Assume that you have selected several sample days for interviewing families at a local campground or trailer park. If you wish to interview six family groups per day, *how* should these groups be selected? List several criteria to be observed that might improve the chances for an unbiased and representative sample.

14-4 Devise an indirect indicator of recreational use and test it against a complete census at a nearby facility. Prepare a report on your findings.

14-5 If aerial photographs of your county are available, make a preliminary survey to locate at least three new potential recreational sites. Then visit these proposed sites on the ground and assess their relative potential, availability, and access. Explain your methods of selection and site evaluation in an illustrated report.

14-6 Locate a tract of land that is currently managed for three or more resource benefits. Summarize yields in a product-mix tabulation; express all benefits in terms of monetary returns, if possible.

REFERENCES

Campbell, Frederick L.
1970. Participant observation in outdoor recreation. *J. Leisure Research* **2:** 226-236.

Ffolliott, Peter F., and Worley, David P.
1965. An inventory system for multiple use evaluations. *U. S. Forest Serv., Rocky Mt. Forest and Range Expt. Sta. Res. Paper* RM-17. 15 pp., illus.

Hendee, John C., and Lucas, Robert C.
1973. Mandatory wilderness permits: a necessary management tool. *J. Forestry* 71:206-209, illus.

Hewlett, John D., and Douglass, James E.
1968. Blending forest uses. *U.S. Forest Serv., Southeast. Forest Expt. Sta., Res. Paper* SE-37. 15 pp., illus.

James, George A., and Henley, Robert K.
1968. Sampling procedures for estimating mass and dispersed types of recreation use on large areas. *U.S. Forest Serv., Southeast. Forest Expt. Sta., Res. Paper* SE-31. 15 pp., illus.

———— and Tyre, Gary L.
   1967. Use of water-meter records to estimate recreation visits and use on developed sites. *U.S. Forest Serv., Southeast. Forest Expt. Sta., Res. Note* SE-73. 3 pp.
———— and Ripley, Thomas H.
   1963. Instructions for using traffic counters to estimate recreation visits and use. *U.S. Forest Serv., Southeast. Forest Expt. Sta., Res. Paper* SE-3. 12 pp., illus.
Litton, R. Burton, Jr.
   1968. Forest landscape description and inventories—a basis for land planning and design. *U.S. Forest Serv., Pacific Southwest Forest and Range Expt. Sta., Res Paper* PSW-49. 64 pp., illus.
MacConnell, William P., and Archey, Warren
   1969. The use of aerial photographs to evaluate the recreational resources of the Connecticut River in New Hampshire. Bulletin 576, College of Agri. Expt. Sta., Univ. of Massachusetts, 81 pp.
Stout, Benjamin B.
   1973. A forest management decision variable. *J. Forestry* **71**: 358-360, illus.
U.S. Department of Agriculture
   1973. National forest landscape management, Vol. 1. Goverment Printing Office, Washington, D.C. 76 pp., illus.

Dendrochronology

15-1 Introduction Dendrochronology is the study of the growth rings in living trees and aged woods for the purpose of establishing a time sequence in the precise dating of past events. Originally developed by astronomer Andrew E. Douglass, the concept of tree-ring dating has been applied in the dating of archeological and geological events that occurred as far back as 8,200 years ago. This expanding science is also being utilized to provide information on past climatic regimes, past variations in water runoff for certain areas, and the effects of past and present environmental factors that are reflected by variations in tree-growth rings (Fritts, 1972).

The resource manager has been traditionally concerned with the management of trees under optimum site conditions, i.e., those trees which display average or above-average growth rates. Thus it is perhaps not surprising that few foresters have been directly involved in the development of dendrochronology, since this science is primarily based on the analysis of growth rings from trees found on severely limiting sites. The purpose of this chapter is to provide the resource manager with an understanding of the fundamentals of dendrochronology and its potential applications.[1]

15-2 Origins of Tree-Ring Dating In the early 1900s, Andrew E. Douglass was an astronomer at the Lowell Observatory in Flagstaff, Arizona. He was primarily interested in the cyclic nature of solar activity, especially sunspots, and the possible relationship of such periodic phenomena to climatic variations on earth. Since records of solar activity extended further back in time than terrestrial weather records, he deduced that past fluctuations in tree-growth rates might provide indications of earlier climatic regimes. During his early studies of 200-to-400-year-old ponderosa pines in northern Arizona, Douglass formulated and verified the following basic premises of tree-ring dating:

1 Precipitation is the most limiting climatic factor affecting tree growth in southwestern United States.
2 The response of trees to limited precipitation is modified by the effects of site.
3 Tree response is best indicated by the relative widths of annual rings, i. e., narrow rings result from low precipitation and accompanying deficiencies in soil mosture.
4 Climatic variations tend to encompass large regions, so that characteristically narrow rings in two or more trees can be matched, provided the trees grew at the same time in the past. Subsequent work has shown that these basic ideas are sound, even though the cause and effect relationships are not so simplistic (Stokes, 1970).

The last premise cited was an especially important concept. As Douglass extended his ponderosa pine growth curves into the past, he noted that similar patterns of wide and narrow annual rings were evident in trees growing as far apart as 160 km and at elevations differing by as much as 300 m. The recognition of this recurring tree-ring pattern over large areas led to the principle of *crossdating*, which has become the foundation of all subsequent dendrochronological investigations (Fig. 15-1).

Douglass possessed the facility of committing entire tree-ring sequences to memory, and he first demonstrated the utility of crossdating in 1904, when he recognized the growth pattern in an old stump and was able to theorize on the year the tree had been felled. When the date was

---

[1] In a strict sense, dendrochronology is not a part of natural resources measurements. However, since the science is based on tree-ring studies, it is a subject of *potential interest* to resource managers. It is hoped that this brief introduction will serve to stimulate that interest. All illustrations in this chapter were supplied by the Laboratory of Tree-Ring Research, University of Arizona.

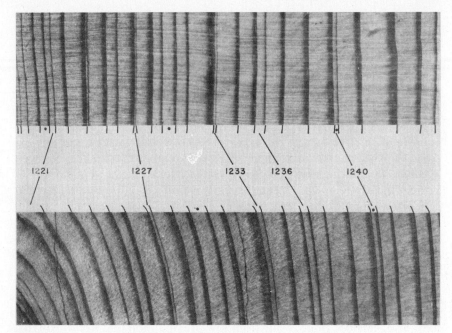

Figure 15-1 Crossdating of a sensitive tree-ring series. Samples were taken from the thirteenth-century Betatakin ruin in northern Arizona.

verified by the man who had cleared the land, the concept of crossdating had been experimentally established (Bannister, 1965). In essence, the technique of crossdating consists of selecting groups of trees or cut timbers of similar ages so that characteristic annual ring patterns overlap one another by 50 to 100 years or more. Through crossdating (precisely matching corresponding growth rings), one may eventually bridge over hundreds of years into the past, and a chronology of ring sequences can be developed and dated by calendar years (Fig. 15-2).

During the following decade, Douglass continued his work on tree rings as climatic indicators and on the establishment of long-term growth curves. He managed to crossdate trees growing as far as 400 km away with ponderosa pines from northern Arizona. He also analyzed tree-ring sequences from northern Europe and devoted considerable attention to California's giant sequoias in the hope that their chronologies could be correlated with the pines of northern Arizona. Although Douglass did not find the giant-sequoia tree-ring chronology to be useful in his study, the crossdated specimens from living trees in nothern Arizona provided a chronology by 1914–1915 that extended back almost 500 years, i.e., to

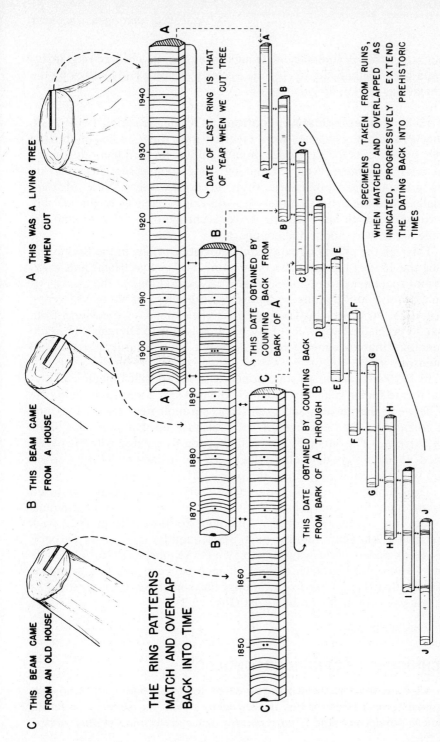

A THIS WAS A LIVING TREE WHEN CUT

DATE OF LAST RING IS THAT OF YEAR WHEN WE CUT TREE

B THIS BEAM CAME FROM A HOUSE

THIS DATE OBTAINED BY COUNTING BACK FROM BARK OF A

C THIS BEAM CAME FROM AN OLD HOUSE

THE RING PATTERNS MATCH AND OVERLAP BACK INTO TIME

THIS DATE OBTAINED BY COUNTING BACK FROM BARK OF B

SPECIMENS TAKEN FROM RUINS, WHEN MATCHED AND OVERLAPPED AS INDICATED, PROGRESSIVELY EXTEND THE DATING BACK INTO PREHISTORIC TIMES

1850 1860 1870 1880 1890 1900 1910 1920 1930 1940

Figure 15-2 Chronology building.

305

about A.D. 1400. A summary of Douglass' early years of tree-ring analyses and their relationship to climatic cycles was published in 1919 by the Carnegie Institution of Washington, D.C.

15-3 Archeological Applications During the period 1914–1930, Douglass and his colleagues were diverted from their studies of climatic cycles by requests for assistance in dating prehistoric Indian ruins in the American Southwest. After examining some sample sections of living trees growing near prehistoric ruins in northwestern New Mexico, Douglass held the belief that these growth-ring sequences might possibly be crossdated with his northern Arizona chronology—even though the sample areas were about 400 km apart.

Through the efforts of many archeologists working in the Southwest during the 1919–1928 period, a large number of pueblo beams and wood charcoal specimens were collected and crossdated among themselves to form a relative, or "floating," prehistoric chronology of about 585 years. As of 1928, however, this floating chronology based on specimens from about 30 prehistoric ruins could not be directly tied to Douglass' absolute chronology that extended from the present back to around A.D. 1400 (Robinson, 1967).

In 1929, an expedition was formed with the specific objective of trying to locate Indian ruins that might yield wood specimens for bridging the gap between the modern and prehistoric chronologies. The charred log that constituted the "missing link" was discovered that year near Show Low, Arizona. The outside rings of the key log crossdated with the oldest rings of Douglass' modern chronology, and the inside annual rings crossdated with the outer rings from the prehistoric chronology.

The joining of the two chronologies constituted a highly significant breakthrough for dendrochronologists, for it provided a continuous, absolute ring chronology for the American Southwest from 1929 back more than 1,200 years into the past. Subsequently, this master chronology was extended all the way back to 59 B.C. (Schulman, 1956). This milestone also established such a close alliance between tree-ring scientists and archeologists that dendrochronology has sometimes been regarded as an exclusive tool of the archeologist (Fig. 15-3).

TECHNIQUES OF DENDROCHRONOLOGY

15-4 Sensitive Tree Rings Most dendrochronological studies in southwestern United States have been based on seven coniferous species: ponderosa pine (*Pinus ponderosa*), pinyon pine (*Pinus edulis*),

Figure 15-3 Part of Betatakin ruin, Navajo National Monument, Arizona, showing roof beams in place; the structure was built around A.D. 1260–1280. The inset shows the annual-ring pattern of a Douglas-fir charcoal specimen; such fragments can often be dated for determining the age of prehistoric structures.

limber pine (*Pinus flexilis*), bristlecone pine (*Pinus aristata*[1]), Rocky Mountain juniper (*Juniperus scopulorum*), Douglas-fir (*Pseudotsuga menziesii*), and giant sequoia (*Sequoia gigantea*). As a general rule, conifers have proved more valuable than hardwoods for tree-ring studies, al-

[1]May also be known as *Pinus longaeva*.

though oaks have been successfully used in Central Europe. Most of the foregoing species tend to display "sensitive" or diagnostic ring sequences when found on limiting sites. Some tree species do not appear to be suitable for dendrochronological studies, even though they may be extremely long-lived.

Trees that grow on good sites under favorable soil moisture and temperature conditions are not likely to show much variation in annual ring growth. There may be a gradual decrease in ring width as such trees reach maturity, but the ring sequences will generally be of a relatively uniform width. Such annual ring sequences, lacking in distinctive character, are termed *complacent* and they are rarely suitable for analysis and inference.

For tree-ring specimens to be truly diagnostic in character, they must be taken from trees that have been severely limited in their development by climatic and/or environmental conditions that vary in intensity from year to year (Fritts, 1972). Precipitation, for example, is the single most limiting factor in the southwestern United States; in northern climates, low temperature is usually the most restrictive element. An unusually dry-hot year in the Southwest will result in narrow tree rings (possibly in the following year instead of in the dry year itself), while those years with greater precipitation and accompanying soil moisture will produce wider ring patterns. This explains why most trees grown in managed forests, i.e., on good sites and in favorable climates, are not as adaptable to dendrochronological studies as those on limiting sites (Fig. 15-4).

15-5 Field-sampling Techniques The field collection of tree-ring specimens is governed by the objective of obtaining the most complete record possible of the ring sequence. With stumps, logs, or beams, it is desirable to obtain a complete cross section of the original stem. Since this ideal record cannot be obtained ordinarily from living trees or from archeological specimens to be preserved, a special kind of increment borer is commonly used instead. The sample trees from which increment cores are extracted would likely display the following characteristics:

   1   Trees on sites that produce sensitive ring series, i.e., sites having internal soil drainage and no subsurface water supply.
   2   Trees that are open-grown and reasonably free from the competitive effects of adjacent crowns.
   3   Trees that are, insofar as possible, free from past injuries or diseases that may have affected growth rates and ring patterns.

In other words, in order to emphasize the effects of the environment on the annual ring pattern, it is necessary to minimize other elements affecting tree growth that may overshadow or distort the climatic response.

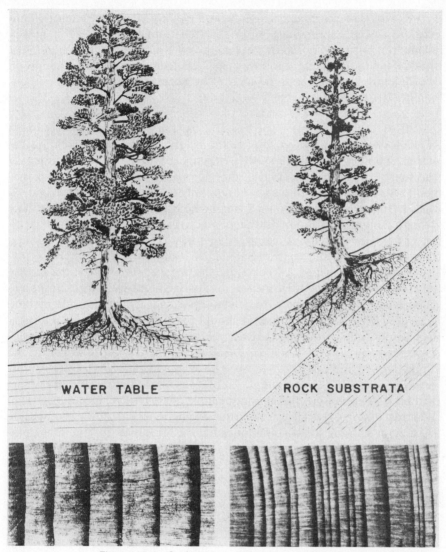

Figure 15-4 Complacent ring series (left) and sensitive series (right).

It is especially important that increment cores be carefully handled in the field and coded as to tree species, geographic location, slope, aspect, soil-site conditions, date, and other factors. After cores are air-dried, they are glued into specially grooved mounts and are then surfaced for detailed study under magnification. By tradition, analysis is made with the bark at the observer's right. The dating of each core (or cross section) is indicated by marking a single dot on each tenth ring; two dots indicate half-centuries, and three dots signify centuries. For convenience, centuries are marked on the core mounts as 19 for 1900, and so on. False or microscopic rings are also noted by year on the core mount, along with the year that the innermost and outermost rings were formed. Additional details on the handling and analysis of increment cores are outlined by Ferguson (1970).

15-6 Crossdating The first and most important step in building a relative or absolute chronology is the establishment of crossdating between sample ring sequences. Where highly sensitive ring series comprise the source of datable specimens, the "Douglass method" is recommended. This system emphasizes (1) abnormally wide or narrow rings and (2) the internal relationship of such rings within the overall ring series. The precise comparison of one ring sequence with another is usually made by one of three methods: memory, skeleton plots, or graphically plotted measurements of ring widths (Bannister, 1963).

Assuming a complete knowledge of the local chronology, the *memory method* simply requires mental comparisons of the ring patterns encountered. Only the most experienced investigators can use this method with confidence, and even then it should be supplemented with comparative wood samples from an existing chronology. As an alternative, photographs of previously dated ring sequences might be used in lieu of the actual wood samples.

The *skeleton plot* is a simple graphical representation of *relative* ring widths, with primary emphasis on the most narrow rings. In the American Southwest, narrow rings are regarded as the most useful for crossdating because trees tend to exhibit a more uniform response in severe or unfavorable years. Thus in a skeleton plot, the greatest value is assigned to a missing ring, and a value nearly as great is recorded for a microscopic ring. More or less "average" ring widths are often ignored completely, but extremely wide ones may be noted.

Since the width of each ring is judged only in relation to nearby rings, the skeleton plot has the advantage of being free of any tree-age trends within the specimen. In other words, the plotting of relative rather than absolute ring widths tends to offset the normal decrease in ring width that occurs as the tree becomes older. The technique also helps in avoiding problems of varying ring widths that have resulted from nonclimatic factors such as competition and/or subsequent "release cuttings." The skeleton plot is regarded as merely one step in the crossdating process. The method must be applied with caution because only certain ring characteristics are taken into consideration. Final dating may depend on additional factors exhibited by the ring patterns (Fig.15-5).

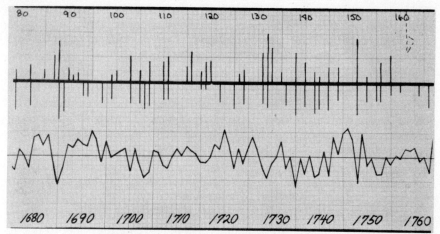

Figure 15-5 (*Above*) The skeleton plot for a single pinyon pine specimen is matched to a master skeleton-plot chronology. Numbers across the top of the illustration indicate the age range of the specimen (79 to 161 years); calendar years are listed at the bottom. (*Below*) The master chronology graphed as percentage deviations from mean ring width. Note that the greatest deviations correspond to the longer lines (i.e., diagnostic narrow rings) of the skeleton plots.

A number of specialized instruments have been devised to *measure and record ring widths* in absolute terms, e. g., to a precision of 0.01 mm. The measurements are then graphically plotted for both visual and statistical comparisons. Since absolute values are recorded, it is sometimes necessary to "standardize" or correct the graphs to remove the effect of tree age before inferences can be drawn on the relationship between climate and ring development (Banister, 1963).

In those instances where a ring sequence cannot be positively dated by one of the three methods described, a computer-programmed correlation routine may sometimes be used to evaluate all possible matches between two series of ring indices. Resulting correlation coefficients tend to be randomly distributed within narrow limits around "zero," except at the match point, where a highly significant positive correlation may be obtained (Ferguson, 1970). This statistical dating technique must be verified by a reexamination of the wood.

15-7 Anomalies in Ring Sequences No matter which method of ring comparison is used, the validity of the results depends on the reliability with which crossdating can be accomplished. Among the principal problems encountered in crossdating are those associated with *missing, false, or microscopic rings*.

During years of severe environmental stresses, portions of tree stems may not exhibit any discernible growth; thus annual rings may be completely missing, or at least not be detectable by ordinary analysis. Such occurrences may require special adjustments in ring counts and verification based on additional specimens before the samples can be dated or incorporated into a chronology. Otherwise, the ring sequences may be out of phase by a year or more as compared with related specimens. The problem is magnified by the extremely slow growth rates shown by older trees on highly sensitive sites. Some specimens of bristlecone pine, for example, have contained more than 80 annual rings per centimeter of radius (Ferguson, 1968).

Under certain circumstances (e. g., defoliation after the start of the growing season, followed by a second flush of leaves), trees may form two or more bands of springwood and summerwood during the same year. The false rings, usually present on only a portion of the ring circumference, can best be detected where complete cross sections are available for study. Identification can be extremely difficult, if not impossible, where analysis is solely dependent upon increment cores. It is believed that for trees of the genus *Pinus*, false rings become more frequent as one moves in a southerly direction (Stokes, 1970). In Mexico, false rings constitute one of the major difficulties in tree-ring studies.

Finally, there are microscopic rings (micro-rings), which are merely very small annual rings. As with false and missing rings, these can be most easily detected when compared with corresponding ring sequences from other specimens. Therefore, crossdating itself is one of the best means of distinguishing anomalies in ring sequences.

15-8 Chronology Building   As previously noted, not all trees in an area can be crossdated with each other; only certain sectors of the earth appear to include crossdatable trees, and crossdating between widely separated regions is usually impossible. Thus a rigorous and rational sampling system for specimen collection is essential, and hundreds (or even thousands) of ring sequences may have to be examined before specimens of various ages can be correctly matched to form a dated and standardized sequence. Such a sequence, once tested and verified, is known as a *master chronology*. The master chronology is unique in its annual ring pattern because year-to-year variations in climate are never precisely repeated over long periods of time.

Once a dated master chronology has been derived for a particular species and region, additional specimens (either wood or charcoal) from similar sites can generally be dated from it, provided there is a minimum ring overlap of 30 to 50 years (Fritts, 1972). Additional ring sequences, if incorporated into the master chronology, may also be used to extend known records further back into the past. For example, wood of the bristlecone pine, especially from remnants that predate the 4000-year-old living trees, has provided a chronology for the White Mountains of east-central California back to around 6200 B.C., a continuous record of nearly 8,200 years (Ferguson, 1972).

15-9   Interpretation The preceding sections have dealt primarily with crossdating techniques and the establishment of chronologies from tree rings. Exactly what one may *infer* from dated wood specimens is another matter. In many instances, questions arise about the time rela-tionships between the dated tree-ring specimens and the event or struc-ture one might hope to place within a time frame. To illustrate this point, Bannister (1963) has described four general classes of interpretation errors that may be encountered by archeologists and others who attempt to assign exact dates to past events in man's history:

1   The association between the dated tree-ring specimen and the archeological manifestation being dated is direct, but the specimen itself came from a tree that died or was cut prior to its use in the situation in question.
2   The association between the dated tree-ring specimen and the archeological manifestation being dated is not direct, the specimen having been used prior to the feature being dated.
3   The association between the dated tree-ring specimen and the archeological manifestation being dated is direct, but the specimen itself represents a later incorporation into an already existing feature.
4   The association between the dated tree-ring specimen and the archeological manifestation being dated is not direct, the specimen having been used later than the feature being dated.

From the foregoing precautions, one may surmise that tree-ring dat-ing is a valuable tool of the earth scientist—a means to an end, but not the end in itself!

TRENDS IN TREE-RING STUDIES

15-10   Dendroclimatology There is an intensified interest in Douglass' original concept of the correlation between tree rings and past climatic variations. The term *dendroclimatology* has been coined to en-compass further studies of this nature.

The width of annual rings from woody plants growing on arid and semiarid sites is visualized as a reliable record of past climates because it tends to vary directly with drought intensity and site temperature. A wide ring indicates a moist and cool year, while a narrow ring results from a dry and hot year (Fritts, 1965). Since it is the climatic information in tree rings that is of interest, dendroclimatological studies in arid regions concentrate on tree sites where moisture is most limiting to growth. In polar regions, where tree sites are mainly limited by low temperatures rather than by high temperatures and low moisture, specimens are preferred from trees that are found within 100 m of the upper climatic timberline.

Studies by Fritts (1965) have shown that the annual ring width for many arid-site trees is influenced more by moisture regimes in fall, winter, and spring than by summer moisture. High-speed computers have been used to assess the relationship between past climates and long-term tree-ring chronologies for large areas of western North America. Abnormal departures in the widths of growth rings can be plotted on maps and then contoured for varying time intervals to indicate growth fluctuations due to past climatic variations.

15-11 Streamflow, Erosion, and Air Pollution It is sometimes feasible to correlate ring-width variations with annual streamflow (representing runoff) from watersheds where climatically sensitive trees grow—and to reconstruct long-term changes in the past annual runoff from tree chronologies. Multivariate statistical techniques may provide extraction of a "climatic signal" from the tree-ring series that corresponds to annual runoff from a river basin (Stockton, 1974). Such investigations have been made in the upper Colorado River basin to determine the long-term variations and average inflow into Lake Powell (Arizona, Utah). A 450-year-old chronology of runoff records has been reconstructed, based on tree-ring series of Douglas-fir, ponderosa pine, pinyon pine, and limber pine. This reconstructed record indicates that:

1 The mean annual inflow into Lake Powell is approximately 13.0 million acre-feet (16,035 million m^3) and *not* 15.0 million acre-feet (18,502 million m^3) as indicated by the 1896–1963 stream-gauge record at Lee's Ferry, Arizona.

2 The gauged record covering 1896–1963 period contains the longest extended period of above-normal runoff in the past 450 years, viz., during 1905–1929.

3 The gauged record does *not* contain any periods of extented drought such as those of the periods 1564–1600 and 1870–1889 as indicated by the analysis of the 450-year-old tree-ring chronology.

It can be seen that, by using dendrochronological techniques, the water resources manager can utilize reconstructed runoff records as best estimates of what actually occurred in the past. He can also use such data for simulation of a reservoir by applying established hydrological rules.

Another use of reconstructed tree-ring records in water resources management has been described by Stockton and Fritts (1973). White spruce trees growing along natural levees of the inflow-outflow channels of Lake Athabasca (Alberta, Canada) have been used to reconstruct long-term lake-level changes. This information was needed because construction of a dam some 1,300 km (800 miles) upstream had seriously deleted annual snowmelt (water inflow) into the lake area. This decrease in inflow resulted in a drop in seasonal lake-level fluctuations, which, in turn, reduced the population of fish and fur-bearing animals.

Because local residents still depend on fish for food and on furs for income, it was desirable to try and restore lake levels to "normal" as a means of maintaining the proper habitat for fish and game. The problem was that only 33 years of lake-level changes had been recorded, but by using a tree-ring chronology, the lake-level records were extended back 180 years. The extended chronology showed that the recordings in the last 33 years included a 20-year period of severe drought—a condition that resulted in greatly diminished variations in seasonal lake-levels. Consequently, it was apparent to resource managers that any construction undertaken to rectify the currently reduced levels would have to reproduce seasonal lake-level variations greater than those in the 33-year record. This was accomplished by building a small dam on one of the inflow-outflow channels to modify the natural, seasonal inflow-outflow regime.

Tree-ring dating can be used to measure erosional rates and to study the frequency of past floods, fires, and earthquakes. LaMarche (1968) used the long-lived bristlecone pine to determine erosional rates in the White Mountains of California. He also utilized destruction of trees by floodwaters along a stream floodplain in northern California to determine the past, long-term frequency of flood occurrence. Such information is vital in modern land-use planning and in enforcing restrictive building codes that are applicable to construction on floodplains.

Fritts (1972) has demonstrated that a tree-ring series from appropriately selected trees can show evidence of damage from air pollution. Evidence of reduced tree-ring growth may be useful in litigation, especially where the establishment of the date of pollution requires verification. Dendrochronological techniques may also be applied in determining the spatial extent of air pollution.

15-12 Future Possibilities As dendroclimatic techniques are extended to new species and to other sectors of the world, it appears likely that tree rings will assume even greater importance in ecological and climatological analyses. The development of new and longer chronologies will be required, and efforts will be made to establish chronologies for nonconiferous species, as well as for species growing in temperate regions.

A promising development is an x-ray technique used to photograph and analyze changes in cell density and wood density within annual rings. It is believed that x-ray analysis will be especially useful for studies of trees in temperate regions and on moderately moist sites. In such areas, it is theorized that environmental fluctuations during the growing season may be more highly correlated with changes in cell structure and wood density than with variations in annual ring widths (Fritts, 1972).

15-13 Laboratory of Tree-Ring Research This research laboratory, founded by A. E. Douglass at the University of Arizona in 1938, constitutes the focal point for continued dendrochronological investigations in the United States. The laboratory serves as a central repository for tree-ring collections and offers instruction and training related to dendrochronology. *The Tree-Ring Bulletin*, the official journal of the Tree-Ring Society, is published in cooperation with the laboratory and may be ordered from

> Laboratory of Tree-Ring Research
> Universtiy of Arizona
> Tucson, AZ   85721

PROBLEMS

15-1 *Field sampling.*   Conduct a study of annual ring patterns for a coniferous species in your locality. Select specimens from trees found on relatively arid or low-temperature (high-elevation) sites. If possible, obtain complete cross sections from stumps *and* increment cores from living trees of widely differing ages. Obtain at least two cores per tree. If you are in a region where previous crossdating has not been established, the species listed here *may* offer crossdating possibilities:

> *Northeast* White spruce (*Picea glauca*) or red spruce (*Picea rubens*) growing in mountainous areas near the timberline
> *Lake States* Tamarack (*Larix laricina*) or red pine (*Pinus resinosa*) growing on marginal sites
> *Southeast* Fraser fir (*Abies fraseri*), red spruce (*Picea rubens*), or eastern hemlock (*Tsuga canadensis*) growing at high elevations in the southern Appalachian Mountains
> *Rocky Mountains* Douglas-fir (*Pseudotsuga menziesii*) or limber pine (*Pinus flexilis*) growing on arid sites or at high elevations

Southwest Douglas-fir (*Pseudotsuga menziesii*), ponderosa pine (*Pinus ponderosa*), or pinyon (*Pinus edulis*) growing on arid sites or at high elevations

Northwest Ponderosa pine (*Pinus ponderosa*) or western hemlock (*Tsuga heterophylla*) growing on semiarid sites

Specimens can often be collected during logging operations or on cut-over areas. If feasible, obtain sample ring patterns from 20 or more trees that are open-grown and free from neighboring competition. Label all materials according to species, date of collection, date of cutting (if known), geographic location, soil-site conditions, slope, aspect, and so on.

15-2 *Laboratory preparation.* Air dry all wood specimens. Mount cores into grooved slats of wood, with cross-section surfaces facing upward. Mark all materials with complete identifying codes. Then sand all sections and cores to produce clearly visible ring sequences.

15-3 *Analysis of ring sequences.* Begin your study with specimens of known cutting age so that outside rings can be precisely dated. If the cross sections and increment cores span varying numbers of years, attempt to crossdate them by visual comparison. Check especially for false, double, or microscopic rings; if any of these are present, they will be most likely discernible on complete cross sections.

If crossdating appears feasible, construct a dated chronology in the form of a simple skeleton plot. Assuming that specimens were selected from trees on sensitive sites, it may be possible to extend the chronology back from the present by at least 80 to 100 years.

If your ring sequences prove to be of normal or relatively uniform widths (a complacent series), and the skeleton plot does not provide a means of crossdating, then attempt to crossdate your more sensitive specimens by plotting actual ring widths on graph paper. If this method also fails, you are likely to be working with a complacent series where local site factors cause differences that do not crossdate.

Prepare a written report of your findings.

REFERENCES

Bannister, Bryant
1965. Andrew Ellicott Douglass. Yearbook of American Philosophical Society. pp. 121-125.

_____

1963. Dendrochronology. In: *Science in Archeology*, Basic Books, Inc., Publishers, New York. Pp. 161-176, illus.

Douglass, A. E.
1919. Climatic cycles and tree growth. Vol. I, *Carnegie Inst. Wash. Pub.* 289, Washington, D. C. 127 pp.

_____

1936. The central pueblo chronology. *Tree-Ring Bulletin* **2** (4):29-33. Tree-Ring Society, Tucson, AZ.

Ferguson, C. W.

1972. Dendrochronology of bristlecone pine prior to 4000 B.C. *Proc.*, 8th *International Conference on Radiocarbon Dating*, Wellington, New Zealand.

───────

1970. Concepts and techniques of dendrochronology. In: *Scientific Methods in Medieval Archeology*, University of California Press, Berkeley. Pp. 183-200, illus.

───────

1968. Bristlecone pine: Science and esthetics. *Science* **159**:839-846, illus.

Fritts, Harold C.

1972. Tree rings and climate. *Scientific American* **226** (5): 92-100, illus.

───────

1971. Dendroclimatology and dendroecology. *Quaternary Research* **1** (4): 419-449, illus.

───────

1965. Tree-ring evidence for climatic changes in Western North America. *Monthly Weather Review* **93** (7): 421-443, illus.

Helley, E. J., and V. C. LaMarche, Jr.

1973. Historic flood information for northern California streams from geological and botanical evidence. *U.S. Geological Survey Professional Paper* 485-E, 16 pp., illus.

LaMarche, V. C., Jr.

1968. Rates of slope degradation as determined from botanical evidence, White Mountains, California. Erosion and sedimentation in a semiarid environment. *U.S. Geological Survey Professional Paper* 352-I, pp. 341-377, illus.

McGinnies, W. G.

1963. Dendrochronology. *J. Forestry* **61**: 5-11, illus.

Robinson, William J.

1967. Tree-ring materials as a basis for cultural interpretations. University of Arizona Ph.D. dissertation, Tucson, AZ. pp. 10-25.

Schulman, E.

1956. Dendroclimatic changes in semiarid America. University of Arizona Press, Tucson. 142 pp., illus.

Stockton, C. W.

1974. Long term streamflow records reconstructed from tree rings. The University of Arizona Press, in press, illus.

─────── **and Fritts, H. C.**

1973. Long-term reconstruction of water level changes for Lake Athabasca by analysis of tree rings. *Water Resources Bulletin*, vol. 9, no. 5, pp. 1006-1027, illus.

Stokes, M. A.

1970. Tree-ring chronologies in Western America. University of British Columbia, Faculty of Forestry, Bull. 7, pp. 86-87.

─────── **and Smiley, Terah L.**

1968. *An Introduction to tree-ring dating*. The University of Chicago Press, Chicago, 73 pp., illus.

Appendix Tables

Appendix Table 1   Selected Conversions: English to Metric Units

LENGTH

Multiply	by	to obtain
Inches	25.40	millimeters (mm)
Inches	2.54	centimeters (cm)
Feet	30.480	centimeters (cm)
Feet	0.3048	meters (m)
Yards	0.9144	meters (m)
Chains (Gunter's)	20.1168	meters (m)
U.S. statute miles	1.6093	kilometers (km)
Nautical miles	1.852	kilometers (km)

AREA

Square inches	645.16	square millimeters (m^2)
Square inches	6.4516	square centimeters (cm^2)
Square feet	929.03	square centimeters (cm^2)
Square feet	0.0929	square meters (m^2)
Square yards	0.8361	square meters (m^2)
Square chains	404.6856	square meters (m^2)
Acres	0.4047	hectares (ha)
Square miles	2.5899	square kilometers (km^2)

VOLUME

Cubic inches	16.387	cubic centimeters (cm^3)
Cubic feet	0.02832	cubic meters (m^3)
Cubic yards	0.7646	cubic meters (m^3)

SPECIAL CONVERSIONS

Square feet per acre	0.2296	square meters per hectare (m^2/ha)
Cubic feet per acre	0.06997	cubic meters per hectare (m^3/ha)
Cubic feet per second	101.941	cubic meters per hour (m^3/h)
Feet per second	1.097	kilometers per hour (km/h)
Gallons per acre	11.2336	liters per hectare (l/ha)
Gallons per minute	0.0757	liters per second (l/s)
Pounds per acre	1.1208	kilograms per hectare (kg/ha)
Pounds per cubic foot	16.0185	kilograms per cubic meter (kg/m^3)
Number (e.g., stems) per acre	2.471	number per hectare (No./ha)

Appendix Table 2   Table for Obtaining Square Roots to Five Significant Digits

OPERATION: Clear-return control towards operator; Carriage in seventh position; Number 7 Tab Key depressed.

N = Number whose root is desired.

1. Beginning at extreme left of Keyboard Dial, enter N and touch Add Bar.
2. Beginning at extreme left of Keyboard Dial, enter Column B number and touch Add Bar.
3. Beginning at extreme left of Keyboard Dial, enter Column C number and touch Division Key.

The square root of N appears in Upper Dials, accurate to five digits.

A	B	C
1.00		
	102	202 00
1.04		
	106	205 92
1.08		
	11	209 77
1.12		
	114	213 55
1.16		
	118	217 26
1.20		
	122	220 91
1.24		
	126	224 507
1.29		
	132	229 79
1.35		
	138	234 954
1.41		
	144	240 01
1.47		
	15	244 956
1.53		
	156	249 806
1.59		
	162	254 56
1.65		
	168	259 235
1.71		
	174	263 82
1.77		
	18	268 33
1.83		
	186	272 77
1.90		
	194	278 575
1.98		
	202	284 26
2.06		

A	B	C
2.06		
	21	289 834
2.14		
	218	295 3
2.22		
	226	300 67
2.30		
	234	305 95
2.38		
	242	311 13
2.46		
	25	316 236
2.55		
	26	322 5
2.65		
	27	328 64
2.75		
	28	334 67
2.85		
	29	340 594
2.95		
	3	346 42
3.05		
	31	352 14
3.15		
	32	357 78
3.25		
	33	363 326
3.36		
	342	369 87
3.48		
	354	376 305
3.60		
	366	382 63
3.72		
	378	388 85
3.84		
	39	394 974
3.96		

A	B	C
3.96		
	402	401 006
4.09		
	416	407 93
4.23		
	43	414 736
4.37		
	444	421 43
4.51		
	458	428 025
4.65		
	472	434 52
4.80		
	488	441 82
4.96		
	504	449 006
5.12		
	52	456 08
5.28		
	536	463 04
5.44		
	552	469 9
5.61		
	57	477 5
5.79		
	588	484 98
5.97		
	606	492 35
6.15		
	624	499 606
6.33		
	642	506 76
6.51		
	66	513 817
6.7		
	68	521 543
6.9		
	7	529 16
7.1		

A	B	C
7.1		
	72	536 66
7.3		
	74	544 065
7.5		
	76	551 37
7.7		
	78	558 575
7.9		
	8	565 69
8.1		
	82	572 72
8.3		
	84	579 66
8.5		
	86	586 52
8.7		
	88	593 3
8.9		
	9	600 00
9.1		
	92	606 63
9.3		
	94	613 19
9.5		
	96	619 68
9.7		
	98	626 1
9.9*		
	1	632 46
10.1		
	102	638 75
10.3		
	104	644 98
10.5		
	106	651 16
10.7		
	108	657 27
10.9		

*For square roots of numbers from 9.9 to but not including 10 enter N in step 1 beginning in *next to leftmost keyboard* dial instead of in leftmost dial.

A	B	C
10.9		
	11	663 33
11.1		
	112	669 33
11.3		
	114	675 28
11.5		
	116	681 18
11.7		
	118	687 03
11.9		
	12	692 82
12.1		
	122	698 57
12.3		
	124	704 28
12.5		
	126	709 93
12.7		
	128	715 54
12.9		
	13	721 11
13.1		
	132	726 64
13.3		
	134	732 12
13.5		
	136	737 57
13.7		
	138	742 97
13.9		
	14	748 33
14.1		
	142	753 66
14.3		
	144	758 95
14.5		
	146	764 2
14.7		
	148	769 42
14.9		
	15	774 6
15.1		
	152	779 75
15.3		
	154	784 86
15.5		
	156	789 94
15.7		

A	B	C
15.7		
	158	794 99
15.9		
	16	800 01
16.2		
	164	809 946
16.6		
	168	819 763
17.0		
	172	829 465
17.4		
	176	839 054
17.8		
	18	848 535
18.2		
	184	857 91
18.6		
	188	867 186
19.0		
	192	876 36
19.4		
	196	885 44
19.8		
	2	894 43
20.2		
	204	903 33
20.6		
	208	912 15
21.0		
	212	920 87
21.4		
	216	929 52
21.8		
	22	938 09
22.2		
	224	946 58
22.6		
	228	954 99
23.0		
	232	963 33
23.4		
	236	971 6
23.8		
	24	979 8
24.2		
	244	987 93
24.6		
	248	996
25.0		

A	B	C
25.0		
	252	100 4
25.4		
	256	101 193
25.8		
	26	101 981
26.2		
	264	102 762
26.6		
	268	103 538
27.0		
	272	104 308
27.4		
	276	105 072
27.8		
	28	105 831
28.3		
	286	106 9587
28.9		
	292	108 075
29.5		
	298	109 1795
30.1		
	304	110 273
30.7		
	31	111 356
31.3		
	316	112 4284
31.9		
	322	113 491
32.5		
	328	114 543
33.1		
	334	115 586
33.7		
	34	116 62
34.3		
	346	117 644
34.9		
	352	118 66
35.5		
	358	119 667
36.1		
	364	120 665
36.7		
	37	121 656
37.3		
	376	122 638
37.9		

A	B	C
37.9		
	382	123 613
38.5		
	388	124 58
39.1		
	394	125 539
39.7		
	4	126 492
40.4		
	408	127 7505
41.2		
	416	128 997
42.0		
	424	130 2313
42.8		
	432	131 454
43.6		
	44	132 666
44.4		
	448	133 866
45.2		
	456	135 056
46.0		
	464	136 236
46.8		
	472	137 405
47.6		
	48	138 565
48.4		
	488	139 7146
49.2		
	496	140 855
50.0		
	504	141 9865
50.8		
	512	143 109
51.6		
	52	144 223
52.4		
	528	145 328
53.2		
	536	146 425
54.0		
	544	147 513
54.8		
	552	148 594
55.6		
	56	149 667
56.5		

A	B	C	A	B	C	A	B	C	A	B	C
56.5			70.5			84.5			98.7		
	57	150 9974		71	168 5235		85	184 391		994	199 4
57.5			71.5			85.5			100.0		
	58	152 316		72	169 706		86	185 473	(not inclusive)		
58.5			72.5			86.5					
	59	153 6236		73	170 881		87	186 548			
59.5			73.5			87.5					
	6	154 92		74	172 047		88	187 617			
60.5			74.5			88.5					
	61	156 2056		75	173 206		89	188 68			
61.5			75.5			89.5					
	62	157 481		76	174 356		9	189 737			
62.5			76.5			90.5					
	63	158 746		77	175 5		91	190 788			
63.5			77.5			91.5					
	64	160 001		78	176 636		92	191 834			
64.5			78.5			92.5					
	65	161 246		79	177 764		93	192 873			
65.5			79.5			93.5					
	66	162 481		8	178 886		94	193 908			
66.5			80.5			94.5					
	67	163 708		81	180 000		95	194 936			
67.5			81.5			95.5					
	68	164 925		82	181 108		96	195 96			
68.5			82.5			96.5					
	69	166 133		83	182 209		97	196 977			
69.5			83.5			97.5					
	7	167 333		84	183 303		98	197 9905			
70.5			84.5			98.7					

SOURCE: Copyright 1952 Marchant Calculators, Inc., reprinted with permission of SCM Corporation.

Appendix Table 3   Scribner Decimal C Log Rule for Logs 6 to 32 Ft in Length

Diameter, in.	Length, ft													
	6	8	10	12	14	16	18	20	22	24	26	28	30	32
	Contents, bd ft in tens													
6	0.5	0.5	1	1	1	2	2	2	3	3	3	4	4	5
7	0.5	1	1	2	2	3	3	3	4	4	4	5	5	6
8	1	1	2	2	2	3	3	3	4	4	5	6	6	7
9	1	2	3	3	3	4	4	4	5	6	6	7	8	9
10	2	3	3	3	4	6	6	7	8	9	9	10	11	12
11	2	3	4	4	5	7	8	8	9	10	11	12	13	14
12	3	4	5	6	7	8	9	10	11	12	13	14	15	16
13	4	5	6	7	8	10	11	12	13	15	16	17	18	19
14	4	6	7	9	10	11	13	14	16	17	19	20	21	23
15	5	7	9	11	12	14	16	18	20	21	23	25	27	28
16	6	8	10	12	14	16	18	20	22	24	26	28	30	32
17	7	9	12	14	16	18	21	23	25	28	30	32	35	37
18	8	11	13	16	19	21	24	27	29	32	35	37	40	43
19	9	12	15	18	21	24	27	30	33	36	39	42	45	48
20	11	14	17	21	24	28	31	35	38	42	45	49	52	56
21	12	15	19	23	27	30	34	38	42	46	49	53	57	61
22	13	17	21	25	29	33	38	42	46	50	54	58	63	67
23	14	19	23	28	33	38	42	47	52	57	61	66	71	75
24	15	21	25	30	35	40	45	50	55	61	66	71	76	81
25	17	23	29	34	40	46	52	57	63	69	75	80	86	92
26	19	25	31	37	44	50	56	62	69	75	82	88	94	100
27	21	27	34	41	48	55	62	68	75	82	89	96	103	110
28	22	29	36	44	51	58	65	73	80	87	95	102	109	116
29	23	31	38	46	53	61	68	76	84	91	99	107	114	122
30	25	33	41	49	57	66	74	82	90	99	107	115	123	131
31	27	36	44	53	62	71	80	89	98	106	115	124	133	142
32	28	37	46	55	64	74	83	92	101	110	120	129	138	147
33	29	39	49	59	69	78	88	98	108	118	127	137	147	157
34	30	40	50	60	70	80	90	100	110	120	130	140	150	160
35	33	44	55	66	77	88	98	109	120	131	142	153	164	175
36	35	46	58	69	81	92	104	115	127	138	150	161	173	185
37	39	51	64	77	90	103	116	129	142	154	167	180	193	206
38	40	54	67	80	93	107	120	133	147	160	174	187	200	214
39	42	56	70	84	98	112	126	140	154	168	182	196	210	224
40	45	60	75	90	105	120	135	150	166	181	196	211	226	241
41	48	64	79	95	111	127	143	159	175	191	207	223	238	254
42	50	67	84	101	117	134	151	168	185	201	218	235	252	269
43	52	70	87	105	122	140	157	174	192	209	227	244	262	279
44	56	74	93	111	129	148	166	185	204	222	241	259	278	296
45	57	76	95	114	133	152	171	190	209	228	247	266	286	304
46	59	79	99	119	139	159	178	198	218	238	258	278	297	317
47	62	83	104	124	145	166	186	207	228	248	269	290	310	331
48	65	86	108	130	151	173	194	216	238	260	281	302	324	346
49	67	90	112	135	157	180	202	225	247	270	292	314	337	359
50	70	94	117	140	164	187	211	234	257	281	304	328	351	374
51	73	97	122	146	170	195	219	243	268	292	315	341	365	389
52	76	101	127	152	177	202	228	253	278	304	329	354	380	405
53	79	105	132	158	184	210	237	263	289	316	341	368	395	421
54	82	109	137	164	191	218	246	273	300	328	355	382	410	437
55	85	113	142	170	198	227	255	283	312	340	368	397	425	453
56	88	118	147	176	206	235	264	294	323	353	382	411	441	470
57	91	122	152	183	213	244	274	304	335	365	396	426	457	487
58	95	126	158	189	221	252	284	315	347	379	410	442	473	505
59	98	131	163	196	229	261	294	327	359	392	425	457	490	523
60	101	135	169	203	237	270	304	338	372	406	439	473	507	541

SOURCE: U.S. Forest Service.

Appendix Table 3   Scribner Decimal C Log Rule for Logs 6 to 32 Ft in Length   (Continued)

Diameter, in.	Length, ft													
	6	8	10	12	14	16	18	20	22	24	26	28	30	32
	Contents, bd ft in tens													
61	105	140	175	210	245	280	315	350	385	420	455	490	525	560
62	108	145	181	217	253	289	325	362	398	434	470	506	542	579
63	112	149	187	224	261	299	336	373	411	448	485	523	560	597
64	116	154	193	232	270	309	348	387	425	464	503	541	580	619
65	119	159	199	239	279	319	358	398	438	478	518	558	597	637
66	123	164	206	247	288	329	370	412	453	494	535	576	617	659
67	127	170	212	254	297	339	381	423	466	508	550	593	635	677
68	131	175	219	262	306	350	393	437	480	524	568	611	655	699
69	135	180	226	271	316	361	406	452	497	542	587	632	677	723
70	139	186	232	279	325	372	419	465	512	558	605	651	698	744
71	144	192	240	287	335	383	430	478	526	574	622	670	717	765
72	148	197	247	296	345	395	444	493	543	592	641	691	740	789
73	152	203	254	305	356	406	457	508	559	610	661	712	762	813
74	157	209	261	314	366	418	471	523	576	628	680	733	785	837
75	161	215	269	323	377	430	484	538	592	646	700	754	807	861
76	166	221	277	332	387	443	498	553	609	664	719	775	830	885
77	171	228	285	341	398	455	511	568	625	682	739	796	852	909
78	176	234	293	351	410	468	527	585	644	702	761	819	878	936
79	180	240	301	361	421	481	541	602	662	722	782	842	902	963
80	185	247	309	371	432	494	556	618	680	742	804	866	927	989
81	190	254	317	381	444	508	572	635	699	762	826	889	953	1016
82	196	261	326	391	456	521	586	652	717	782	847	912	977	1043
83	201	268	335	401	468	535	601	668	735	802	869	936	1002	1069
84	206	275	343	412	481	549	618	687	755	824	893	961	1030	1099
85	210	281	351	421	491	561	631	702	772	842	912	982	1052	1123
86	215	287	359	431	503	575	646	718	790	862	934	1006	1077	1149
87	221	295	368	442	516	589	663	737	810	884	958	1031	1105	1179
88	226	301	377	452	527	603	678	753	829	904	979	1055	1130	1205
89	231	308	385	462	539	616	693	770	847	924	1001	1078	1155	1232
90	236	315	393	472	551	629	708	787	865	944	1023	1101	1180	1259
91	241	322	402	483	563	644	725	805	886	966	1047	1127	1208	1288
92	246	329	411	493	575	657	739	822	904	986	1068	1150	1232	1315
93	251	335	419	503	587	671	754	838	922	1006	1090	1174	1257	1341
94	257	343	428	514	600	685	771	857	942	1028	1114	1199	1285	1371
95	262	350	437	525	612	700	788	875	963	1050	1138	1225	1313	1400
96	268	357	446	536	625	715	804	893	983	1072	1161	1251	1340	1429
97	273	364	455	546	637	728	819	910	1001	1092	1183	1274	1365	1456
98	278	371	464	557	650	743	835	928	1021	1114	1207	1300	1392	1485
99	284	379	473	568	663	757	852	947	1041	1136	1231	1325	1420	1515
100	289	386	482	579	675	772	869	965	1062	1158	1255	1351	1448	1544
101	295	393	492	590	688	787	885	983	1082	1180	1278	1377	1475	1573
102	301	401	502	602	702	803	903	1003	1104	1204	1304	1405	1505	1605
103	307	409	512	614	716	819	921	1023	1126	1228	1330	1433	1535	1637
104	313	417	522	626	730	835	939	1043	1148	1252	1356	1461	1565	1669
105	319	425	532	638	744	851	957	1063	1170	1276	1382	1489	1595	1701
106	325	433	542	650	758	867	975	1083	1192	1300	1408	1517	1625	1733
107	331	442	553	663	773	884	995	1105	1216	1326	1437	1547	1658	1768
108	337	450	563	675	788	900	1013	1125	1238	1350	1463	1575	1688	1800
109	344	459	573	688	803	917	1032	1147	1261	1376	1491	1605	1720	1835
110	350	467	583	700	817	933	1050	1167	1283	1400	1517	1633	1750	1867
111	356	475	594	713	832	951	1069	1188	1307	1426	1545	1664	1782	1901
112	362	483	604	725	846	967	1087	1208	1329	1450	1571	1692	1812	1933
113	369	492	615	738	861	984	1107	1230	1353	1476	1599	1722	1845	1968
114	375	501	626	751	876	1001	1126	1252	1377	1502	1627	1752	1877	2003
115	382	509	637	764	891	1019	1146	1273	1401	1528	1655	1783	1910	2037
116	389	519	648	778	908	1037	1167	1297	1426	1556	1686	1815	1945	2075
117	396	528	660	792	924	1056	1188	1320	1452	1584	1716	1848	1980	2112
118	403	537	672	806	940	1075	1209	1343	1478	1612	1746	1881	2015	2149
119	410	547	683	820	957	1093	1230	1367	1503	1640	1777	1913	2050	2187
120	417	556	695	834	973	1112	1251	1390	1529	1668	1807	1946	2085	2224

Appendix Table 4   International Log Rule, 1/4-In. Saw Kerf, for Logs 8 to 20 Ft in Length

Diameter (small end of log inside bark), inches	Length of log, feet							Diameter, inches
	8	10	12	14	16	18	20	
	Volume, board feet							
4	.....	5	5	5	5	5	10	4
5	5	5	10	10	10	15	15	5
6	10	10	15	15	20	25	25	6
7	10	15	20	25	30	35	40	7
8	15	20	25	35	40	45	50	8
9	20	30	35	45	50	60	70	9
10	30	35	45	55	65	75	85	10
11	35	45	55	70	80	95	105	11
12	45	55	70	85	95	110	125	12
13	55	70	85	100	115	135	150	13
14	65	80	100	115	135	155	175	14
15	75	95	115	135	160	180	205	15
16	85	110	130	155	180	205	235	16
17	95	125	150	180	205	235	265	17
18	110	140	170	200	230	265	300	18
19	125	155	190	225	260	300	335	19
20	135	175	210	250	290	330	370	20
21	155	195	235	280	320	365	410	21
22	170	215	260	305	355	405	455	22
23	185	235	285	335	390	445	495	23
24	205	255	310	370	425	485	545	24
25	220	280	340	400	460	525	590	25
26	240	305	370	435	500	570	640	26
27	260	330	400	470	540	615	690	27
28	280	355	430	510	585	665	745	28
29	305	385	465	545	630	715	800	29
30	325	410	495	585	675	765	860	30
31	350	440	530	625	720	820	915	31
32	375	470	570	670	770	875	980	32
33	400	500	605	715	820	930	1,045	33
34	425	535	645	760	875	990	1,110	34
35	450	565	685	805	925	1,050	1,175	35
36	475	600	725	855	980	1,115	1,245	36
37	505	635	770	905	1,040	1,175	1,315	37
38	535	670	810	955	1,095	1,245	1,390	38
39	565	710	855	1,005	1,155	1,310	1,465	39
40	595	750	900	1,060	1,220	1,380	1,540	40
41	625	785	950	1,115	1,280	1,450	1,620	41
42	655	825	995	1,170	1,345	1,525	1,705	42
43	690	870	1,045	1,230	1,410	1,600	1,785	43
44	725	910	1,095	1,290	1,480	1,675	1,870	44
45	755	955	1,150	1,350	1,550	1,755	1,960	45
46	795	995	1,200	1,410	1,620	1,835	2,050	46
47	830	1,040	1,255	1,475	1,695	1,915	2,140	47
48	865	1,090	1,310	1,540	1,770	2,000	2,235	48
49	905	1,135	1,370	1,605	1,845	2,085	2,330	49
50	940	1,185	1,425	1,675	1,920	2,175	2,425	50
51	980	1,235	1,485	1,745	2,000	2,265	2,525	51
52	1,020	1,285	1,545	1,815	2,080	2,355	2,625	52
53	1,060	1,335	1,605	1,885	2,165	2,445	2,730	53
54	1,100	1,385	1,670	1,960	2,245	2,540	2,835	54
55	1,145	1,440	1,735	2,035	2,330	2,640	2,945	55
56	1,190	1,495	1,800	2,110	2,420	2,735	3,050	56
57	1,230	1,550	1,865	2,185	2,510	2,835	3,165	57
58	1,275	1,605	1,930	2,265	2,600	2,935	3,275	58
59	1,320	1,660	2,000	2,345	2,690	3,040	3,390	59
60	1,370	1,720	2,070	2,425	2,785	3,145	3,510	60

SOURCE: U.S. Forest Service.

Appendix Table 5 Doyle Log Rule for Logs 6 to 20 Ft in Length

Diameter (small end of log inside bark), inches	Length of log, feet							
	6	8	10	12	14	16	18	20
	Volume, board feet							
8	6	8	10	12	14	16	18	20
9	9	13	16	19	22	25	28	31
10	14	18	23	27	32	36	41	45
11	18	25	31	37	43	49	55	61
12	24	32	40	48	56	64	72	80
13	30	41	51	61	71	81	91	101
14	38	50	63	75	88	100	113	125
15	45	61	76	91	106	121	136	151
16	54	72	90	108	126	144	162	180
17	63	85	106	127	148	169	190	211
18	74	98	123	147	172	196	221	245
19	84	113	141	169	197	225	253	281
20	96	128	160	192	224	256	288	320
21	108	145	181	217	253	289	325	361
22	122	162	203	243	284	324	365	405
23	135	181	226	271	316	361	406	451
24	150	200	250	300	350	400	450	500
25	165	221	276	331	386	441	496	551
26	182	242	303	363	424	484	545	605
27	198	265	331	397	463	529	595	661
28	216	288	360	432	504	576	648	720
29	234	313	391	469	547	625	703	781
30	254	338	423	507	592	676	761	845
31	273	365	456	547	638	729	820	911
32	294	392	490	588	686	784	882	980
33	315	421	526	631	736	841	946	1,051
34	338	450	563	675	788	900	1,013	1,125
35	360	481	601	721	841	961	1,081	1,201
36	384	512	640	768	896	1,024	1,152	1,280
37	408	545	681	817	953	1,089	1,225	1,361
38	434	578	723	867	1,012	1,156	1,301	1,445
39	459	613	766	919	1,072	1,225	1,378	1,531
40	486	648	810	972	1,134	1,296	1,458	1,620

SOURCE: U.S. Forest Service.

Appendix Table 6   The Distribution of *t*

df	Probability								
	0.5	0.4	0.3	0.2	0.1	0.05	0.02	0.01	0.001
1	1.000	1.376	1.963	3.078	6.314	12.706	31.821	63.657	636.619
2	0.816	1.061	1.386	1.886	2.920	4.303	6.965	9.925	31.598
3	0.765	0.978	1.250	1.638	2.353	3.182	4.541	5.841	12.941
4	0.741	0.941	1.190	1.533	2.132	2.776	3.747	4.604	8.610
5	0.727	0.920	1.156	1.476	2.015	2.571	3.365	4.032	6.859
6	0.718	0.906	1.134	1.440	1.943	2.447	3.143	3.707	5.959
7	0.711	0.896	1.119	1.415	1.895	2.365	2.998	3.499	5.405
8	0.706	0.889	1.108	1.397	1.860	2.306	2.896	3.355	5.041
9	0.703	0.883	1.100	1.383	1.833	2.262	2.821	3.250	4.781
10	0.700	0.879	1.093	1.372	1.812	2.228	2.764	3.169	4.587
11	0.697	0.876	1.088	1.363	1.796	2.201	2.718	3.106	4.437
12	0.695	0.873	1.083	1.356	1.782	2.179	2.681	3.055	4.318
13	0.694	0.870	1.079	1.350	1.771	2.160	2.650	3.012	4.221
14	0.692	0.868	1.076	1.345	1.761	2.145	2.624	2.977	4.140
15	0.691	0.866	1.074	1.341	1.753	2.131	2.602	2.947	4.073
16	0.690	0.865	1.071	1.337	1.746	2.120	2.583	2.921	4.015
17	0.689	0.863	1.069	1.333	1.740	2.110	2.567	2.898	3.965
18	0.688	0.862	1.067	1.330	1.734	2.101	2.552	2.878	3.922
19	0.688	0.861	1.066	1.328	1.729	2.093	2.539	2.861	3.883
20	0.687	0.860	1.064	1.325	1.725	2.086	2.528	2.845	3.850
21	0.686	0.859	1.063	1.323	1.721	2.080	2.518	2.831	3.819
22	0.686	0.858	1.061	1.321	1.717	2.074	2.508	2.819	3.792
23	0.685	0.858	1.060	1.319	1.714	2.069	2.500	2.807	3.767
24	0.685	0.857	1.059	1.318	1.711	2.064	2.492	2.797	3.745
25	0.684	0.856	1.058	1.316	1.708	2.060	2.485	2.787	3.725
26	0.684	0.856	1.058	1.315	1.706	2.056	2.479	2.779	3.707
27	0.684	0.855	1.057	1.314	1.703	2.052	2.473	2.771	3.690
28	0.683	0.855	1.056	1.313	1.701	2.048	2.467	2.763	3.674
29	0.683	0.854	1.055	1.311	1.699	2.045	2.462	2.756	3.659
30	0.683	0.854	1.055	1.310	1.697	2.042	2.457	2.750	3.646
40	0.681	0.851	1.050	1.303	1.684	2.021	2.423	2.704	3.551
60	0.679	0.848	1.046	1.296	1.671	2.000	2.390	2.660	3.460
120	0.677	0.845	1.041	1.289	1.658	1.980	2.358	2.617	3.373
∞	0.674	0.842	1.036	1.282	1.645	1.960	2.326	2.576	3.291

source: This table is abridged from Table III of Fisher and Yates, "Statistical Tables for Biological, Agricultural, and Medical Research," published by Longman Group, Ltd., London (previously published by Oliver and Boyd, Edinburgh), and by permission of the authors and publishers.

Appendix Table 7 Random Numbers

11 80	30 08	62 82	83 11	17 09	86 68	64 32	45 97	67 13	63 18
96 53	77 12	13 55	28 97	38 09	18 62	02 25	81 46	73 29	82 79
14 48	58 73	54 81	89 31	67 22	04 86	87 74	30 61	52 16	78 19
57 87	73 26	25 87	28 46	24 39	45 27	94 00	80 19	98 86	95 14
69 24	20 53	62 29	34 60	23 77	76 88	89 49	94 27	26 21	40 60
00 03	75 21	52 97	45 90	69 14	79 61	82 14	96 04	05 14	79 63
30 33	74 63	34 13	31 20	70 05	03 82	06 65	70 20	92 22	73 58
86 42	98 02	07 99	88 73	33 49	59 95	71 99	81 20	62 17	20 88
46 30	16 61	33 24	56 35	21 32	59 07	88 88	48 56	58 41	19 61
86 07	40 87	29 88	23 89	31 50	76 44	56 03	97 79	11 95	14 43
46 46	96 07	33 97	95 30	51 79	73 91	64 78	55 29	64 36	08 22
22 93	80 82	70 69	09 60	44 04	49 51	26 55	45 13	55 37	44 94
83 21	62 35	05 20	36 68	41 14	64 39	13 49	80 54	92 08	06 98
84 34	52 87	26 59	09 63	71 37	70 26	45 79	65 11	87 94	30 06
07 82	85 08	30 22	94 85	49 44	44 23	71 98	01 09	40 30	83 02
00 78	58 86	52 29	65 48	96 79	93 74	91 23	38 59	61 16	26 00
09 13	65 12	92 84	52 31	47 45	15 12	81 67	71 04	16 42	09 82
06 33	39 17	07 47	34 08	40 17	81 49	28 89	93 81	89 86	51 15
66 83	04 52	99 49	39 47	02 70	33 10	46 93	70 28	95 32	06 42
46 04	48 79	59 38	46 75	73 02	54 52	99 97	56 40	13 19	48 11
18 35	65 96	41 13	60 47	41 04	19 18	58 80	21 23	54 77	67 07
15 04	32 70	21 79	23 47	06 92	60 40	34 67	18 98	35 18	97 72
95 69	27 78	66 25	13 68	30 07	32 65	36 63	23 36	35 50	36 87
99 26	05 29	82 66	46 87	09 66	95 93	24 10	63 31	78 37	57 02
30 08	17 28	76 70	47 39	15 10	17 32	46 58	56 16	55 34	54 02
45 60	97 97	15 84	67 21	04 78	43 50	02 32	27 60	51 87	73 89
35 16	27 73	40 95	42 37	43 14	58 20	24 00	71 07	37 99	11 15
41 54	25 79	68 36	78 41	38 94	30 67	62 44	21 82	72 71	07 86
17 01	51 78	45 46	64 00	85 15	83 50	77 85	01 14	78 74	56 25
42 56	77 46	69 20	36 96	78 85	23 06	70 97	94 30	92 22	77 34
62 61	43 35	60 70	25 66	34 91	87 06	65 38	04 45	80 87	11 65
69 88	92 47	70 49	79 00	01 16	23 57	64 84	99 32	44 88	28 98
99 18	66 14	99 05	97 21	04 19	64 82	54 76	91 17	25 85	81 75
40 80	16 02	33 64	22 13	86 52	15 43	63 00	97 34	37 79	84 63
00 13	27 80	31 17	52 58	28 51	39 20	16 08	68 56	76 02	71 41
54 11	00 34	83 96	18 04	23 48	33 29	53 67	30 59	10 01	89 41
91 88	14 48	27 52	18 29	99 65	75 65	52 99	30 19	80 98	49 38
75 72	47 73	42 37	44 17	95 56	46 45	20 36	80 36	38 04	56 55
55 50	22 73	06 05	84 67	50 79	33 89	17 60	46 66	03 59	67 47
19 13	66 43	08 97	77 69	47 73	91 64	20 07	08 05	49 81	17 64

Index

Index